Teens
A to Z

Teens

A to Z

A Manual for Developing Mature, Godly Teenagers

Steve Damron

XULON PRESS ELITE

Xulon Press Elite
2301 Lucien Way #415
Maitland, FL 32751
407.339.4217
www.xulonpress.com

Paperback ISBN-13: 978-1-66285-314-2
Ebook ISBN-13: 978-1-66285-315-9

Dedication

To all the teens, youth groups, and youth rallies that helped me develop my love of working with young people, I deeply thank all of you. It has been quite a journey together. May God continue to raise up young people who love His Word and His work. Stay faithful until He comes again.

Contents

Introduction

It is a fact that adults do not always have the highest admiration and respect for young people. Therefore, Paul wrote to Timothy, "Let no man despise thy youth" (I Tim. 4:12). Timothy faced a real problem as a young leader because adults immediately "turned him off" as they do young people today. As youth leaders and parents of teens, we must work to help our young people instead of criticizing them. We should consider the following regarding our young people. Are our young people trying to stretch their minds, or are they trying to find the easiest and shortest books for a book report? Do they exercise their minds in academics and in spiritual learning, or are they focused on the cares of this world? Are our young people implementing character traits that will develop a biblically strong life? The intent of this book is to help parents, pastors, and youth pastors with some guidelines and direction for instilling character, morals, and guidance for young people today.

As revealed in I Timothy 4, God has blessed teenagers with abundant energy, ample time, and an alert mind. As parents and as leaders in churches, let's make sure that we don't underestimate the youth that God has given us, and let's use the teenage years to advance their training so that they can be equipped for God's purpose for their lives.

In His Service

Steve Damron

Chapter 1

A - Authority in the Home

"F rank & Ernest" cartoons have many humorous comic strips that indicate the idea of questioning authority. One particular strip shows a sign that says, "Don't feed the bears." A bear is standing with a t-shirt with the slogan, "Question authority."[1] Americans think that questioning or defying authority is our inalienable constitutional right. If our president begins to act as if he were the king, we rally to throw him out of office. It carries down through our society, all the way to rebellion on the family level. We resist the concept of authority. We don't like submitting to anyone.

> Now the serpent was more subtil than any beast of the field which the LORD God had made. And he said unto the woman, Yea, hath God said, Ye shall not eat of every tree of the garden? And the woman said unto the serpent, We may eat of the fruit of the trees of the garden: But of the fruit of the tree which is in the midst of the garden, God hath said, Ye shall not eat of it, neither shall ye touch it, lest ye die. And the serpent said unto the woman, Ye shall not surely die: For God doth know that in the day ye eat thereof, then your eyes shall be opened, and ye shall be as gods, knowing good and evil. And when the woman saw that the tree was good for food, and that it was pleasant to the eyes, and a tree to be

---

[1] https://www.cartoonistgroup.com/store/add.php?iid=70333. Accessed on June 22, 2018.

desired to make one wise, she took of the fruit thereof, and did eat, and gave also unto her husband with her; and he did eat. And the eyes of them both were opened, and they knew that they were naked; and they sewed fig leaves together, and made themselves aprons. And they heard the voice of the LORD God walking in the garden in the cool of the day: and Adam and his wife hid themselves from the presence of the LORD God amongst the trees of the garden. And the LORD God called unto Adam, and said unto him, Where art thou? (Gen 3:1–9)

We want to look at the biblical concept of authority with youth as the focus. For this reason, we will not dwell on the establishment of authority in society; that discussion is for another time. We want to start with the passage in Genesis to show that God was the authority to Adam and Eve. We see a pattern established at the beginning of time—authority is derived from God. This is true in society, in churches, and in a home. For this reason, if a society disregards God's Word, then there will be a breakdown in authority. It has always been the devil's aim to get human beings to question authority. He did this as revealed in Scripture in Isaiah. Let's refresh ourselves on this passage.

How art thou fallen from heaven, O Lucifer, son of the morning! how art thou cut down to the ground, which didst weaken the nations! For thou hast said in thine heart, I will ascend into heaven, I will exalt my throne above the stars of God: I will sit also upon the mount of the congregation, in the sides of the north: I will ascend above the heights of the clouds; I will be like the most High. (Isa. 14:12–14)

In this passage, we see that Satan's desire has always been to ascend to the place of God. He does not want any authority above himself. J. Vernon McGee says the following about this passage: In this passage there are five "I wills." Lucifer was setting his will over against the will of God. This is sin in its embryo. This is the evolution of evil. It began by a creature setting his will against the will of God."[2]

The devil's desires have not changed for today—he desires each of us to be our own law unto ourselves. This is a fundamental difference between Christianity and the pagan world. In a society that screams, "I have my rights," Christians should be crying out that God has my rights and my life. It is important that we see these differences and do not conform to the world's mindset when it comes to authority.

In the passage in Genesis 3, the devil wanted to get Adam and Eve to disobey God's direct commands. Notice he did this by saying that God knew that they would be like gods if they partook of the fruit of the tree. Authority is always compromised when we have a wrong view of self. Satan is a master at making us think more highly than we ought to think of ourselves.

Biblically, what is the authority in the home? The greatest passages to look at are in Ephesians 5 and 6.

> *Submitting yourselves one to another in the fear of God. Wives, submit yourselves unto your own husbands, as unto the Lord. For the husband is the head of the wife, even as Christ is the head of the church: and he is the saviour of the body. Therefore as the church is subject unto Christ, so let the wives be to their own husbands in every thing. (Eph. 5:21–24)*

> *Children, obey your parents in the Lord: for this is right. Honour thy father and mother; (which is the first commandment with promise;) That it may be well with thee, and thou mayest live long on the earth. And, ye fathers, provoke not your children to wrath: but bring them up in the nurture and admonition of the Lord. (Eph. 6:1–4)*

---

[2] J. Vernon McGee, *Thru the Bible with J. Vernon McGee: Volume 3 (Proverbs-Malachi)* (Nashville, Tennessee: Thomas Nelson Publishers, 1982), 234.

We see, in these passages, the order God has given to a home. Christ is the spiritual head, the father is the physical head, the mother is next in authority, and children are final in the pecking order. This does not seem hard to understand. However, most fathers do not understand that they must submit to Christ. If the father does not have proper submission to Christ, there will always be authority issues in the home. There are many fathers who have a "caveman" mentality of their authority. This type of father will "thump his chest" and "wave his club" and think that the minions in the house should cower and submit to him. His thought is that he has all-encompassing power and authority and can do whatever he wants. This is not a biblical view of authority. A father must submit to the lordship of Christ; and then, from that humble position, he is the head of the home.

The wife, then, must submit to her husband, and together they are united as a team to work in rearing their children for the Lord. The burden for the nurture and admonition of the home is on the father. This is shown in Ephesians 6:4. Authority for the home is established by God, and this order must be followed for a godly home to exist. Our society has placed an overemphasis on female leadership and child's rights. We have seen so much deterioration in the home, and it is evident the average citizen of America does not even understand what a good, godly home is like. Authority is essential to having a good home. We must understand the biblical design for authority and how it helps in bringing order to the home and to society. Consider the following from a book by Noah Webster written in 1832:

> It is not only proper that children should obey their parents, but their obedience should be prompt and cheerful . . . But a cold and unwilling obedience, with a murmuring disposition, alienates affection, and inclines the parent to rigor and severity in the exercise of his authority.[3]

---

[3] Noah Webster, *Noah Webster's Advice to the Young and Moral Catechism* (Aledo, Texas: Wallbuilders Press, 1993), 22.

Biblical authority brings peace of mind to the children in the home. As the children mature into teenagers, they will have a balanced philosophy of life and will be spiritually and socially fitted to being a benefit to God's kingdom.

Let me close with a few simple points on godly authority in the home and society:

- All authority originates from God.

- Authority is designed by God for blessing and protection.

- Authority does mean superiority.

- Proper authority needs accountability either to God or another chain of command.

- Proper authority means one is responsible to the leadership they have.

Nowhere does the Bible say authority is always right. Only Christ is perfect! Aside from this, you will be able to see imperfections in the authority that has been placed in your life. Does this mean that we do not have to obey authority? No, it does not. Character is an important part of proper authority, but we must realize that we live in a finite, fleshly world where bosses, parents, pastors, and teachers have imperfections. This does not give us a right to rebel. There may be some proper channels that we can take to rectify erring leadership, but we should never allow rebellion into our lives. Biblically, opening the door to rebellion will allow the works of Satan into a young person's life.

Chapter 2

B - Bible

As we begin looking at the importance of the Word of God in our homes, let's first consider some familiar typologies for the Word of God. The Bible is compared to a sword in Ephesians 6:17: "And take the helmet of salvation, and the sword of the Spirit, which is the word of God." The Word of God is a weapon that has been given to us to defend our homes. As fathers, we are not left helpless in guiding our young people as they face this ever-changing wicked world. We can equip and train them in the right use of the Sword of the Lord.

The Bible is also compared to a two-edged sword and a probing instrument in Hebrews 4:12: *"For the word of God is quick, and powerful, and sharper than any twoedged sword, piercing even to the dividing asunder of soul and spirit, and of the joints and marrow, and is a discerner of the thoughts and intents of the heart."* The Bible is a living and powerful book, which is such an encouragement to those rearing children. The Word of God is alive, and it is relevant to any time or season of our lives. It is sharper than any two-edged sword, indicating that this Bible can penetrate the heart more than the body. How far will this Bible probe? The Bible will probe all the way to the soul and spirit and to the joints and marrow. This means that the Bible can access farther than joints, inside the bones, and reach the marrow.[4] Reading, teaching, and studying God's Word in our homes will do more than any lecture.

---

[4]   Albert Barnes, *Commentary on Hebrews* (Nashville, Tennessee: Baker Books, 2005), 102.

The Bible is also mentioned as a crushing hammer in Jeremiah 23:29, *"Is not my word like as a fire? saith the LORD; and like a hammer that breaketh the rock in pieces?"*

A woman had often been urged by Christians to receive the Lord. In spite of their persistent efforts, she continued to harden her heart. One day she threw a Bible and several tracts someone had given her into the blazing fireplace. One of the leaflets fell out of the flames, so she cast it in again. A second time, it slipped down, and once more she put it back in. Again, her evil intentions were frustrated. The third time, however, part of it became scorched. That night, when the fire had died down, she picked up the portion that remained and exclaimed, "Surely the devil must be in that paper for it will not burn!" Out of curiosity, she began to read the partially destroyed tract. Because it was a message on salvation, it brought deep conviction to her heart. Finally, through that half-charred leaflet, she was led to Christ![5]

The Word of God can mold and make a young, immature boy into a strong, bold, and reliable man. It reminds me of a blacksmith that would take a useless piece of metal or iron and mold it into something useful. This is the power of the Word of God. Our homes should be saturated with it, and we must strive to implement the Bible into every area of our homes and lives. Referring to Titus 1:9, *"Holding fast the faithful word as he hath been taught, that he may be able by sound doctrine both to exhort and to convince the gainsayers."* Let me give an illustration from a pastor from years gone by:

> The other day I received a communication from a lawyer, who says that a very large property owner has discovered that a very small piece of property belongs to him and not to the small proprietor in whose possession it has for a very long time remained. The matter seemed a trifling one. We had a conference, and there came the steward with the

---

[5] http://www.wayoftruth.org/media//issues/13–02.pdf. Accessed on June 29, 2018.

lawyers. He was furnished with maps, and, putting on his spectacles, examined them with great care. Why? It was a small matter to him, but because he was a steward, he was expected to be faithful. And when he found that this small piece of ground belonged to his lord he was determined to have it. So let me say, as stewards of the gospel of God, we must never give up one verse, one doctrine, or one word of the truth of God. Let us be faithful to that which has been committed to us; it is not ours to alter. We have but to declare that which we have received.[6]

Titus 1 lists the qualifications of a pastor. One of those qualifications is to be faithful to the Word of God. You will notice in this text that he is taught the Word. The application is very good for parents of young people. It is important that we, as parents, are students of the Word of God. As we grow in our knowledge of the Word of God, then can we implement it into the lives of our own children. Here are three important areas where we should assimilate the Word of God in our lives.

We Should Study the Word of God

As parents and authority in the lives of our young people, we need to be students of the Word of God ourselves. A "do-as-I-say and not-as-I-do" attitude will ruin a young person in this area of the learning the Word of God. Our young people should see us reading, studying, and memorizing the Word of God. Consider this verse in Romans 15:4, *"For whatsoever things were written aforetime were written for our learning, that we through patience and comfort of the scriptures might have hope."* Notice that the Scriptures are given to us for learning. What have you learned from the Word of God over the past few weeks? Remember that I Timothy 3:16 tells us all Scripture is profitable and is for our instruction.

---

[6] J. L. Nye, *Anecdotes on Bible Texts, The Gospel According to St. Luke* (Charleston, South Carolina: Nabu Press, 2012), 86.

What are some of your favorite passages? Have you learned from the Word of God? According to the text, we can learn so that we can have hope. This world does not offer much hope; but we can go to His Word and find hope for today.

We Should "Soak Up" the Word of God

What exactly does this mean in the life of a young person? As a parent, I should be listening, reading, memorizing, and assimilating the Word of God into my life. In other words, my whole life should be permeated with the Word of God. When someone is in love with sports, it is easy to tell; and it is easy to tell when someone is in love with politics. In the same manner, it should be easy for our young people to see that we are in love with the Word of God because wherever we are, the Word of God must be evident there. Listen to what Daniel Webster said regarding the Word of God:

> From the time that, at my mother's feet or on my father's knee, I first learned to lisp verses from the sacred writings, they have been my daily study and vigilant contemplation. If there be any thing in my style or thoughts to be commended, the credit is due to my kind parents in instilling into my mind an early love of the Scriptures.[7]

We Should Share the Word of God

How often do you share Christ with others? This is a critical part of our life being saturated with the Word of God. When our life is filled up with God, it will overflow into our conversations with others. We will be looking for the lost and asking the Holy Spirit to lead us into conversations with them. We will be sharing Christ with our young people, and

---

[7]   Elon Foster, *6000 Sermon Illustrations* (Nashville, Tennessee: Baker Book House, 1972), 56.

we will always be looking for opportunities to share biblical principles for them to live by.

How are you undertaking the task of assimilating the Word of God into your life? God desires us to be faithful in heeding and keeping the Word of God. Make sure that you are setting aside daily times to personally read and study the Bible. Then, take that knowledge and give it to your children. As we started this chapter, we thought on what the Word of God is to us. It is a sword, a two-edged sword, a probing instrument, and a hammer. We have been given some mighty tools to help us in our child-rearing. Don't let your tools and weapons lay unused and gather rust. Take full advantage of the Word of God.

Chapter 3

C - Communication

After doing extensive research on the family, marriage, and the home, it is amazing to me how many different opinions there are on these subjects. I have come to realize that we must be careful in our study and research because we do not want to get drawn in by worldly influences. I am listing just a few of the many ideas that are out there today when it comes to our topic of communication.

- Instead of lecturing, listen. Lecturing just doesn't work.

- Try not to judge. If your teen feels judged, they won't approach you to tell you about serious problems.

- Encourage your teen to develop their own solutions to problems. You can make suggestions, but often you need to step back and allow your teen to work things out. Do intervene if the situation is unsafe.

- Yelling and intimidation may produce short-term compliance; but, in the long run, they are ineffective and unkind strategies.

- Do something different if you have been using the same old scripts that haven't worked before.

- Say something nice.

- Ask questions, but don't "grill" your child.

- Create private times your child can count on, like a weekly trip to the ice cream store or a daily walk. If you have younger kids, put them to bed earlier so your teen can have some "adult" time with you.

- Turn off the TV or, at least watch some programs together and discuss them. TV can create some excellent teachable moments.

- Take turns talking—don't monopolize the conversation.

- Ask your teen's opinion—then be careful that what you consider "discussion" doesn't sound like criticism to your teen.

- Ask for your teen's help and expertise, for example, with using your computer on a project.

- Praise your teen in front of others but not to the point of embarrassment. ("Chris really helped me today when my computer wasn't working properly. I had no idea he had such great skills!").

- Don't pry. You need enough information to help your teen stay safe, but you certainly shouldn't expect to know everything. Trust me; you don't want to know everything!

- Watch the tone of your voice. Teens tend to be hypersensitive, even if they don't show it. If necessary, take a few minutes to calm down.

These are some of the websites for the above-mentioned list:

- "10 Ways to Improve Your Communication Skills" (https://www.right.com/wps/wcm/connect/right-us-en/home/thoughtwire/categories/career-work/10-Ways-to-Improve-Your-Communication-Skills)

- "Worst Mistakes Parents Make When Talking to Kids" (https://www.psychologytoday.com/us/blog/the-mindful-self-express/201209/worst-mistakes-parents-make-when-talking-kids)

- "Feeling Hopeless? Learn How to Talk so Your Kids Will Listen" (https://childdevelopmentinfo.com/how-to-be-a-parent/communication/talk-to-kids-listen/)

I listed just a few examples of the worldly philosophy being taught and practiced in our society today. While somethings may not necessarily be wrong, we need to be careful, as parents, that we do not follow a worldly, unbiblical line of thinking and substitute true biblical guidelines with today's psychological babble in our homes. Every bit of advice must be judged by scripture.

Let's look at what the Bible has to say about our communication with our children and young people, beginning with Deuteronomy 6:3–9.

> *Hear therefore, O Israel, and observe to do it; that it may be well with thee, and that ye may increase mightily, as the LORD God of thy fathers hath promised thee, in the land that floweth with milk and honey. Hear, O Israel: The LORD our God is one LORD: And thou shalt love the LORD thy God with all thine heart, and with all thy soul, and with all thy might. And these words, which I command thee this day, shall be in thine heart: And thou shalt teach them diligently unto thy children, and shalt talk of them when thou*

sittest in thine house, and when thou walkest by the way, and when thou liest down, and when thou risest up. And thou shalt bind them for a sign upon thine hand, and they shall be as frontlets between thine eyes. And thou shalt write them upon the posts of thy house, and on thy gates. (Deut. 6:3–9)

A Good Home Has Its Foundation in God

You will notice a few guidelines for parents in this text. The first is that a good home has its foundation in God. As parents, our foundation must be in loving the Lord with all of our heart. We cannot expect our teenagers to be godly teenagers when we ourselves have no desire to be godly. I was recently studying the idea of having passion in one's life. It intrigued me how we can tie our passion or desire with the direction of our heart. In looking at Scripture, God convinced me that if my heart is in the wrong direction, my passion or desire will be heading in the wrong direction also. This may seem juvenile to you as a reader, but you cannot deny that there are numerous examples of folks in this world who are passionate about something that is trivial. They have let their heart take them in a path that is insignificant when it comes to eternity. Many Christians today are running after possessions, positions, or pettiness; and they cannot figure out why they are empty. Our young folks must see that we are passionate about Christ and seeking Him first. In this passage, I believe God addresses our heart's desires first, so we will align our desires properly toward God.

Parents Are to Teach Their Children and Teenagers.

Second, we see that parents are to sit down and teach their children and teenagers. This seems to indicate that a family will sit down together and talk. This is a lost art today. There is a constant hustle and bustle in which a parent has to set an appointment with their teenager to have a chance to talk with them. This is a false concept of a home. I want my children and our young people to work and be busy; but there seems to be this concept, in the average home, that there can never be a time to sit down and eat as a family to discuss what has happened through the day or through the week.

Let me give you a few items to consider about your week or month when it comes to your time with your young person.

1. Have Family Devotions

This is one of the most important times that you can have with your children. If you say you love God and you never read the Bible and pray as a family but instead watch television and sporting events, then what is the priority in your family? You must make an effort to read the Bible and pray with your family. Dad must be proactive in the area of Bible instruction.

Listen to what one author says about the failings that can happen in Christian homes:

> Many parents grasp the importance of raising obedient, respectful children, but fail to understand the significance of raising them to be lovers of God and others... As followers of Christ, we must raise children who not only have the virtue of self-control, but who are lovers of God and true lovers of their families, neighbors, and enemies.[8]

What is the point of the author? Families that don't implement sound biblical teaching through times in the Word of God will not have successful results with their young people.

While a youth group and a strong church are very important, parents should not outsource their teenager's spiritual development to the youth group alone. I love youth groups, and I have been involved with

---

[8] Reb Bradley, *Child Training Tips: What I Wish I Knew When My Children Were Young* (New York, New York: WND Books, 2014), 189–190.

youth in churches for over thirty years! I still love the excitement and energy that a youth group can bring to a church. Church youth groups have been a huge help to my own children. They have been motivated to serve the Lord and have grown in their maturity in the Lord; however, it is still my job as a dad to sit down and deal with the spiritual direction of my children.

2. Have Family Meetings

Besides family devotions, there should be times where you sit together as a family and talk. This could be a family dinner, a family outing, or a family vacation. All of these are family meetings, but there should be times where you sit down and talk about things that are going on in society, in school, and in your church. I believe that sitting down and eating dinner together as a family as much as possible is very important. Many scoff at this and say, "This will not make that much of a difference." By itself, maybe not, but combined with many other items that we have mentioned in rearing our young people, having family dinnertime is important. It is a time where Dad and Mom and children are all together and life is calm, and the family can interact with one another.

3. Have Family Outings or Activities

Many may think this means spending a lot of money, but that is not what I am talking about. For over twenty years, we made a practice of having a family event or activity almost every week of our children's lives. If I had planned on spending money for every event, I would be in the "poor house." Family events for smaller children can be going to a park, playing ball in your backyard, playing board games, even cleaning the yard together. As the children get older, you may find that doing something that costs a little money is fun; however, if you have a limited budget, find things that do not blow your budget. You will find that some of the things that cost the least are the most enjoyable.

4. <u>Have Family Vacations</u>

Some may dread this aspect of spending time with their young people. Often this is because a parent has not spent any time in disciplining and teaching their young person how to behave around others. Going on vacation for some families means spending time with a self-centered ego-maniac. This would be torture; but if you have worked at bringing up your children in the nurture and admonition of the Lord, you will find having an extended time with them is enjoyable. Even if there has been much training in the home, these longer times together help bring out bad habits or areas that need to be worked on. Thank God for having the experience to reveal the areas in which improvement is needed. Training involves time. There are many activities that having a little more time together will help. You can take a historical trip, a camping trip, an over-night trip, or an adventurous trip. There are so many things you can do together, and you will find that planning and working together toward the trip helps build strong relationships in your family.

5. <u>Have Family Church Attendance</u>

Even though church attendance is last on the list, it is certainly not the least on the list. Going to church together is very important to the proper spiritual communication of a young person. As a dad, you are sending a large nonverbal message of where you believe God should be in their life. Church attendance should not be an optional item in the home. It should be a staple for the building of the family's spiritual life. How important is it that you attend church as a family? Many folks claim the family is more important than the church, but after time, they have lost all of their children. The family and church are important in every home. There should not be a conflict. This illustration is appropriate with this final point of church attendance. It is a reminder that consistency and faithful attendance are a very important, but mundane part of a family's growth.

In a recent issue of *GLASS Window,* a contributor recalls that several years ago, *The British Weekly* published this provocative letter:

> Dear Sir: It seems ministers feel their sermons are very important and spend a great deal of time preparing them. I have been attending church quite regularly for thirty years, and I have probably heard 3,000 of them. To my consternation, I discovered I cannot remember a single sermon. I wonder if a minister's time might be more profitably spent on something else?

For weeks a storm of editorial responses ensued . . . finally ended by this letter:

> Dear Sir: I have been married for thirty years. During that time, I have eaten 32,850 meals—mostly my wife's cooking. Suddenly I have discovered I cannot remember the menu of a single meal. And yet . . . I have the distinct impression that without them, I would have starved to death long ago.[9]

---

[9] Craig Brian & Leadership Journal, *750 Engaging Illustrations for Preachers, Teachers, and Writers* (Grand Rapids, Michigan: Baker Books, 2002), 555.

Chapter 4

D - Dating

There has been a lot of discussion over the past two decades in the area of dating. Much of the dialogue is just on the term *dating*. Many have decided to use different terms, such as courting, courtship, betrothal, and so on. Much of the discussion has come from the failure in most churches and homes to teach young people about relationships with the opposite gender. Listen to what one author, a pastor for over forty years, mentions about the problems he has faced in dating relationships in his ministry.

> In looking back over the years, I have counseled many people; and in doing so, I heard many sad stories. For instance, after a daughter experiences a horrible marriage situation, I have heard dads say, "I knew they were making a serious mistake, but I didn't want to rock the boat," or "I felt it was their decision," which, by the way, is one of the worst ideas anyone can have. I say that because marriage had better be God's decision and not yours or your children's. If it is not, your children are very likely headed for a lifetime of heartache, and so are you. I cannot say this enough: fathers need to get involved in helping to prepare their children for marriage.[10]

---

[10] Larry Youngblood, *Biblical Principles for Parenting: How God Trained My Wife and Me to Raise Our Children* (Fleming Island, Florida: Berean Publications, 2011), 28.

I would like to look at some guidelines that should be established early in the home with boys and girls. We will then move on to the teen years.

<u>There Must Be a Clear Distinction Between the Genders</u>

Consider some important principles to be established at an early age. First, there must be a clear distinction between the genders. This means clothing, activities, and behavior toward the opposite gender. Right away this will help establish that boys and girls are different. America is reaping the result of equality of genders. We now have boys and girls who are saying they don't know what gender they are. This is a direct result of bad training in the home. In Genesis, the Bible clearly tells us that He created them male and female. This distinction needs to be clearly established in the home at an early age. This will help you as a parent later when you begin putting principles in place for touching, for conversation, and for interaction with the opposite gender. There are those who will disagree with some of my conclusions, but I would ask that you consider where we are heading. The end result is a godly home for your young son or daughter.

What are the clear distinctions that should be put into place? First, have distinctions in the home between dad and mom. There is considerable non-biblical teaching in this regard. Some say that authority must be equally divided, some say that there should be job sharing, and some say that there is no real distinction given between dad and mom. This is not seen in the Bible. The Bible does not teach a Neanderthal-age philosophy where the dad is a caveman pounding his chest and mom is the hired kitchen help. However, there are clear definite roles concerning the husband and wife in the home.

It should be evident in your home that the man is the spiritual head. This does not belittle the mother. It should not be that dad "brings home the bacon" and mom runs basically everything else. Dads should be engaged in the home on a constant basis. This will help develop a balanced child and also help later in life when the young son or daughter is maturing to an age where they are starting to look for a mate.

In America, we have a society that is continually saying, "women are belittled." In the Bible, we do not see the responsibility of being a mother scorned. The world has rejected the biblical model in many social areas. As a result of this, we shouldn't be surprised when they don't respect the mother's place in the home. I have been involved in churches as a member, a staff member, and a pastor. I have seen that there is great joy in children whose mothers enjoy fulfilling their biblical role. I am sure that those children, who are now grown adults, do not look at their moms as second-class citizens.

So, the first thing parents can do in preparing their children in the area of dating is presenting a good example of a biblical home and having the proper roles for dad and mom.

<u>There Must Be Training in Behavior</u>

Let's consider another area that will help your children in preparing for dating—behavior training. You may think, what does behavioral training have to do with dating? Believe it or not, proper table manners, treating their brothers or sisters as human beings, learning to do their chores, and learning conversational skills will help them when their dating life begins. These skills and behavioral attributes need to be started at an early age, such as three to five years old. A young child who learns that life does not exist for their pleasure is well on their way to becoming a great mate for someone someday. Etiquette and proper manners are becoming a lost art. A young boy should learn that his sisters and his mother are special in the house and should be respected. Dad needs to show this by his actions.

Meg Meeker is a doctor who wrote a book to encourage dad involvement in a society that is trying to do everything to stop boys from becoming men. She relates the following:

A boy watches his father to see what he does with his strength. He watches to see how his father controls his temper when he is angry, how he talks with people when he is irritated by them. He watches how his father spends his money and spends his time. He watches to see how committed he is toward his loved ones. Does he discipline himself to go to work when he is sick? Does he continue to be patient with the boy's mother when they're arguing? When a boy sees how self-control benefits his father, and everyone in the family, he learns an important lesson.[11]

This should be taught in the home both from Bible training and example. My favorite time growing up was around the dinner table where we could practice some of the table manners and discuss some of the proper etiquette that should be used. We did this with our own children also. It is fun to put this into practice with their friends and acquaintances. In our church, we try to put resources in the hands of our families so that this can be accomplished. Repetition is key to this character training. We all must work at character and manners. We must not get frustrated when our seven-year-old son or daughter forgets to pick up after themselves, forgets where to put their napkin, or forgets to write a thank-you card right after receiving a gift from someone. Keep at it. Keep training in this even through the teen years.

One of the greatest victories you can gain over a man is to beat him at politeness.[12]

There Must Be Modesty and Distinction regarding Dress

Third, let's consider modesty and distinction regarding dress. This can be touchy for some folks, but when we go to the Bible, we see that God

---

[11] Meg Meeker, M.D., *Boys Should Be Boys: 7 Secrets to Raising Healthy Sons* (New York, New York: Ballantine Books, 2008), 163.

[12] Croft M. Pentz, *The Complete Book of Zingers* (Wheaton, Illinois: Tyndale House Publishers, Inc., 1990), 187.

made men and women differently. There is nothing wrong with boys understanding that women are made to be pretty and beautiful. Because of the twisted society we live in, we tend to think even saying that a woman is pretty or complimenting a lady is leading down a dangerous road. It should be developed in the nature of boys that are becoming men that prettiness is a trait distinctive to a lady. An overemphasis in this area in a man will lead to his becoming effeminate. This is not saying that a man should be unkempt, but that prettiness and beauty are biblically distinctive of a lady. In training our young men, careful attention should be given to make sure the boy is not getting caught up in the world's latest styles. The world's styles confuse the sexes.

In training our ladies, the Bible talks about modesty in I Timothy 2:9–19. "*In like manner also, that women adorn themselves in modest apparel, with shamefacedness and sobriety; not with broided hair, or gold, or pearls, or costly array; but (which becometh women professing godliness) with good works.*" Verse nine is not necessarily talking about the distinction between dresses and pants. It is saying, however, that a biblical lady does not dress to draw attention to herself, but she is modest. This means that in the style of clothing, in the amount of jewelry, and in other areas a biblical lady is not drawing attention to her person. These are important items to make clear with our young boys and girls. In a day and age when five-year-olds are paraded across a stage to be the next young model, we should be trying in our Christian homes to oppose these wrong actions.

Chapter 5

E - Education of Youth

The entrance of thy words giveth light; it giveth understanding unto the simple" (Ps. 119:130).

Harvard University was founded in 1636 by the General Court of Massachusetts only sixteen years after the landing of the Pilgrims and is the oldest university in the United States. Originally called the College at Cambridge, being established in Cambridge, Massachusetts, it was renamed after its first major benefactor, Reverend John Harvard (1607–1638), who donated his library and half of his estate. The declared purpose of the college was "to train a literate clergy."

The Rules and Precepts observed at Harvard, September 26, 1642, stated:

1. When any scholar . . . is able to make and speak true Latin in verse and prose . . . and decline perfectly the paradigms of nouns and verbs in the Greek tongue . . . [he is able] of admission into the college.

2. Let every student be plainly instructed, and earnestly pressed to consider well, the main end of his life and studies is, to know God and Jesus Christ which is eternal life, John 17:3, and therefore to lay Christ in the bottom, as the only foundation of all sound knowledge and learning. And seeing the Lord only giveth wisdom,

let everyone seriously set himself by prayer in secret to seek it of him. (Proverbs 2:3)

3. Everyone shall so exercise himself in reading the Scriptures twice a day, that he shall be ready to give such an account of his proficiency therein, both in theoretical observations of language and logic, and in practical and spiritual truths, as his tutor shall require, according to his ability; seeing the entrance of the Word giveth light, it giveth understanding to the simple. (Psalm 119:130)

4. That they eschewing all profanation of God's name, attributes, Word, ordinances, and times of worship, do study with good conscience carefully to retain God, and the love of His truth in their minds, else let them know, that (notwithstanding their learning) God may give them up to strong delusions, and in the end to a reprobate mind. (II Thessalonians 2:11,12; Romans 1:28)

5. That they studiously redeem the time; observe the general hours . . . diligently attend the lectures, without any disturbance by word or gesture.

6. None shall . . . frequent the company and society of such men as lead an unfit, and dissolute life. Nor shall any without his tutors leave, or without the call of parents or guardians, go abroad to other towns.

7. Every scholar shall be present in his tutor's chamber at the 7th hour in the morning, immediately after the sound of the bell, at his opening the Scripture and prayer, so also at the 5th hour at night, and then give   account of his own private reading . . . but if any . . . shall absent himself from prayer or lectures, he shall be liable to admonition, if he offend above once a week.

8. If any scholar shall be found to transgress any of the laws of God, or the school . . . he may be admonished at the public monthly act.[13]

Ten of the twelve presidents of Harvard, prior to the Revolutionary War, were ministers, and according to reliable calculations, over fifty percent of the seventeenth-century Harvard graduates became ministers. Of note is the fact that 106 of the first 108 schools in America were founded on the Christian faith.

The dedication inscribed on the wall by the old iron gate at the main entrance to Harvard University campus, as well as in the catalog of the Harvard Divinity School, reads:

> After God had carried us safe to New England and we had builded our houses, provided necessaries for our livelihood, reared convenient places for God's worship and settled the civil government, one of the next things we longed for and looked after was to advance learning and perpetuate it to posterity, dreading to leave an illiterate ministry to the churches when our present ministers lie in the dust.[14]

Isn't it interesting that schools, such as Harvard, Princeton, and Brown University, which seem now to despise Christianity, find their origins in that which they hate—Christianity. It has always been a Christian tenet to educate their youth. As the verse in Psalm 119 says, the words of God give light. A Christian parent and a strong Bible-believing church are in the business of educating their youth to open their mind to the words of God.

I would like us to consider the importance of education for young people. Most who study the Bible know that every verse in Psalm 119

---

[13] https://constitution.org/1-History/primarysources/harvard.html Accessed on June 22, 2018.

[14] https://hds.harvard.edu/about/history-and-mission. Accessed on June 22, 2018.

has some reference to the Word of God. This is important as we think of educating our young people whether in our homes or in our churches. The Word of God cannot be forsaken or set aside. Let's consider a couple of important truths brought out by Psalm 119:130.

The word *entrance* is used to illustrate that any attempt at educating or opening our young people's minds with knowledge without the use of the Word of God is futile. That word *entrance* means "to open, to illuminate, or to enlighten." It is interesting that the Psalmists consider the Word of God as the tool necessary to help enlighten an individual.

> There is an interesting story told of a ranger in Yellowstone National Park. A park ranger was so intent on telling the hikers about the flowers and animals that he considered the messages on his two-way radio distracting, so he switched it off. Nearing the tower, the ranger was met by a nearly breathless lookout, who asked why he hadn't responded to the messages on his radio. A grizzly bear had been seen stalking the group, and the authorities were trying to warn them of the danger.[15]

The point of this story helps us in understanding how important the Word of God is to illuminate the path of our life, the perils in life, and the purpose to our life. Any time we turn away from the message God has sent us, we put our lives in danger. This entrance of the Word of God is guaranteed to give results. The verse says that light will be given, and understanding will be obtained. This has happened in men that we are familiar with in history. Consider the following examples of men that were devout Christians.

---

[15] https://drbillmcconnell.blog/2015/07/31/teach-me-to-pray/. Accessed on July 12, 2018.

<u>Johann Kepler</u>

He published tables for tracking star motions; he eventually was able to develop principles of calculus. He studied for two years in seminary, leaving only with reluctance to enter the study and teaching of astronomy when the Lord opened that door. Kepler wrote in one of his books: "Since we astronomers are priests of the highest God in regard to the book of nature, it befits us to be thoughtful, not of the glory of our minds, but rather, above all else, of the glory of God."[16]

<u>Francis Bacon</u>

He developed what is known as the "scientific method" in science, stressing experimentation and induction from data rather than philosophical deduction in the tradition of Aristotle. It is believed that Francis Bacon was a believer. His writings can be confusing on the subject of religion, but the following quote does seem to indicate a strong belief in God.

> It is true, that a little philosophy inclineth man's mind to atheism, but depth in philosophy bringeth men's minds about to religion; for while the mind of man looketh upon second causes scattered, it may sometimes rest in them, and go no further; but when it beholdeth the chain of them confederate, and linked together, it must needs fly to Providence and Deity.[17]

---

[16] http://hyperphysics.phy-astr.gsu.edu/Nave-html/Faithpathh/Kepler.html. Accessed on June 29, 2018.

[17] https://www.bartleby.com/3/1/16.html. Accessed on June 29, 2018.

Isaac Newton

He was responsible for development of the laws of universal gravitation, the formulation of the three laws of motion which make possible the discipline of dynamics and all its subdivisions as well as many other important laws that have helped in the scientific world. This man of gigantic intellect was also a genuine believer in Christ as his Savior and in the Bible as God's Word. He wrote many books on biblical subjects. In one book entitled *Principia*, he stated, "The most beautiful system of the sun, planets, and comets could only proceed from the counsel and dominion of an intelligent and powerful Being."[18]

Michael Faraday

He discovered electromagnetic induction and introduced the concept of magnetic lines of force. Faraday also invented the generator. He fully believed in the official doctrine of his church, which said: "The Bible, and it alone, with nothing added to it nor taken away from it by man, is the sole and sufficient guide for each individual, at all times and in all circumstances."[19]

In our modern society, Christianity is mocked and scoffed. Those that hold to the belief system of the Bible, whether it is in regard to creation, earth sciences, or astronomy, are considered out of date and out of touch. These men of the past show us that having a Bible-based education gave light to their path. Christianity has always helped a young man or woman excel. The Bible gives freedom of thought; it does not constrain thought.

As you consider giving your young person a proper education, please don't forget to include God's Word. This is of the utmost importance for the education of young people. How much emphasis do you place in your

---

[18] http://www.creationstudies.org/es/articles/intelligent-design/388-dawkins-ben-carson. Accessed on June 29, 2018.

[19] D. Kennedy and Jerry Newcombe, *What If the Bible Had Never Been Written?* (Nashville, Tennessee: Thomas Nelson Publishers, 1998), 104.

young person truly knowing the Word of God? I have stepped foot onto college campuses that claim to be Bible based, but you would have never known it. Why do they call themselves Christian or have Bible in their name? They do not hold to any of the tenets of Scripture. The source for the education must come from the Word of God. If we vary away from the Bible, our homes, churches, and schools will just be safe places for them to attend so that they might have a little discipline. But remember knowledge without direction will result in humanism.

Chapter 6

F - Family Life in the Home

In trying to help parents and youth pastors, I want to look at three areas in the family life of a young person and discuss some helps in establishing guidelines for them.

I would like us to consider the idea of contentment. The apostle Paul tells us in Philippians 4 that he found contentment. We live in a day that is contrary to contentment. In the material world, we must have a bigger car, boat, or house. In the job market, we must climb the ladder, ask for more pay, or be looking for some type of advancement. I understand that we should strive for the mastery, but many have taken this idea of never being content with where God has placed them or with what God has given them. Let's consider the story of Jacob and Esau.

Develop Contentment

And he said, Thy brother came with subtilty, and hath taken away thy blessing. And he said, Is not he rightly named Jacob? for he hath supplanted me these two times: he took away my birthright; and, behold, now he hath taken away my blessing. And he said, Hast thou not reserved a blessing for me? (Gen. 27:35–36)

There are a few important thoughts here for a parent to consider as they develop contentment in their home. A young person must learn to develop contentment for what they have. This must start early in the developmental years, but it will be magnified in the teen years. A young person must not come to the place where nothing will satisfy. Many teenagers today will only work if they are being paid. I have had parents tell me this numerous times over my years in the ministry. The conversation will progress something along these lines: "I can't believe how hard they work for money. I just wish they would be interested in doing some work around the house."

We must be careful that we do not develop in a young person's heart a covetous desire for materialism. If they will work "like a dog" for money but you can't get them to do anything around the house, they have a problem with contentment. The Bible instructs us to be content with such things as we have. One person put it this way, "A Christian is one who does not have to consult his bank book to see how wealthy he really is."[20] This is not always true for the average teenager. Some teens feel that their material possessions give them a status in life.

I have encountered both pros and cons to giving an allowance to a young person. In your home, you must settle on what God wants you to do. Either decision you come to will not eliminate the covetous nature of the heart. Some that are given too much become spoiled brats and develop an entitlement philosophy. On the other hand, I have seen young people who are not given anything, work with their own hands, and become covetous. In all these cases, the truth in I Timothy 6:6 that *godliness with contentment is great gain*" must be studied and lived out in the home. Our young people must have a biblical philosophy toward possessions.

The next item that I find in this passage to help with contentment is that a young person should be secure in their love at home. I don't want to get into psychological babble, but a young person who is not shown love at home and who is not accepted or noticed at home will find this attention in other places. The biblical love that parents should show their young people in their own home will help them in understanding God's love in that He gives them all that they need or should desire. Without

---

[20] Croft M. Pentz, *The Complete Book of Zingers* (Wheaton, Illinois: Tyndale House Publishers, Inc., 1990), 206.

biblical love and training, possessions can become a young person's entire focus for getting the love and attention. Jobs and work opportunities are great for young people, but those environments should not become the social hangouts for young people outside of the home or their church. Many teens' parents are so busy with their own lives that they do not see the needs that their children have. It is important to note that both daughters and sons need proper attention from their father. Lack of attention is one of the contributing facts to the rampant immorality and rebellious teenagers, often leading to the growing problem with gangs in our culture. Worldly discontentment will always lead the teen to look elsewhere besides their home, church, and school environment to find acceptance.

The second concept we want to consider in regard to family life is the implementing of integrity in the home. Let's consider the biblical example of Joseph.

> *And Joseph was brought down to Egypt; and Potiphar, an officer of Pharaoh, captain of the guard, an Egyptian, bought him of the hands of the Ishmeelites, which had brought him down thither. And the LORD was with Joseph, and he was a prosperous man; and he was in the house of his master the Egyptian. And his master saw that the LORD was with him, and that the LORD made all that he did to prosper in his hand. And Joseph found grace in his sight, and he served him: and he made him overseer over his house, and all that he had he put into his hand. And it came to pass from the time that he had made him overseer in his house, and over all that he had, that the LORD blessed the Egyptian's house for Joseph's sake; and the blessing of the LORD was upon all that he had in the house, and in the field. And he left all that he had in Joseph's hand; and he knew not ought he had, save the bread which he did eat. And Joseph was a goodly person, and well favoured. And it came to pass after these things, that his master's wife cast her eyes upon Joseph; and she said, Lie with*

me. But he refused, and said unto his master's wife, Behold, my master wotteth not what is with me in the house, and he hath committed all that he hath to my hand; There is none greater in this house than I; neither hath he kept back any thing from me but thee, because thou art his wife: how then can I do this great wickedness, and sin against God? And it came to pass, as she spake to Joseph day by day, that he hearkened not unto her, to lie by her, or to be with her. And it came to pass about this time, that Joseph went into the house to do his business; and there was none of the men of the house there within. (Gen. 39:1–11)

Although this biblical example does not take place in the home, I believe his integrity was developed many years before this. It is integral in a boy's life that he be taught the importance of honesty and integrity. To live an honest life is natural to a young man rather than living a life of deception.

Living honestly feels better to boys than living with deception, even if that deception is meant to get them what they want. Boys like feeling strong and courageous, and telling the truth demands strength and honesty. Lying feels grungy. Lying makes boys fearful because they know it is a weakness. The liar is someone who is afraid of the truth.[21]

How do we instill integrity into a young person so that when they are faced with strong temptation, they can resist?

---

[21] Meeker, 206.

<u>Do not tolerate a lying tongue</u>

There are countless Scriptures which indicate God's intolerance of a lying tongue. You cannot allow a lying tongue in your home, and this must start at a very early age. I would recommend disciplining a lying tongue in a strong way. In dealing with folks who despise God, I have learned that lying is not an issue with them. They have no conscience when it comes to twisting the facts and misrepresenting the truth. They have no "integrity."

Some fathers in Christian homes are raising a similar generation. Do not allow your sons or daughters to pull the wool over your eyes and lie to you without consequences. I have had folks say that we should have mercy and grace in our homes. I agree with this, but mercy should not start with the acceptance of lying because it is contrary to God's standard given to us in His Word. Discipline for lying should be swift and unforgettable! Having them read their Bible or talking your young person to death is not discipline. A young person knows that if they endure the spiritual rant and act like they are spiritual by putting on some tears or if they go to their room to read their Bible, you will be buffaloed into thinking your son is now John Wesley.

God hates lying, and a parent that excuses lying is actually displeasing God. I have never read in the Scriptures where God disciplined lying with Bible reading or a long talk. It was action. Consider the following biblical examples: Adam and Eve were kicked out of the garden for lying; Jacob, the supplanter, was punished by having to work for fourteen years for his wife; King Saul lied about obeying God to the prophet Samuel and lost the kingdom; Ananias and Sapphira lied and both died on the spot. Parents, we cannot be soft on lying. It develops a deceptive character!

We can use the example of Joseph as a Bible example of someone who had integrity. Going back to that story, note his words to Potiphar's wife. You will see that Joseph's allegiance was not just to his father or mother. More importantly, it was to God. This is a most crucial point when we are training our young people. A young person's allegiance ultimately must be tied to God. Although this is a daunting task as a parent (or youth worker), our young people must develop their own relationship with the Lord. Here is a list of a few things that might be a help to a parent or youth minister:

1.   Have Daily Bible Reading Resources for Young People.

These can be journals for filling out information or be actual daily devotional thoughts. They do not have to be complicated but can be a resource to start developing the habit of a daily walk with the Lord. There are classics, such as Spurgeon's *Morning and Evening* and *Faith's Checkbook*, as well as Oswald's Chamber's *My Utmost for His Highest*. These have stood the test of time. The daily devotionals do not necessarily have to be all through the year. You, as a parent, youth pastor, or pastor, can develop a couple months of devotionals to help in directing a young person's thoughts to a book of the Bible or a specific area of study through the Bible.

2.   Have Teaching on What Daily Walk Entails

As a parent, I am glad we have a youth group in our church that has times specifically for teaching on Bible study and prayer. This is so important for the growth of young people—but it doesn't end there. There must also be teaching in the home. This is obviously referring to those who have Christian homes. As you know, there are people reached through ministries in the church whose parents are not saved and who have no concern for a daily walk with the Lord. Other ways must be implemented to help in these types of situations. However, Christian parents play the most important role in developing the prayer life and Bible study of their young people. Listen to what one doctor who deals with young children has observed in relation to parents who discount the existence of God and the authenticity of faith:

When boys mature and hear adults ridicule their faith or those representing a faith, they become more uncomfortable with their own beliefs about God. One of the greatest offenses an adult can commit against a boy is to crush his childlike, honest, and very real belief about God. Many adults squelch a child's faith often under the guise of wanting him to "decide for himself." Ironically, that takes the very decision away from the boy.[22]

3. Have Young People Journal Their Walk with the Lord

This is helpful as they mature from a young person at the age of ten or twelve up to the age of eighteen or twenty. They will have a record of high times and low times, times of extra prayer, times of extra Bible study, and times of barrenness. I have made it a practice to journal a couple of times through a month for close to two decades. This helps me to ponder the path that I am taking with my life. Every so often, I look back through a year or two to see if there is a pattern of wandering or weakness that I need to address.

Develop Courage in a Young Person

One of the most important character traits needed in a young person is *courage*. We live in a day of weakening standards and loss of spiritual strength. How can we make sure we are implementing courage in the lives of our young people?

Again, let's go to Scripture and consider the Biblical example of David.

And the Philistine said, I defy the armies of Israel this day; give me a man, that we may fight together. When Saul and all Israel heard those words of the Philistine, they were

---

[22] Ibid., 185.

dismayed, and greatly afraid. Now David was the son of that Ephrathite of Bethlehem-judah, whose name was Jesse; and he had eight sons: and the man went among men for an old man in the days of Saul. And the three eldest sons of Jesse went and followed Saul to the battle: and the names of his three sons that went to the battle were Eliab the firstborn, and next unto him Abinadab, and the third Shammah. And David was the youngest: and the three eldest followed Saul. But David went and returned from Saul to feed his father's sheep at Bethlehem. (I Sam. 17:10–15)

And all the men of Israel, when they saw the man, fled from him, and were sore afraid. And the men of Israel said, Have ye seen this man that is come up? surely to defy Israel is he come up: and it shall be, that the man who killeth him, the king will enrich him with great riches, and will give him his daughter, and make his father's house free in Israel. And David spake to the men that stood by him, saying, What shall be done to the man that killeth this Philistine, and taketh away the reproach from Israel? for who is this uncircumcised Philistine, that he should defy the armies of the living God? (I Sam. 17:24–26)

And David said to Saul, Let no man's heart fail because of him; thy servant will go and fight with this Philistine. And Saul said to David, Thou art not able to go against this Philistine to fight with him: for thou art but a youth, and he a man of war from his youth. And David said unto Saul, Thy servant kept his father's sheep, and there came a lion, and a bear, and took a lamb out of the flock: And I went out after him, and smote him, and delivered it out of his mouth: and when he arose against me, I caught him by his beard, and smote him, and slew him. Thy servant slew both the lion and the bear: and this uncircumcised Philistine shall be as one of them, seeing he hath defied the armies of the living God. David said moreover, The LORD that delivered me out of the paw of the lion, and out of the paw of the bear, he will deliver me out of the hand of this Philistine. And Saul said unto David, Go, and the LORD be with thee. (I Sam. 17:32–37)

1. Courage Is Built in the Heart of a Young Person

Courage is not found in a quotation or in a motivational picture. Courage is built in the heart of a young person. It does take time, patience, and practice; but I believe all Christian teens can have courage through knowing and serving God. Courage starts with a fear of God. The right fear of God, which stems from a biblical fear of Dad, will develop courage— courage to stand up against those who offend God. An offense against God will eventually be such a great cause for that teen that he cannot sit still or stand down.

2. Courage Continues with Strenuous Spiritual Exercise

You will not develop courage in young people who are lazy in their work ethic. In the chapters preceding this story in I Samuel 16, you understand that David was in the outdoors and had exercised his sling, his weapon of warfare, so that coming up to Goliath was a challenge but not overwhelming. He had exercised himself in combat. If we desire courage in our young people, they must be exercised in the disciplines of spiritual warfare and learn to use the Christian weapons that God has given us in a way that will make them victorious.

3. Courage Is Demonstrated by Actions, Not Words

Eventually, David had to "put his money where his mouth was." This is not always easy, but actions in the life of a young person are where courage is built. Talk is cheap and talk is easy to deliver if there is never any follow-through. The story is told of a conversation between John Wesley and his brother Charles. Charles was lamenting on the toughness of the ministry that God had called them both to do. It was in the early years of both of their ministries, and things were not always smooth or easy. Charles told John, "If the Lord would give me wings, I'd fly." John answered his brother saying, "If God bids me fly, I will trust him for the wings."[23] Simply put, God will enable a young person to endure the tests of each given day. He may not give the answer or solution months in advance, but God will supply the need in that given moment. The toughness comes in the battleground of life. There must be continual engaging with the Sword of the Spirit in order to see if one is ready and useful in the attacks that the enemy engages us in.

---

[23] https://bible.org/illustration/if-god-bids-me-fly-i-will-trust-him-wings. Accessed on July 12, 2018.

Chapter 7

G - Giving: The Value of Sacrifice

Developing an unselfish attitude in young people is not an easy task. It is innate in our desires to take care of "numero uno." We do not like to be in want or lack anything. For this reason, we will get odd jobs, work overtime, and even volunteer for extra strenuous labors to take care of ourselves. This was true in my life as I became a teenager. I wanted some extra items for school, and I wanted a moped. My parents could not afford this when I was a teen, so they let me get some extra jobs to be able to buy those items on my own. I worked shampooing carpets, filing as a clerk in a hospital, working in a lighting distribution factory, and painting for a professional painter. I never complained (too much) about the long hours and hard work because I was doing this for my own benefit.

I am glad that along the way in this process, and for many years to come afterward, I had parents who directed my thinking in the area of sacrificial giving to the Lord. Through Bible study, prayer, and godly living, my parents were able to steer my focus off myself and my wants. It has been said that Christians show what they are by what they do with what they have.[24] I learned that godliness in a person is shown by a giving spirit. Let's consider two thoughts in Scripture in this regard.

---

[24] Pentz, 120.

The Lad with the Lunch

One of his disciples, Andrew, Simon Peter's brother, saith unto him, There is a lad here, which hath five barley loaves, and two small fishes: but what are they among so many? And Jesus said, Make the men sit down. Now there was much grass in the place. So the men sat down, in number about five thousand. And Jesus took the loaves; and when he had given thanks, he distributed to the disciples, and the disciples to them that were set down; and likewise of the fishes as much as they would. When they were filled, he said unto his disciples, Gather up the fragments that remain, that nothing be lost. Therefore they gathered them together, and filled twelve baskets with the fragments of the five barley loaves, which remained over and above unto them that had eaten. (John 6:8–13)

I love this story because there are so many ideas that are conveyed in this text. The lad wanted to see Jesus, which is noteworthy, because it shows a spiritual inclination in this young man. I am sure that this young boy would have had friends in the neighborhood who would have loved to go fishing or go to their favorite swimming hole, but he wanted to go see Jesus. Seeing his desire to be with Jesus at the outset will help us in developing an unselfish attitude in our young people. Make sure that your young person wants to be around the things of God. Work at developing a yearning for the things of God. A major part of developing this desire is being at all church events. When your children see a parent thrilled to be serving God, they will also have the same desires.

We see that this young man did not hesitate to offer his lunch up for Christ's use. The conversation is not recorded between the disciple and the young lad. However, we do know that when they wanted to feed the multitude, this young man stepped up to offer his lunch to the Lord. I have been involved with youth work for over twenty-five years, and I love the idea of this lad volunteering for service. This is a great attitude to have in a young person. Most youth of our day are only concerned with receiving rather than giving. It is so important that they come to the point of giving all of their desires, ambitions, and wants to the Lord. Many readers may remember the old biblical term of consecration. *Consecration* simply is giving our whole life to be used of God as He would see fit. That is diligent in our business, losing no moment of time, filling our days with tasks and duties that God would be happy with in our life.

> Living thus, holding our whole life to be used by the Master as he would use it, diligent in our business, losing no moment of time, we are to fill our day with tasks and duties well and faithfully done. This is consecration. No other kind of living is worthy of the name. We cannot be always at prayer, or always reading our Bible; and it is a mistake to think that consecration has to do only with these spiritual acts and exercises. It has to do quite as much with the secularities of life, although, indeed, this spirit makes all our duties holy.[25]

This lad who surrendered his lunch did not have any promise of future reimbursement, but he saw that there was a need and wanted to help in meeting the need. In essence, his lunch was consecrated to the things of God just as his own being was consecrated to God. All that a young person has should be given over to our Savior's use.

The last thought concerning this lad is that the need was met, and he was filled up to overflowing. This is amazing when you consider the vastness of the multitude and the little that this lad had to offer. Can you imagine his astonishment as he saw what the Lord did with his lunch? This story is encouraging for parents and youth ministers as we consider the vastness of the need in church and mission work. The youth God has

---

[25] J. R. Miller, *Young People's Problems: Help and Hope for Today's Teen* (Birmingham, Alabama: Solid Ground Christian Books, 2008), 66.

placed in our care can be used to supply the need if they are completely given over to God. How is it possible to meet all the needs of the ministry? A life given over to God can be multiplied to meet the needs.

David and the Threshingfloor

And the king said unto Araunah, Nay; but I will surely buy it of thee at a price: neither will I offer burnt offerings unto the LORD my God of that which doth cost me nothing. So David bought the threshingfloor and the oxen for fifty shekels of silver. (II Sam. 24:24)

The background of the verse is that David wanted to buy a threshing floor from a man in order to give offerings to the Lord. The man wanted to give the threshing floor to David free of charge. David made this statement found in verse 24. King David had learned by this time of his life that something will mean much more to you when you have given something of your own to obtain it. There is a sad illustration from days gone by that illustrates how many sacrifice to their false gods. It is instructive for us in helping us understand that God demands no less.

This is a touching story a missionary tells of a Hindu mother who had two children, one of them blind. The mother said her god was angry, and must be appeased, or something worse would come to pass. One day the missionary returned, and the little bed had but one child in it. The mother had thrown the other into the Ganges. "And you cast away the one with good eyes?" "Oh, yes," she said; "my god must have the best." Alas! Alas! The poor mother had a true doctrine, but she put it to a bad use.

Let us try to give God the best. Too long already have we put Him off with the drippings from life's overfull cup.[26]

As parents and leaders of youth, we can use this example to help us in the training of our teenagers. If we are not careful, we will forget this lesson and raise spoiled brats. David knew there is value in investing one's own personal assets into a cause in order for it to be truly meaningful. This principle is very important for our youth. If the young people who grow up in a church do not learn to sacrifice on their own, they will become spoiled. They will never have a deep-rooted attachment to their home or church if they do not learn to give of themselves.

I nickname it the "Paris Hilton" syndrome. Most of us who watch the news will laugh at her stupidity and then become disgusted because she acts like a spoiled brat. She represents someone who has been given to and given to and given to but was never taught the value of self-service. We may laugh at Paris Hilton; but in many of our churches, we have raised a generation who expect dad, mom, their teachers, and church staff to give and give and give with no sacrifice or gratefulness in return. They bristle up when anyone dares to ask them to stand up and serve God. As youth leaders and parents, we must always be looking for areas in which our teenagers and our children can learn the value of serving. It is through service that a Christian finds fulfillment and satisfaction.

Learning to Give Back

In conclusion, let me give some ideas of ways that a teenager can learn to give back to those who invested in their lives without getting something in return.

1. Have your teenager find a job once a month or semester at church that needs done. This should be done without prompting by a

---

[26] Joseph S. Exell, *The Biblical Illustrator: I & II Samuel and I & II Kings* (Grand Rapids, Michigan: Baker Book House, 1977), 401.

staff member or raising a banner. As parents, we need not to act as though this is a wonderful event.

2. Find another young person in the youth group, who is hurting financially and have your teenager work to get some funds for them anonymously; for instance, money for a teen trip or some funds for some personal items.

3. As a family, find a staff member to pray for and do something for once a semester or every three to four months. The kids can leave notes and special tokens of appreciation. These all should be done anonymously also.

4. Find a missionary overseas to send letters and gifts to.

5. Spend some time with an elderly person or widow in your church. This could be in the form of outside work or inside work—checking up on them, doing some mowing, or just simply bringing a game or book to their house and talking with them.

We all have selfish tendencies, and as we learn the biblical way of giving, our selfish tendencies will be weakened. Becoming more like Christ means to give as He gave Himself. Are you helping your youth to be unselfish, God-honoring people in the preaching, teaching, and activities of your church?

Let me close with a story from Russian folklore entitled "Fortune and the Beggar" by Ivan Krylov.

> One day a ragged beggar was creeping along from house to house. He carried an old wallet in his hand and was asking at every door for a few cents to buy something to eat. As he was grumbling at his lot, he kept wondering

why it was that folks who had so much money were never satisfied but were always wanting more.

Here, thought he, is the master of the house—I know him well. He was always a good businessman, and he made himself wondrously rich a long time ago. Had he been wise he would have stopped then. He would have turned over his business to someone else, and then he could have spent the rest of his life in ease. But what does he do instead? He began building ships and sending them to sea to trade with foreign lands. He thought he would get mountains of gold, but there were great storms on the water. His ships were wrecked, and his riches were swallowed up by the waves. Now the hopes all lie in the bottom of the sea, and his great wealth has vanished like the dreams of a night. There are many such cases. Men never seem to be satisfied unless they can gain the whole world. As for me if I had only enough to eat and to wear, I would not want anything more.

Just at that moment Fortune came down the street. She saw the beggar and stopped. She said to him, "Listen! I have long wished to help you. Hold your wallet, and I will pour this gold into it. But I will pour only on this condition: All that falls into the wallet will be pure gold, but every piece that falls upon the ground shall become dust. Do you understand?"

"Oh, yes; I understand," said the beggar. "Then have a care," said Fortune. "Your wallet is old, so do not load it too heavily." The beggar was so glad that he could hardly wait. He quickly opened his wallet, and a stream of yellow coins was poured into it. The wallet soon began to grow heavy.

"Is that enough?" asked Fortune. "Not yet." "Isn't it cracking?" "Never fear." The beggar's hand began to tremble. Ah, if the golden stream would only pour forever! "You are the richest man in the world now!" "Just a little more" said the beggar. "Add just a handful or two." "There, it's full. The wallet will burst." "But it will hold a little more, just a little more!"

Another piece was added, and the wallet split. The treasure fell upon the ground and was turned to dust and Fortune had vanished. The beggar had nothing now but his empty wallet, and it was torn from top to bottom. He was as poor as before.[27]

---

[27] http://www.saibhaktiradio.com/wp/fortune-and-the-beggar/. Accessed June 22, 2018.

Chapter 8

H - Holy Spirit in the Home

What are some requirements for the filling of the Holy Spirit? First, you must be born again. In Galatians 4:6 the Bible says, *"Because ye are sons, God hath sent forth the Spirit of His Son into your hearts."* There also must be evidence of faith in one's life. John 7:39 says that the Spirit is given to those who believe. The next step in obtaining the Holy Spirit's filling is obedience. Acts 5:32 says that God gives the Holy Spirit to those who obey Him. It is clear that the Holy Spirit will not guide contrary to the Scriptures. If there is some spirit that is leading us to do that which is against the Word of God, then we can be sure that it is not the Holy Spirit.[28]

The last item that I want to include in our list is prayer. According to Luke 11:13, the Holy Spirit is given to those who seek Him. There are other qualities that the Bible seems to indicate must either be in place or must be sought after for the Holy Spirit to have free reign in a believer's life, but these characteristics are some of the preeminent items that a young person must acquire to develop a relationship with Him.

Nowhere in Scripture is there a certain age indicated for the filling of the Holy Spirit. I believe that many limit the work of the Holy Spirit to age twenty-five and older. This concept has limited the work that the Holy Spirit can do in a young person's life. The Holy Spirit's work is marginalized in most homes regarding the work that He can do in changing a teen into the image of Christ. The Holy Spirit can guide and lead a young

---

[28] R. A. Torrey, *The Person & Work of the Holy Spirit* (Springdale, Pennsylvania: Whitaker House, 1996), 144.

person into spiritual maturity. Without the proper teaching and preeminence of the Holy Spirit, young people will wander aimlessly through their teen years. By focusing young people on the person of the Holy Spirit, a parent or leader in the church can help stabilize the "roller coaster years" of youth.

The one great secret that is essential for a young person regarding the leading of the Holy Spirit is surrender—surrendering our wills, bodies, possessions, and every other aspect of our lives to His control. All of my children have received lifeguard training. They can testify that they are instructed to approach someone drowning cautiously. They are taught different holds and approaches because normally the drowning victim will fight their rescuer.[29] In a similar case, the average young person fights the rescue and security that the Holy Spirit can give to their life. This aspect is very hard for a young person, but once they give their life over to the Spirit's control, they will see amazing results. The Bible gives great insight into this thought of surrender. I would like us to consider one of the most common passages found in Romans 12. "*I beseech you therefore, brethren, by the mercies of God, that ye present your bodies a living sacrifice, holy, acceptable unto God, which is your reasonable service*" (Rom. 12:1).

I Beseech You

That word *beseech* is a term that means "to implore, to entreat, to beg, or to encourage."[30] The apostle Paul is saying to the church in Rome that he was challenging them to be accountable in this area of surrender. The word was used in military circles and was used to indicate a military leader's call of soldiers to action. When the troops were on their way to war, the commander would call them together because they were preparing to do battle. This is what we must understand when we are helping our

---

[29] https://lifevesthub.com/save-drowning-swimmer/. Accessed on July 12, 2018.

[30] Noah Webster, *An American Dictionary of the English Language: Intended to Exhibit, I. The Origin, Affinities and Primary Signification of English Words, as Far as They Have Been Ascertained; II. the Genuine Orthography and Pronunciation of Words, According to General*. S. Converse, Printed by Hezekiah Howe, 1828.

young people in this area of surrender to the Holy Spirit's leading. It will be a battle, so we must rally with them for the war that will take place.

Mercies of God

There is no singular word used for mercy in the Old Testament, so there is a match here to the Old Testament word *mercies,* which is true for you and me when we consider what the Lord has done for us. It is not a singular mercy. These mercies, which means "undeserving or unwarranted" or "God in his mercies multiplied in our undeserving."

Present

This word is picturesque of the Old Testament sacrificial system in which an Israelite would bring in hand their gift to the Lord. We see this illustrated in the Pentateuch when it describes a person coming leading their animal or carrying their offering in hand to the Lord. Likewise, this is a personal task that a young person must do themselves. They must come to a point that they bring their life in hand to the altar.

Holy

This means "to set it aside for God's use" and God's use only. Remember that Paul in the book of Corinthians explains that we are bought with a price, the precious blood of Christ; therefore, we are not our own. We must realize that our bodies belong to God because he claimed ownership when He saved us.

Reasonable Service

The word *reasonable* comes from the Greek word *logikos,* which means, "logical by reason or dictated by thinking."[31] The apostle Paul is saying that we should present our bodies to the Lord because through research and study, it is the most logical explanation. In other words, it makes common sense to give our lives as a Christian to the Lord.

---

[31] Albert Barnes, *Barnes' Notes on the New Testament* (Grand Rapids, Michigan: Baker Books, 2005), 264.

After one considers the text of Romans 12:1, there is clear evidence that we should surrender to the leading and working of the Holy Spirit in our life. The infilling of the Spirit is indispensable for a young person desiring to live a holy life. The Holy Spirit quickens the intellect, affections, conscience, will, and personality. The filling is the secret of abiding or obeying and having a God-honoring trust in the Word of God.

The Results of the Spirit's Control

We have looked at some of the foundational thoughts about the doctrine of the Holy Spirit and how important it is. I would like to conclude by looking at some practical results that a young person can see when they surrender to the Spirit and let Him take control.

1. Guidance

Yet thou in thy manifold mercies forsookest them not in the wilderness: the pillar of the cloud departed not from them by day, to lead them in the way; neither the pillar of fire by night, to shew them light, and the way wherein they should go. Thou gavest also thy good spirit to instruct them, and withheldest not thy manna from their mouth, and gavest them water for their thirst. (Neh. 9:19–20)

The LORD is my shepherd; I shall not want. He maketh me to lie down in green pastures: he leadeth me beside the still waters. He restoreth my soul: he leadeth me in the paths of righteousness for his name's sake. Yea, though I walk through the valley of the shadow of death, I will fear no evil: for thou art with me: thy rod and thy staff they comfort me. Thou preparest a table before me in the presence of mine enemies: thou anointest my head with oil: my cup runneth over. Surely

goodness and mercy shall follow me all the days of my life:
and I will dwell in the house of the LORD for ever. (Ps. 23)

I believe these passages help us to understand one of the great results of having the Holy Spirit's presence in a young person's life. Many young people find themselves experiencing a time of wandering like the children of Israel. They almost seem lost, and the way seems hard and weary. The passage in Nehemiah tells us that God gave the children of Israel a cloud by day and a pillar of fire by night. The Holy Spirit will not leave us alone. It may seem like we are in a wandering period of life, but God's Spirit can still guide our everyday steps. This is comforting in helping a young person through the treacherous times of learning to make decisions on their own. As parents and youth leaders, we do not have to work alone. We can help that young person get a personal relationship with the Holy Spirit, and He will guide them daily.

2. <u>Chastening</u>

Nevertheless I tell you the truth; It is expedient for you that I go away: for if I go not away, the Comforter will not come unto you; but if I depart, I will send him unto you. And when he is come, he will reprove the world of sin, and of righteousness, and of judgement: of sin, because they believe not on me; of righteousness, because I go to my Father, and ye see me no more; of judgement, because the prince of this world is judged. (John 16:7–11)

In the passage in John, we see that the Holy Spirit is on this earth to rebuke and reprove. Most young people do not appreciate being told that what they are doing is wrong. Individuals involved in developing young people can take heart that the Holy Spirit is there to assist our training and the reproof that we are trying to give to our youth. The Holy Spirit will nudge a young person toward righteousness and toward the image of Christ. This is the reason that the teaching on the Holy Spirit and the development of a relationship with the Holy Spirit is vital for growth in a young person. When those in authority are not present, the Holy Spirit, who is always with that young person, will convict and chasten when they start to walk in the flesh.[32] Another great passage to study out regarding chastening of the Holy Spirit is Acts 5.

3. Alertness

When Elihu saw that there was no answer in the mouth of these three men, then his wrath was kindled. And Elihu the son of Barachel the Buzite answered and said, I am young, and ye are very old; wherefore I was afraid, and durst not shew you mine opinion. I said, Days should speak, and multitude of years should teach wisdom. But there is a spirit in man: and the inspiration of the Almighty giveth them understanding.

Behold, now I have opened my mouth, my tongue hath spoken in my mouth. My words shall be of the uprightness of my heart: and my lips shall utter knowledge clearly. The Spirit of God hath made me, and the breath of the Almighty hath given me life.

Yea, surely God will not do wickedly, neither will the Almighty pervert judgment. Who hath given him a charge over the earth? or who hath disposed the whole world? If he set his heart upon man, if he gather unto himself his spirit and his breath; All flesh shall perish together, and man shall turn again unto dust. (Job 32:5–8; 33:2–4; 34:12–15)

---

[32] Michael P. Green, *1500 Illustrations for Biblical Preaching* (Grand Rapids, Michigan: Baker Books, 2005), 191.

The passages above, along with Genesis 2, indicate that the Spirit's job is to produce life. Most young people believe that life comes through worldliness and through the satisfaction of the flesh. By developing a relationship with the Holy Spirit, the young person will start to understand that only God can produce life. Just like at creation, the breath or the Spirit of God brings life into a dead soul.

For this reason, parents need to be careful not to maintain the world's philosophy in the home. The world creates the idea that this world is all there is to live for. As a young person sees this world, they do not have the perspective that life is short. In their eyes, they don't see death and wasted lives that often. This world seems so promising and seems to have so much to offer even if it is not necessarily the evils of this world but rather the promise of future employment, future pay, future love to a godly mate, and future enjoyment. These are not all horrible things in the future, but they should not be the primary focus of a godly young person. Our young people need to seek God first. This will come as we help them grow in their relationship with the Holy Spirit. The Holy Spirit will work to breathe spiritual life into their souls and into their hearts.

4. <u>Godliness</u>

This I say then, Walk in the Spirit, and ye shall not fulfil the lust of the flesh. For the flesh lusteth against the Spirit, and the Spirit against the flesh: and these are contrary the one to the other: so that ye cannot do the things that ye would. But if ye be led of the Spirit, ye are not under the law. Now the works of the flesh are manifest, which are these; adultery, fornication, uncleanness, lasciviousness, idolatry, witchcraft, hatred, variance, emulations, wrath, strife, seditions, heresies, envyings, murders, drunkenness, revellings, and such like: of the which I tell you before, as I have also told you in time past, that they which do such things shall not inherit the kingdom of God. But the fruit of the Spirit is love, joy, peace,

*longsuffering, gentleness, goodness, faith, meekness, temper-
ance: against such there is no law. And they that are Christ's
have crucified the flesh with the affections and lusts. If we
live in the Spirit, let us also walk in the Spirit. Let us not be
desirous of vain glory, provoking one another, envying
one another. (Gal. 5:16–26)*

True godliness will only occur if there is the Spirit's indwelling in the
home. Without this indwelling, a home will produce a pious hypocrite
who will become critical of true Spirit-filled living. Long lists of rules and
regulations without the understanding that the Spirit desires us to be led
by Him will result in a false piety. Our rules and regulations will be our
spirituality instead of a close, personal relationship with the Holy Spirit.
In the passage in Galatians, we see that walking in the Spirit will produce
fruit. It is interesting that the Bible uses the word *walking*. This is an
action verb which indicates that we need our young people to be active
in their pursuit of a Spirit-filled life. We may talk of being close to God
and speak of the Spirit's leading, but only our walk will reveal the true
existence of this in our lives to others. Make sure to reveal the pathway for
a young person to walk so that they may find the Holy Spirit as a com-
panion on the path of life. He will guide them into holiness.

5. Seriousness

*Now the God of hope fill you with all joy and peace in
believing, that ye may abound in hope, through the power
of the Holy Ghost. And I myself also am persuaded of you,
my brethren, that ye also are full of goodness, filled with all
knowledge, able also to admonish one another. Nevertheless,
brethren, I have written the more boldly unto you in some
sort, as putting you in mind, because of the grace that is given
to me of God, that I should be the minister of Jesus Christ to
the Gentiles, ministering the gospel of God, that the offering*

*up of the Gentiles might be acceptable, being sanctified by
the Holy Ghost. (Rom. 15:13–16)*

*Know ye not that your bodies are the members of Christ?
shall I then take the members of Christ, and make them the
members of an harlot? God forbid. What? know ye not that
he which is joined to an harlot is one body? for two, saith
he, shall be one flesh. But he that is joined unto the Lord is
one spirit. Flee fornication. Every sin that a man doeth is
without the body; but he that committeth fornication sinneth
against his own body. What? know ye not that your body is
the temple of the Holy Ghost which is in you, which ye have
of God, and ye are not your own? For ye are bought with a
price: therefore glorify God in your body, and in your spirit,
which are God's. (I Cor. 6:15–20)*

This implies a passion. As parents, we will have a passion for proper discipline because all matters of discipline are important. There is a passion to see your children reared in the right way. The character that parents and authority are working to build will be important in the young person's life. The Bible reveals to us that our bodies are the temples of the Holy Ghost. This fact will put seriousness in our walk on this earth. A young person, who understands that everywhere they step they will have the Holy Spirit with them, will have a different perspective in life. They will not be so flippant with loose lips, with loose actions, and with loose living. As parents and youth leaders, we need to stress that the eyes of the Lord are everywhere; but we should also stress that where a Christian goes, so does the Spirit of the Lord. We need to encourage our young people to be in the business of fellowshipping with the Holy Spirit throughout the day rather than quenching His influence in their life.

Let me end with a story that helps us understand the concept of surrender. It is the story of a meeting between two men of God in history, J. Wilbur Chapman and General Booth of the Salvation Army.

When J. Wilbur Chapman was in London, he had an opportunity to meet General Booth, who at that time was past 80 years of age. Dr. Chapman listened reverently as the old general spoke of the trials and the conflicts and the victories he had experienced.

The American evangelist then asked the general if he would disclose his secret for success. "He hesitated a second," Dr. Chapman said, "'and I saw the tears come into his eyes and steal down his cheeks," and then he said, "I will tell you the secret. God has had all there was of me. There have been men with greater brains than I, men with greater opportunities; but from the day I got the poor of London in my heart, and a vision of what Jesus Christ could do with the poor of London, I made up my mind that he would have all of William Booth there was. And if there is anything of power in the Salvation Army today, it is because God has all the adoration of my heart, all the power of my will, and all the influence of my life."

Dr. Chapman said he went away from that meeting with General Booth knowing "that the greatness of a man's power is the measure of his surrender."[33]

---

[33] Ted Kyle and John Todd, *Bible Illustrations: A Treasury of Bible Illustrations* (Chattanooga, Tennessee: AMG Publishers, 1998), 242.

Chapter 9

I - Independence in a Teen

The most effective way that we as parents can develop independence in a young person is to teach them to be responsible for their actions. Responsibility is defined as "the state of being accountable or answerable, as for a trust or office, or for a debt. It is used in the plural; as heavy responsibilities."[34]

There is a story told about Mr. Brown who was a worker in a healthcare facility in the state of Georgia. Mr. Brown once worked in a hospital where a patient knocked over a cup of water, which spilled on the floor beside the patient's bed. The patient was afraid he might slip on the water if he got out of the bed, so he asked a nurse's aide to mop it up. The patient didn't know it, but the hospital policy said that small spills were the responsibility of the nurse's aides while large spills were to be mopped up by the hospital's housekeeping group.

The nurse's aide decided the spill was a large one, and she called the housekeeping department. A housekeeper arrived and declared the spill a small one. An argument followed.

It's not my responsibility," said the nurse's aide, "because it's a large puddle." The housekeeper did not agree. "Well, it's not mine," she said, "The puddle is too small."

The exasperated patient listened for a time, then took a pitcher of water from his night table and poured the whole thing on the floor. "Is

---

34 http://sorabji.com/1828/words/r/responsibility.html. Accessed on July 23, 2018.

that a big enough puddle now for you two to decide?" he asked. It was, and that was the end of the argument.[35]

<u>Teach Responsibility</u>

What was the problem? Neither person wanted to take responsibility to do the job. This is a growing problem that is found with the youth of America. We are raising a generation that has been "babied" and taught not to make decisions or take responsibility for their actions.

As a youth pastor, I have often used funny lawsuits in our society to add some humor at the beginning of a message, but what I am finding is that many of our parents will present the same silly deflecting excuse making when confronted with their teenager's problem. What can we do as parents, pastors, and youth pastors to work at overcoming this tragic trend?

When you look at Scripture, you find many instances where someone tried to shift the blame. We see the example of Adam in the book of Genesis.

> *And the LORD God called unto Adam, and said unto him, Where art thou? And he said, I heard thy voice in the garden, and I was afraid, because I was naked; and I hid myself. And he said, Who told thee that thou wast naked? Hast thou eaten of the tree, whereof I commanded thee that thou shouldest not eat? And the man said, The woman whom thou gavest to be with me, she gave me of the tree, and I did eat. And the LORD God said unto the woman, What is this that thou hast done? And the woman said, the serpent beguiled me, and I did eat. (Gen. 3:9–13)*

We see another example of shifting the blame in the life of Aaron in the book of Exodus.

---

[35] Fr. Mark Burger, *Falling Awake* (Morrisville, North Carolina: Lulu Publishing Services), 2015.

And it came to pass, as soon as he came nigh unto the camp, that he saw the calf, and the dancing: and Moses' anger waxed hot, and he cast the tables out of his hands, and brake them beneath the mount. And he took the calf which they had made, and burnt it in the fire, and ground it to powder, and strawed it upon the water, and made the children of Israel drink of it. And Moses said unto Aaron, What did this people unto thee, that thou hast brought so great a sin upon them? And Aaron said, let not the anger of my lord wax hot: thou knowest the people that they are set on mischief. For they said unto me, Make us gods, which shall go before us: for as for this Moses, the man that brought us up out of the land of Egypt, we wot not what is become of him. And I said unto them, whosoever hath any gold, let them break it ff. So they gave it me: then I cast it into the fire, and there came out this calf. (Exod. 32:19–24)

As stated, there are many other instances we could point to such as Eve, Cain, Joseph's brothers, King Saul; and this is just the start of the list in the Bible. We listed the previous examples because in both, you see that shifting the blame limited their spiritual life. As parents and leaders, we must start requiring personal responsibility.

There is a story of a college professor who had his class evaluate his course. One of his students wrote, "I think this is an excellent class, but I am concerned that the professor puts too much responsibility for learning on the students."[36]

We must stop letting folks make excuses. I have noticed that when dealing with a parent, they will readily admit how bad all the other teens are in the youth group and may even suggest restriction of contact for their teen with these other worldly teenagers. However, when you suggest that maybe their teenagers could be wrong or worldly, the conversation is over.

---

[36] Michael Hodgin, *1001 Humorous Illustrations for Public Speaking* (Grand Rapids, Michigan: Zondervan Publishing House, 1994). 131.

One of the most amazing examples of God's mercy is found in the life of David.

> *And David's anger was greatly kindled against the man; and he said to Nathan, As the LORD liveth, the man that hath done this thing shall surely die: And he shall restore the lamb fourfold, because he did this thing, and because he had no pity. And Nathan said to David, Thou art the man. Thus saith the LORD God of Israel, I anointed thee king over Israel, and I delivered thee out of the hand of Saul. And David said unto Nathan, I have sinned against the LORD. And Nathan said unto David, The LORD also hath put away thy sin; thou shalt not die. (II Sam. 12:5–7. 13)*

God blessed David because he was willing to take personal responsibility for his actions.

Daniel Webster was asked once what was the greatest concept that overwhelmed him. His answer was, "My greatest thought is my accountability to God."

R.G. Lee when asked "Can I be a Christian without joining the church?": replied, "Yes, it is as possible as being: A student who will not go to school. A soldier who will not join an army. A citizen who does not pay taxes or vote. A salesman with no customers. An explorer with no base camp. A seaman on a ship without a crew. A businessman on a deserted island. An author without readers. A tuba player without an orchestra. A parent without a family. A football player without a team. A politician who is a hermit. A scientist who does not share his findings. A bee without a hive."[37]

Irresponsibility breeds irresponsibility. We must not let our feelings get involved in the rearing of our young folks so that we try to give them everything. Make a young person learn to be dependable by having

---

[37] https://www.sermoncentral.com/sermons/christian-responsibility-jerry-flury-sermon-on-growth-in-christ-70987?ref=SermonSerps. Accessed on June 29, 2018.

some responsibility in the home, at school, and at his church. Then have someone else check up on this young person. I believe it is good to have others besides dad and mom to check up on the young person because they will learn that there are other authorities in life beside dad and mom.

Teach to Have Foresight

There is another aspect that we must think about in developing independence in young people. Parents and other authority figures need to teach responsibility, but then they need to work at teaching young people to have common sense and the ability to have foresight. "*A prudent man foreseeth the evil, and hideth himself: but the simple pass on, and are punished*" *(Prov. 22:3.* Common sense is not as common as people think. Children are not born with common sense. They must learn it by making mistakes or by witnessing the mistakes of others. It's difficult for an adult to teach common sense to a child; you may be more effective by creating opportunities for responding to incidents that allow the child to develop common sense.

Here are a few ways parents multiply a child's lack of common sense:

- Give him a big weekly allowance.

- Give him a brand-new car when, as a teenager, he turns sixteen.

- Protect him from the consequences of his bad decisions.

- Lay out all activities and choices so that they never have to make a decision.

One of the most familiar stories in the Bible is the parable of the prodigal son—about a young man who lacked common sense. The young man asked his father for his inheritance in advance, and the father gave him everything he desires. The prodigal then did what many young men with easy money would do: he squandered his wealth in wild living and wound up penniless.

I found this quote from an author who wrote a book in the 1950s. The author said the following: "The perfect bureaucrat everywhere is the man who manages to make no decisions and escape all responsibility." This sometimes is what we are doing with our young folks. They must learn to make a decision. They must learn that each decision has consequences and that they need to learn to weigh and foresee what the decision will ultimately lead to.

I read the story of a young man inherited a lot of money long before he was able to handle the consequences of it. He was a teenager living in Florida where he found some jewelry alongside a railroad track. An honest boy, he did the right thing and turned the jewels over to the police. After six months and several newspaper articles, no one claimed the prize, so the police gave the jewels back to the young man. They were valued at more than $1 million. This young man was living with his aunt, and she hired a lawyer to help manage the money, but as soon as he turned eighteen, he had complete legal control of his wealth.

A responsible adult wanted to try to help this young man and invited him to the opening of a new Chick-fil-A restaurant in his town. Afterward, the young man went to this adult's house to talk. As soon as he stepped inside, he lit a cigarette. The adult learned that evening that this young man was a high school dropout and that he had worked odd jobs around the neighborhood. Much of his newly found money was going for drugs. He already was beginning to realize the truth of his new situation. "I wish I hadn't found that jewelry," he told the man who was trying to help him. "Whenever I go out with friends, they expect me to pick up the tab for drinks and food." In other words, he was realizing the true value his friends placed in him.

Later, this young man's aunt said the money was "the worst thing that could have happened to him. I had him outside weed-eating grass one day, and the next-door neighbor called over, 'Why is a millionaire doing a job like that?'" The aunt had a hard time getting that boy to do any work after that.

The story does not end there. The same adult who tried to help this young man when he was a teenager was asked by relatives many years later to try to help. Now, however, twenty years had passed. After a twenty-year gap in time, this young man, who had been a millionaire, was broke. He had lost every tooth in his mouth, and at middle age, he looked like he was ready for a nursing home. Why did this modern story of a prodigal happen? He was given something and not taught to have common sense in handling decisions in life. We need to be careful of being "the fixer" for our young people, always trying to get them out of their messes. Sometimes, they need to learn that the mess they made must be lived with.[38]

We should help our young people to look ahead and see signs of trouble coming. A wise son or daughter starts to see signs that will help them to avoid wrong doing. I have noticed a positive trend when a young person is in a godly environment. These young people stay out of a lot of trouble because godly parents teach them to not be out late "partying." These young people are being taught to foresee trouble. When do most drunk driving accidents occur? When do most sexual misconducts occur? When do most fights or brawls occur—these occur at hours and places which promote limited self-control and promote self-gratification. Avoiding these types of institutions enable our young people to notice signs of evil and avoid the harm that is involved with that activity.

Teach to Make Wise Decisions

Let's look at one final stage to help our young people become independent. This stage is the idea of decision-making. Young people need guidance in learning to make wise decisions, and this comes by making some decisions on their own. This phase is hard because the parent will

---

[38] https://www.smp.org/dynamicmedia/files/d8782c894d37499e2a46239a0e114bd7/TX005786–2-K-A_ Modern_Parable_of_the_Prodigal_Son.pdf. Accessed on June 29, 2018.

want to fix the problem or stop the consequences of the bad decision when their young person makes some wrong decisions.

> *Yea doubtless, and I count all things but loss for the excellency of the knowledge of Christ Jesus my Lord: for whom I have suffered the loss of all things, and do count them but dung, that I may win Christ, And be found in him, not having mine own righteousness, which is of the law, but that which is through the faith of Christ, the righteousness which is of God by faith: That I may know him, and the power of his resurrection, and the fellowship of his sufferings, being made conformable unto his death; If by any means I might attain unto the resurrection of the dead. Not as though I had already attained, either were already perfect: but I follow after, if that I may apprehend that for which also I am apprehended of Christ Jesus. Brethren, I count not myself to have apprehended: but this one thing I do, forgetting those things which are behind, and reaching forth unto those things which are before, I press toward the mark for the prize of the high calling of God in Christ Jesus. (Phil. 3:8–14)*

The passage above helps a young person to find the correct direction when they are trying to spread their wings. They need to understand that they should be striving to better themselves in the knowledge of the Lord Jesus Christ. This should be every Christian's goal in life—to be more like our Savior. All decisions ultimately need to align with that goal. As parents and authority, we need to help our young people develop decision-making skills. When your young person needs to make a decision, you can help them develop skills by:

1. Presenting them with different options and letting them make a choice. I would not start out with life-and-death situations, but there are options

that all of us decide on daily, and a young person can start feeling the effects of simple decisions.

2. Taking some time to talk about the pros and cons of different actions once decisions are made. This will help them in the future to see that all decisions have consequences.

3. Teaching them how to weigh the pros and cons to make the best decision. This goes along with foreseeing the wrong path. There are indicators that we as authority figures and parents take for granted that a young person needs to be able to see before making decisions. Pausing and evaluating may seem archaic and not practical, but over time they will find the prudence in weighing decisions.

4. Helping them learn what brainstorming means. This is a fun exercise to do with ministry, family activities, and recreation; and you will find a host of other things that this exercise can be used for. Brainstorming is getting a few people together and throwing out ideas and talking about options vocally together.

5. Including your young person in family decision-making when possible. This is another chance to boost your child's decision-making skills and shows them that you value their input. I am not talking about whether to pay your mortgage or what vehicle should you buy. There are some decisions that are easy to include your young person's input and you will find that they have an opinion.

Many folks in authority seem to believe that the most important work in the training of a child or young person is to be always commanding and prohibiting. They are always telling a young person to do this or that, and not to do this or that. But this nagging of a young person is not training; on the contrary, it is destructive to the development of the decision-making mind of a young person. Don't be always "don't-ing," is a good instructive reminder to parents of young folks.

THE ROAD NOT TAKEN
by Robert Frost

Two roads diverged in a yellow wood
And sorry I could not travel both
And be one traveler, long I stood
And looked down one as far as I could
To where it bent in the undergrowth;

Then took the other, as just as fair,
And having perhaps the better claim,
Because it was grassy and wanted wear;
Though as for that the passing there
Had worn them really about the same,

And both that morning equally lay
In leaves no step had trodden black.
Oh, I kept the first for another day!
Yet knowing how way leads on to way,
I doubted if I should ever come back.

I shall be telling this with a sigh
Somewhere ages and ages hence:
Two roads diverged in a wood, and I—
I took the one less traveled by,
And that has made all the difference.

Chapter 10

J - Jealousy: The Evil of Envy

M urder. Grand theft. Rape. Jay walking. Drug trafficking. Pedophilia. Driving with a blinker out. As we read through the list, our minds begin to categorize these chargeable offenses as either "bad" or "not so bad." In our finite minds, murder and jay walking are not comparable crimes. Neither is drug trafficking compared to driving with a blinker out. In a similar fashion, Christians weigh various sins differently—fornication, envy, witchcraft, idolatry. Doesn't envy seem almost harmless compared to the other three? As Christians, we convince ourselves that some sins are not as offensive to God as other sins; however, we need to be reminded about God's view of sin.

Know ye not that the unrighteous shall not inherit the kingdom of God? Be not deceived: neither fornicators, nor idolaters, nor adulterers, nor effeminate, nor abusers of themselves with mankind, nor thieves, nor covetous, nor drunkards, nor revilers, nor extortioners, shall inherit the kingdom of God. And such were some of you: but ye are washed, but ye are sanctified, but ye are justified in the name of the Lord Jesus, and by the Spirit of our God. (I Cor. 6:9–11)

Now the works of the flesh are manifest, which are these; Adultery, fornication, uncleanness, lasciviousness, Idolatry, witchcraft, hatred, variance, emulations, wrath, strife, seditions, heresies, envyings, murders, drunkenness, revellings, and such like: of the which I tell you before, as I have also told you in time past, that they which do such things shall not inherit the kingdom of God. (Gal. 5:19–21)

But fornication, and all uncleanness, or covetousness, let it not be once named among you, as becometh saints; Neither filthiness, nor foolish talking, nor jesting, which are not convenient: but rather giving of thanks. For this ye know, that no whoremonger, nor unclean person, nor covetous man, who is an idolater, hath any inheritance in the kingdom of Christ and of God. (Eph. 5:3–5)

God looks at envy as a deep sin. Biblically, we can trace its evil influence even before the fall of man. It began with Lucifer, Son of the Morning, who was envious of the praise that was being directed to God. Lucifer was then able to lead other angelic beings in this envy. In addition, it was the sin of envy that caused our "first" parents to fall. The devil replaced their happiness with envy by tempting Eve, who then tempted Adam, who brought sin into the human race. Envy causes unhappiness. Because David was so popular and successful, it was envying that motivated Saul to want to murder him. It was envy that caused the scribes and pharisees to persecute Christ, have Him condemned, and finally have Him crucified on Calvary. Envy is an age-old sin that can lead us as finite humans into a spiral that will bear evil fruit in our lives.

In today's era, many may argue that envy is one of the "Seven Deadly Sins"; however, this phrase is not found in the Bible. There are lists of sins in the Bible, but never is the term "Seven Deadly Sins" used. This phrase was likely the creation of a Catholic church monk who lived around the fourth century AD, and the term was retained by the church's theologians starting in the Middle Ages (1913 Catholic Encyclopedia article on Sin). However, envy is a spiritual deadly sin.

A little snail that lived by the ocean noticed with envy the big, beautiful shell in which the lobster lived. "What a grand palace the lobster carries on his back! I wish I lived in his place," whined the little snail. "Oh, wouldn't my friends admire me in that shell!" In time, a wonderful thing occurred. The watching, envious snail beheld the lobster walk right out of his shell to grow up in another, larger one. When the empty lobster shell lay neglected on the beach the snail said, "Now I shall have my wish." And he boasted to all his friends that he was going to take up residence in a grand palace.

The birds and the animals then watched the snail pull himself loose from his own little shell and proudly crawl into the towering lobster shell. He huffed, puffed, blew, and gasped in an effort to make himself fit. But with all his efforts he felt very small inside the grand lobster shell. He grew tired too. That night he died because the large empty shell was so cold. A wise old crow then said to the younger crows, "You see! That's what comes of envy. What you have is enough. Be yourself and save yourself from a lot of trouble. How much better to be a little snail in a comfortable shell than to be a little snail in a big shell and freeze to death!"[39]

Envy and Jealousy Defined

EN'VY, verb transitive [Latin invideo, in and video, to see against, that is, to look with enmity.]

1. To feel uneasiness, mortification or discontent, at the sight of superior excellence, reputation or happiness enjoyed by another; to repine at another's prosperity; to fret or grieve one's self at the real or supposed superiority of another, and to hate him on that account.

2. To grudge; to withhold maliciously.

---

[39] Ted Kyle and John Todd, *Bible Illustrations: A Treasury of Bible Illustrations Book 2* (Chattanooga, TN: AMG Publishers, 1995), 312.

EN'VY, noun pain, uneasiness, mortification or discontent excited by the sight of another's superiority or success, accompanied with some degree of hatred or malignity, and often or usually with a desire or an effort to depreciate the person, and with pleasure in seeing him depressed. Envy springs from pride, ambition or love, mortified that another has obtained what one has a strong desire to possess.

1. Rivalry; competition. [Little used.]

2. Malice; malignity.

JEALOUS, adjective jel'us.

1. Suspicious; apprehensive of rivalship; uneasy through fear that another has withdrawn or may withdraw from one the affections of a person he loves or enjoy some good which he desires to obtain; followed by of, and applied both to the object of love and to the rival. We say, a young man is jealous of the woman he loves, or jealous of his rival. A man is jealous of his wife, and the wife of her husband.

2. Suspicious that we do not enjoy the affection or respect of others, or that another is more loved and respected than ourselves.

3. Emulous; full of competition.[40]

The Bible on These Subjects

1. **Jealousy**

---

[40] http://webstersdictionary1828.com/Dictionary/Envy. Accessed on December 27, 2018.

*"Thou shalt not bow down thyself to them, nor serve them: for I the LORD thy God am a **jealous** God, visiting the iniquity of the fathers upon the children unto the third and fourth generation of them that hate me." (Exod. 20:5)*

*"For thou shalt worship no other god: for the LORD, whose name is **Jealous**, is a **jealous** God." (Exod. 34:14)*

*"And the spirit of jealousy come upon him, and he be **jealous** of his wife, and she be defiled: or if the spirit of jealousy come upon him, and he be **jealous** of his wife, and she be not defiled." (Num. 5:14)*

*"Or when the spirit of jealousy cometh upon him, and he be **jealous** over his wife, and shall set the woman before the LORD, and the priest shall execute upon her all this law." (Num. 5:30)*

*"For the LORD thy God is a consuming fire, even a **jealous** God." (Deut. 4:24)*

*"Thou shalt not bow down thyself unto them, nor serve them: for I the LORD thy God am a **jealous** God, visiting the iniquity of the fathers upon the children unto the third and fourth generation of them that hate me." (Deut. 5:9)*

*"And Joshua said unto the people, Ye cannot serve the LORD: for he is an holy God; he is a **jealous** God; he will not forgive your transgressions nor your sins." (Josh. 24:19)*

*"Therefore thus saith the Lord GOD; Now will I bring again the captivity of Jacob, and have mercy upon the whole house of Israel, and will be **jealous** for my holy name." (Ezek. 39:25)*

*"God is **jealous**, and the LORD revengeth; the LORD revengeth, and is furious; the LORD will take vengeance on his adversaries, and he reserveth wrath for his enemies."* (Nah. 1:2)

*"For I am **jealous** over you with godly jealousy: for I have espoused you to one husband, that I may present you as a chaste virgin to Christ." (II Cor. 11:2)*

2. <u>**Envy**</u>

*For wrath killeth the foolish man, and **envy** slayeth the silly one." (Job 5:2)*

***Envy** thou not the oppressor, and choose none of his ways." (Prov. 3:31)*

*"A sound heart is the life of the flesh: but **envy** the rottenness of the bones." (Prov. 14:30)*

*"Let not thine heart **envy** sinners: but be thou in the fear of the LORD all the day long." (Prov. 23:17)*

*"Wrath is cruel, and anger is outrageous; but who is able to stand before **envy**?" (Prov. 27:4)*

*"Also their love, and their hatred, and their **envy**, is now perished; neither have they any more a portion for ever in any thing that is done under the sun." (Eccles. 9:6)*

*For he knew that for **envy** they had delivered him." (Matt. 27:18)*

*"And the patriarchs, moved with **envy**, sold Joseph into Egypt: but God was with him."* (Acts 7:9)

*"But when the Jews saw the multitudes, they were filled with **envy**, and spake against those things which were spoken by Paul, contradicting and blaspheming."* (Acts 13:45)

*"But the Jews which believed not, moved with **envy**, took unto them certain lewd fellows of the baser sort, and gathered a company, and set all the city on an uproar, and assaulted the house of Jason, and sought to bring them out to the people."* (Acts 17:5)

*"Being filled with all unrighteousness, fornication, wickedness, covetousness, maliciousness; full of **envy**, murder, debate, deceit, malignity; whisperers;"* (Rom. 1:29)

*"Some indeed preach Christ even of **envy** and strife; and some also of good will."* (Phil. 1:15)

*"He is proud, knowing nothing, but doting about questions and strifes of words, whereof cometh **envy**, strife, railings, evil surmisings,"* (I Tim. 6:4)

*"For we ourselves also were sometimes foolish, disobedient, deceived, serving divers lusts and pleasures, living in malice and **envy**, hateful, and hating one another;"* (Titus 3:3)

*"Do ye think that the scripture saith in vain, The spirit that dwelleth in us lusteth to **envy**?"* (James 4:5)

As you can see, the Bible has much to say on this subject. Biblically, you will not find that the word *jealousy* is used in a bad light. It seems as if jealousy comes when something that is rightfully ours is taken away or given to someone else (God's right to demand worship, the husbands right to be jealous of his wife, etc.). Over time in our culture, we have intertwined the idea of jealousy and envy. The definitions are almost identical when we are considering the modern idea of jealousy and that of envy. Here is an explanation that may help in differentiating between the two.

They differ in the fact that jealousy consists of an excessive love of one's own good accompanied by the fear of being deprived of it by others. A top-ranked student, for example, upon noticing the progress of another student, may become jealous of him because he fears the latter will take away his rank. Jealousy often abounds among professionals, among writers, and even among priests. The essential difference between envy and jealousy is this: we are envious of another's good, and jealous of our own.[41]

In this study, we are going to consider the concept of envy. Many would believe this to be a study of jealousy; but as I have analyzed the Scripture, most instances of what we would label as jealousy is simply selfishness or a non-giving spirit. The Bible deals with this many times but does not necessarily call it jealousy.

There was an ambitious young student that was in attendance at Stanford University. While attending, he was given the opportunity to go visit the Far East one summer. While there, he came to meet a group of Buddhists. The group encouraged him to change. They said that he was ambitious, and that this ambitious lifestyle would be the ruin of him. They told him that he studied hard, but not to learn, but only to get better grades than his friends. He worked very hard, but not to better society, but only to purchase more than his peers. He dated the most beautiful ladies, not to find true love, but only to be seen with the most admired woman. The young man came to grips with this realization internally and admitted that all of this was true. From Tokyo, he called his parents and told them he was dropping out of school and entering a Buddhist monastery. Six months later, his parents received the following letter:

---

[41] http://www.pravdareport.com/history/01–08–2012/121809-envy-0/. Accessed on November 27, 2018.

"Dear Dad and Mom,

I know you weren't happy with my decision to stay here, but I want to tell you how happy I am with my decision to stay. I am at peace for the first time in my life, living in an environment without competition or envy. Here, we all share, and life is equal. This way of life is so much in harmony with the inner essence of my soul that in six months I've become the Number Two Disciple in the monastery, and I think I can be Number One by June."[42]

Principles Drawn from Study

According to Exodus 34, God is called Jealous. What does this mean?

For the Lord whose name is Jealous, is a jealous God; his name and nature answer to one another; he admits of no rival or competitor in worship; he will not give his glory to another god, or one so called, nor his praise to graven images; and in this he is distinguished from all nominal and fictitious gods, who have many joined with them, and are rivals of them, which gives them no concern, because insensible; but it is otherwise with the Lord, who knows the dishonor done him, and resents it, and is as jealous of any worship being given to another, as the husband is of the honor of his marriage bed; for idolatry is spiritual adultery, as is suggested in the following verse.[43]

The book of Proverbs deals heavily with wisdom for youth. Repeatedly, there is an emphasis to a young person to not be envious of the wicked.

---

[42] Robert Morgan, *Preacher's Sourcebook of Creative Sermon Illustrations* (Nashville, TN: Thomas Nelson Publishers, 2007), 273.

[43] https://www.biblestudytools.com/commentaries/gills-exposition-of-the-bible/exodus-34-14.html.

This is seen in Proverbs 3, 23, and 24. We also see David mentioning this plight for the righteous in Psalm 37 and 73.

> *Fret not thyself because of evildoers, neither be thou* **envious** *against the workers of iniquity."* (Ps. 37:1)

> *For I was* **envious** *at the foolish, when I saw the prosperity of the wicked."* (Ps. 73:3).

> **Envy** *thou not the oppressor, and choose none of his ways."* (Prov. 3:31)

> *Let not thine heart* **envy** *sinners: but be thou in the fear of the LORD all the day long."* (Prov. 23:17)

> *Be not thou* **envious** *against evil men, neither desire to be with them."* (Prov. 24:1)

> *"Fret not thyself because of evil men, neither be thou* **envious** *at the wicked."* (Prov. 24:19)

The plea is simple. There will be a longing in the soul of the believer to see the prosperity and success that seems to come from living wickedly in this temporal world. There are numerous historical examples.

> The Roman Empire—All one has to do is pick up a simple history book regarding this time period, and they will be disgusted with the vulgarity, immorality, and the complete infatuation with gross violence; yet it seems that the worse that the Roman oligarchs became, the more money they seemed to garner into their coffers. Historically, though, do you really think that now? Is there not an amazing justice that seems to come to all of these evil leaders?

Emperor Nero—Nero was born in 37 A.D., the nephew of the emperor. After his father's death, his mother married his great uncle, Claudius, and persuaded him to name Nero his successor. Nero took the throne at 17, rebuffed his mother's attempts to control him, and had her killed. He spent lavishly and behaved inappropriately. He began executing opponents and Christians. In 68, he committed suicide when the empire revolted.[44]

Vladimir Lenin—Vladimir Lenin founded the Russian Communist Party, led the Bolshevik Revolution and was the architect of the Soviet state. He was the posthumous source of "Leninism," the doctrine codified and conjoined with Marx's works by Lenin's successors to form Marxism-Leninism which became the Communist worldview. He has been regarded as the greatest revolutionary leader and thinker since Marx. In late 1917, Lenin led what was soon to be known as the October Revolution but was essentially a coup d'état. Three years of civil war followed. The Lenin-led Soviet government faced incredible odds. The anti-Soviet forces, or Whites, headed mainly by former tsarist generals and admirals, fought desperately to overthrow Lenin's Red regime. They were aided by World War I Allies who supplied the group with money and troops, but the Russia he presided over was reeling from the bloody civil war he'd helped instigate. Famine and poverty shaped much of society. In 1921, Lenin now faced the same kind of peasant uprising he'd ridden to power. From May 1922 to March 1923, he suffered three strokes which resulted in his death.[45]

Hitler—With millions unemployed, the Great Depression in Germany provided a political opportunity for Hitler. Germans were ambivalent to the parliamentary republic and increasingly

---

[44] https://www.biography.com/people/nero-9421713. Accessed on November 27, 2018.

[45] https://www.biography.com/people/vladimir-lenin-9379007. Accessed on November 27, 2018.

open to extremist options. Adolf Hitler was chancellor of Germany from 1933 to 1945, serving as dictator and leader of the Nazi Party, or National Socialist German Workers Party, for the bulk of his time in power. Hitler's policies precipitated World War II and led to the genocide known as the Holocaust which resulted in the deaths of some six million Jews and another five million non-combatants. With defeat on the horizon, Hitler committed suicide with wife Eva Braun on April 30, 1945, in his Berlin bunker.[46]

Consider the wicked entertainment industry. Their laughing and joyful appearances seem to lure our youth into immoral and debauched lifestyles. What is the plight of these entertainers? Let's list a few examples.

Marilyn Monroe—Monroe's death caused a lot of controversy in the media, not just because of her celebrity status, but because of her curious relationship with President John F. Kennedy. Her death was ruled a suicide by drug overdose. Many thought she was going to go public about an alleged affair with JFK which would give someone the motive to silence her. The actress and model was only 36 when she passed away.

Bob Crane—Bob Crane was an actor and a drummer who was brutally murdered with an electrical cord tied around his neck in 1978 in his Arizona apartment. The main suspect was Crane's friend John Henry Carpenter who had flown out to Arizona to spend time with the actor just days before his death. Smears of Crane's blood were found inside Carpenter's rental car. Carpenter was acquitted in trial, and Cranes' murder still remains unsolved.

---

[46] https://www.biography.com/people/adolf-hitler-9340144. accessed on November 27, 2018.

Tupac Shaku—Tupac's death still reigns as one of the most controversial celebrity deaths in history, simply because no one was ever charged for his murder. Tupac was shot four times while sitting in his car at a red light in Las Vegas in 1996. A rival gang member named Orlando Anderson was the primary suspect, but the police only questioned him once. The rapper was only 25 years old when he died.

David Carradine—Known for his iconic roles in Kung Fu and Kill Bill, Carradine was found dead in his hotel in Bangkok in 2009. A hotel maid found him with a noose around his neck. Police deemed it an obvious suicide case. Later, a private autopsy was done that showed he died from asphyxiation, ruling out suicide, but his murder was never solved.

Phil Hartman—The Saturday Night Live comedian was shot in 1998 by his wife, Brynn Hartman. Phil and his wife had argued over her drug problems which had been a common problem between the couple. Phil went to bed and soon after, Brynn followed him then shot him twice in the head and once on the side of his body. She then locked herself in a room as police arrived and shot herself.[47]

The lists could go on, but the end of the lives of these famous historical and Hollywood figures should help us to understand that we need to be careful in allowing envy to creep into our souls for the prosperity of the wicked. We must continually seek the Lord's guidance through Scripture to help us understand that evil does not ultimately triumph.

---

[47] https://twentytwowords.com/haunting-and-mysterious-hollywood-deaths/. Accessed on November 28, 2018.

1. **The Bible indicates that envy can lead a person into dangerous territory.**

   Envy made Joseph's brothers sell him into bondage. Envy led King Saul to hate David so much that he wanted to kill him and chased him into the wilderness. Because of envy, King Saul ended up despising his own son's achievements. Envy led the Jewish religious leaders to kill our Savior according to Matthew 27.

2. **There can be physical problems with the body because of the effects of envy.**

   Consider what Charles Bridges, the classic commentary on Proverbs says regarding envy being the rottenness of the bones.

   The wise man teaches that wisdom is the life of the flesh. (Chap. iii. 7, 8.) And surely a sound heart, freed from corroding passions, and imbued with Christian habits, though it will not bring immortality, must be eminently conducive to health.† The contrast, however, here distinguishes a sound heart by the absence of selfishness,‡ and rejoicing in another's happiness or honor. (Num. xi. 29.) Envy, on the other hand, is wounded by our neighbor's prosperity. (Gen. xxvi. 14.1 Sam. xviii. 9.) His ruin, or at least his injury, would give pleasure. It sickens at hearing of his praises, and repines at his very virtues. Something is always wrong in his conduct, something at least, which, if it does not deserve blame, greatly detracts from his intolerable praise. This evil is indeed the deadliest fruit of selfishness. Nothing flourishes under its shade.[48]

---

[48] https://faculty.gordon.edu/hu/bi/ted_hildebrandt/otesources/20-proverbs/text/books/bridges-proverbscommentary/bridges-proverbs.pdf. Accessed on November 27, 2018.

3. There is an escalation that envy allows that can lead to horrible sins of the flesh.

Again, Charles Bridges expresses the evil of envy in his comments on Proverbs 27:4.

Well then might it be asked—Who is able to stand before envy? Even the perfect innocence of paradise fell before it. Satan lost his own happiness. Then he envied man, and ceased not to work his destruction. (See Wis. ii. 23, 24.) It shed the first human blood that ever stained the ground. (1 John; iii. 12.) It quenched the yearnings of natural affection, and brought bitter sorrow to the patriarch's bosom1 Even the premier of the greatest empire in the world was its temporary victim.2 Nay more—the Savior in his most benevolent acts was sorely harassed, 3 and ultimately sunk under its power.4 "His servants therefore must not expect to be above their Master." The good that a person is doing can be done out of a heart of envy.

Traits That Will Develop in the Envious Heart

We find these traits expressed to us in the actions of those that acted upon their envy in the pages of Scripture.

1. Self-Importance

The very first act of envy was when Satan desired the praise that was designated for God alone. This in turn caused Satan to stir up a rebellion against heaven itself. There is an important characteristic that can be seen from this mutiny. The envious person will even feel invincibility against God Himself.

2. <u>Family Hatred</u>

The book of Acts records for us that it was envy that drove Joseph's brothers to sell him into slavery. Genesis tells us the account of how Rachel was envious of her sister's ability to bear children and cried out to the Lord. This evil of envy will be seen by our children if it is present in our home and may be duplicated if we are not careful.

3. <u>Selfishness</u>

Selfishness is one of the many roots that spread from the evil tree of envy and jealousy. We must learn to crucify this old Adamic flesh that wants to have the preeminence. It should never be a joy to see either a friend or enemy go through hardship. We must learn to have the spirit of Christ in us.

4. <u>Covetousness</u>

Thou shalt not covet thy neighbor's house, thou shalt not covet thy neighbor's wife, nor his manservant, nor his maidservant, nor his ox, nor his ass, nor any thing that is thy neighbor's" *(Exod. 20:17)*

Thou shalt not covet" is one of the Ten Commandments. Consider these three areas where envy could creep into our lives:

Personal Possessions—*"Thou shalt not covet thy neighbor's house."* If we are not careful, the seed of envy may be cultivated if we become disgruntled with what God has given others. If we are envious of other's possessions, we cannot be satisfied with our own. We may begin to question God and His ability to provide for us.

Personal Relationships—*"Thou shalt not covet they neighbor's wife."* How often have we looked enviously at someone else's family? Maybe we look at someone and ask God, "Why don't I have a wife as beautiful as him?," "Why do they get to have those children?" or "Why do they get to get married, and I don't?" Be careful of the spirit of envy! It is deadly and can lead to discontentment.

Personal Achievements—Achievement can be found in the phrase, *"nor his manservants, nor his maidservants, nor his ox, nor his ass (donkey.)"* Maybe this man had been able to achieve a status that many of us may not ever be able to reach. This could be in notoriety or position within a business or church. Envy may cause us to stop considering the goodness of God in our lives and start to believe that God is not being fair to us because of what others around us are able to achieve.

How Does One Overcome Envy and Jealousy

A great example in the Old Testament is that of Joseph. This story is an amazing tribute to a man who stayed true to God and did not yield to the sin of envy. One will not find a negative statement about Joseph in the Bible. He is an Old Testament type of Christ. Joseph is an example of one who had been dealt all the wrong this world could afford, yet he still trusted in a loving God that had a plan and purpose for his life.

The New Testament reveal to us the root sins that surround envy.

> *This I say then, Walk in the Spirit, and ye shall not fulfil the lust of the flesh. For the flesh lusteth against the Spirit, and the Spirit against the flesh: and these are contrary the one to the other: so that ye cannot do the things that ye would. But if ye be led of the Spirit, ye are not under the law. Now the works of the flesh are manifest, which are these; Adultery, fornication, uncleanness, lasciviousness, Idolatry, witchcraft, hatred, variance, emulations, wrath, strife, seditions, heresies, envyings, murders, drunkenness, revellings, and such like: of the which I tell you before, as I have also told you in time past, that they which do such things shall not inherit the kingdom of God. But the fruit of the Spirit is love, joy, peace, longsuffering, gentleness, goodness, faith, meekness, temperance: against such there is no law. And they that are Christ's*

have crucified the flesh with the affections and lusts. If we live in the Spirit, let us also walk in the Spirit. Let us not be desirous of vain glory, provoking one another, envying one another. (Gal. 5:16–26)

This I say therefore, and testify in the Lord, that ye henceforth walk not as other Gentiles walk, in the vanity of their mind, Having the understanding darkened, being alienated from the life of God through the ignorance that is in them, because of the blindness of their heart: Who being past feeling have given themselves over unto lasciviousness, to work all uncleanness with greediness. But ye have not so learned Christ; If so be that ye have heard him, and have been taught by him, as the truth is in Jesus: That ye put off concerning the former conversation the old man, which is corrupt according to the deceitful lusts; And be renewed in the spirit of your mind; And that ye put on the new man, which after God is created in righteousness and true holiness. (Eph. 4:17–24)

How do we remove the wicked sin of envy from our hearts? According to Galatians 5, the first thing we must learn to do is walk in the Spirit. If we are walking in the Spirit, it will be evidenced by some distinct characteristics. This same passage tells us that a believer must be active in "crucifying the flesh." This may seem almost barbaric and "cultic" in one sense, but what does it actually mean? Those listed sins of the flesh must be always crucified. Physically, a man will die if starved. So, starve those sinful traits. Don't give in to feeding them in any way. Don't allow your righteous soul to be vexed by continually subjecting yourself to wrong behavior—be it where you go, what you watch, or what you listen to. Don't allow any satisfaction of your flesh.

According to Ephesians 4, a believer must work at changing his mind. The passage in Ephesians 4 says that the sinful man walks in the vanity of his mind. A believer must learn to renew his mind. We are also told that a believer must put on the new man.

In Romans 12, we are told to develop a biblical love for the brethren. One way to defeat envy is to develop the biblical attitude of charity. The apostle Paul said, *"Rejoice with those who rejoice, weep with those who weep" (Rom. 12:15).* The person who is filled with envy tends to do just the opposite: He is saddened by another's good fortune and rejoices at his failure. This attitude is a contradiction of the Christian spirit that should be a part of the regenerated heart. In both envy and jealousy, love of neighbor is displaced by love of possessions, whether the possessions be tangible, such as money, houses, vehicles, and clothing, or intangible such as fame, talent, and position.

As we close out this study on the sin of envy, let's review some of the horrific results of envy found throughout Scripture.

1. The downfall of the human race was the result of Satan's envy.

2. Cain killed his brother Abel because of envy since the Lord looked favorably on Abel's sacrifice but not on his own (Gen. 4:3–8).

3. Joseph was sold into slavery by his brothers who were envious of the affection given to him by his father (Gen. 37:28).

4. Moses's sister Miriam was struck with leprosy because she was envious of the fact that God spoke through Moses and not through her and Aaron (Num. 12:2, 9).

5. King Saul became envious of the praise given to David as the giant killer, and King Saul tried to kill him (I Sam. 18:6–11).

6. Because of envy, the attendants of King Darius encouraged him to order Daniel to be thrown into the den of lions (Dan. 6:3f).

7. Pilate perceived that it was because of envy that the members of the Sanhedrin were seeking Christ's death (Matt. 27:18; Mark 15:10).

Henry Varley is the well-known man who said to D. L. Moody, "The world has yet to see what God will do with a man who is fully committed to him." That statement challenged Moody and he made it his life's motto. Ultimately, he did shake the world for Christ.

What is not so well known about Henry Varley is that he was a renowned evangelist and pastor himself. In the biography about Henry Varley's life, the author talks about a struggle that Pastor Varley had with another pastor in his area. The other pastor began to gain some of Varley's church members and envy welled up in his heart. Pastor Varley wrote in his own words how he dealt with it.

> I shall never forget the sense of guilt and sin that possessed me over that business. I was miserable. Was I practically saying to the Lord, "Unless the prosperity of Thy church and thy people come in this neighborhood by me, success had better not come"? Was I really showing inability to rejoice in another worker's service? I felt that it was a sin of a very hateful character. I asked the Lord to resolve this in my heart before I went to heaven and by his grace give me victory over this foul enemy of envy.[49]

We need to be wary of the sin of envy that will turn God's goodness in our lives into a lack of contentment. The devil is a master at making us discontent with what God has given us and letting us think that God is somehow slighting us by not giving us more and more.

---

[49] Robert Morgan, *Preacher's Sourcebook of Creative Sermon Illustrations* (Nashville, TN: Thomas Nelson Publishers, 2007), 272.

Chapter 11

K - Kindness

For I say, through the grace given unto me, to every man that is among you, not to think of himself more highly than he ought to think; but to think soberly, according as God hath dealt to every man the measure of faith." (Rom. 12:3)

Be kindly affectioned one to another with brotherly love; in honor preferring one another." (Rom. 12:10)

If it be possible, as much as lieth in you, live peaceably with all men." (Rom. 12:18)

One day, a great lion lay asleep in the sunshine. A little mouse ran across his paw and awakened him. The great lion was just going to eat him when the little mouse cried, "Oh, please, let me go, sir. Someday I may help you." The lion laughed at the thought that the little mouse could be of any use to him. But he was a good-natured lion, and he set the mouse free.

Not long after, the lion was caught in a net. He tugged and pulled with all his might, but the ropes were too strong. Then he roared loudly. The little mouse heard him and ran to the spot. "Be still, dear lion, and I will set you free. I will gnaw the ropes." With his sharp teeth, the mouse cut the ropes, and the lion came out of the net.

You laughed at me once," said the mouse, "You thought I was too little to do you a good turn. But see, you owe your life to a poor little mouse."[50]

I share this story to illustrate that there is a measure of kindness that even the mighty, which seemingly need nothing, should show. We that hold to the mighty Scriptures need to apply this teaching of kindness in our ministries.

The Bible has much to say about kindness, generosity, and caring. The following passages deal with kindness in a believer's life:

- Leviticus 19:34

- Psalm 85:10

- Proverbs 3:3–4

- Proverbs 11:17

- Proverbs 14:21–22

- Matthew 5:7, 42

- Matthew 25:34–36

- Acts 20:35

- Romans 12

- Romans 15:1

- I Corinthians 13

- Galatians 6:10

---

[50] William J. Bennett, *The Book of Virtues: A Treasury of Great Moral Stories* (New York, NY: Simon & Schuster, 1993), 110.

As you can see, numerous passages discuss kindness. As Christians, we should be exemplary in spreading abroad the love of God to those who have not been saved, but we should also be especially kind to our fellow brothers and sisters in Christ. This can be hard for a teenager. They do not look at their peers and think they need to apply kindness to them. Galatians 6:10 says that we should especially show love to those who are of the "household of faith." It is true and good that the elderly need kindness shown to them, but it is also true that teens need kindness shown to them as well. As those that guide the lives of young people, we must be clear to help them understand a biblical definition of kindness. They need to see kindness from us toward them.

Let's consider the entire twelfth chapter of Romans to gain specific instruction for developing kindness.

Let the Lord Transform Your Mind

I beseech you therefore, brethren, by the mercies of God, that ye present your bodies a living sacrifice, holy, acceptable unto God, which is your reasonable service. And be not conformed to this world: but be ye transformed by the renewing of your mind, that ye may prove what is that good, and acceptable, and perfect, will of God (Rom. 12:1–2).

Transformation is changing from the "old way" of doing things. The old nature is concerned primarily with self-gratification. It is not shocking when an unsaved person wants to cheat, push down, and connive to get ahead of others. However, once someone gets saved, this old nature should become a thing of the past. The new nature takes charge. The Spirit of God has liberty in a believer's life by residing within. This process of transformation will only come as we surrender ourselves to the Spirit's leading. The old man will not surrender to the Spirit. Romans 12:1 instructs the believer to place himself at the mercy of the Holy Spirit and let the process of transformation begin.

Realize the Source of Your Gifts

For I say, through the grace given unto me, to every man that is among you, not to think of himself more highly than he ought to think; but to think soberly, according as God hath dealt to every man the measure of faith. For as we have many members in one body, and all members have not the same office: so we, being many, are one body in Christ, and every one members one of another. Having then gifts differing according to the grace that is given to us, whether prophecy, let us prophesy according to the proportion of faith; or ministry, let us wait on our ministering: or he that teacheth, on teaching; or he that exhorteth, on exhortation: he that giveth, let him do it with simplicity; he that ruleth, with diligence; he that sheweth mercy, with cheerfulness. (Rom. 12:3–8)

Commentator John Gill provided some interesting thoughts on this passage. Consider his statements:

"Not to think of himself more highly: that is, either not to arrogate to himself what does not belong to him, and detract from others, who may have equal, if not superior, abilities to him; or not to glory in what he has, as if he had not received it, and as if it was altogether owing to his own sagacity, penetration, diligence, and industry.

But to think soberly, according as God hath dealt to every man the measure of faith: such ought to consider that what gifts, abilities, light, and knowledge they have, they have then, not of themselves, but from God."[51]

When we understand that God has given us the gifts we have, it is then hard to take credit for achievements and accolades bestowed on us. The worldly person lives for himself; so even his acts of kindness are an attempt to gain some type of favor or recognition. Our purpose as Christians is to bring glory to God. We have been given gifts to use for God's glory, not our own. This mentality will also help us to better appreciate our fellow brethren. By gaining the right perspective of our God-given gifts, we will have the right opinion of ourselves. Not thinking too highly of us is indicative of godly humility which portrays the Spirit of Christ. Knowing from whom our gifts are given helps us to keep our pride in check. Remembering that God is the giver of the gifts helps us to love our fellow brethren. How? By understanding that God in His wisdom has given to each member of the body of Christ differing gifts within each local church so that we can accomplish His will and bring glory to our Savior. Understanding that one will have a gift that differs from another helps us to appreciate their gifts and not be envious of them.

Develop a Genuine Love for Others

"Let love be without dissimulation. Abhor that which is evil; cleave to that which is good" (Rom. 12:9). The phrase, "without dissimulation" means "without hypocrisy" or "having a genuine love." Alexander Maclaren says the following about having genuine love:

> It means, hiding what one is; but there is simulation, or pretending to be what one is not. There are words of love which are like the iridescent scum on the surface veiling the black depths of a pool of hatred. A Psalmist complains

---

[51] https://www.biblestudytools.com/commentaries/gills-exposition-of-the-bible/romans-12–3.html. Accessed on June 29, 2018.

of having to meet men whose words were "smoother than butter" and whose true feelings were as "drawn swords"; but, short of such consciously lying love, we must all recognize as a real danger besetting us all, and especially those of us who are naturally inclined to kindly relations with our fellows, the tendency to use language just a little in excess of our feelings. The glove is slightly stretched, and the hand in it is not quite large enough to fill it. There is such a thing, not altogether unknown in Christian circles, as benevolence, which is largely cant, and words of conventional love about individuals which do not represent any corresponding emotion. Such effusive love pours itself in words, and is most generally the token of intense selfishness. Any man who seeks to make his words a true picture of his emotions must be aware that few harder precepts have ever been given than this brief one of the Apostle's, "Let love be without hypocrisy."[52]

Developing a kind heart is a process for the believer. It does not come naturally. Our natural man is self-centered, egotistical, and vengeful toward others. We, in our natural state, tend toward those that have similar ideas as we do. They bolster us; however, when someone opposes our ideas, we tend to malign and denigrate "their ideas." The new man works to transform his mind, surrenders to the leading of the Spirit, understands that God gives differing gifts, and then works at developing genuineness. Genuineness (some may call it transparency) is a characteristic that must be developed all through one's life. Many folks are scared to let others see who they really are because they may find flaws. This is silly because there are no "perfect" people. We all have flaws. Having transparency helps a person to feel comfortable among others.

---

[52] Alexander MacLaren, *Expositions of Holy Scripture: The Acts* (Grand Rapids, Michigan: Baker Book House, 2014), 262.

This passage is not teaching to be a flatterer. Flattery is not kindness. *"He that rebuketh a man afterwards shall find more favour than he that flattereth with the tongue" (Prov. 28:23),* and *"A man that flattereth his neighbour spreadeth a net for his feet" (Prov. 29:5).* These verses demonstrate that the use of flattery is not kindness. A flatterer is self-serving. The only reason that someone uses flattery is to gain something for themselves, not to prefer someone above himself.

Christians should develop proper decorum. We should not be "a loudmouth," rude, uncouth, or vulgar. We should have a "filter." But it is refreshing when you can sit down with someone that is not "prickly." They make you relax, and you have a true sense that this person is genuine. A believer will have to work at this because we, like the Pharisees, want to have an air of superiority—an air of righteousness.

I would like us to consider two words as we look at this idea of hating evil and loving good. The first is the word *abhor*; it is a verb meaning "to have an intense dislike." This is the only time it is used in the New Testament. It is in the present tense which means that it is an ongoing action. Abhorring that which is evil must be at the forefront of daily life. Another word in the text is *cleave.* This same idea appears in I Corinthians 6 where the Bible says, "But he that is joined unto the Lord is one spirit."[53]

These two words (abhor and cleave) provide instruction as we pursue kindness. A Christian must have a disdain for evil. This disdain is an intense dislike. Evil must not be tolerated in our lives, and we must seek to rid our lives of its influence. To help us in the right hatred of evil, we are to cleave to that which is good. The word cleaving gives the idea of "super glue." We are attached to truth and righteousness with a bond that cannot be separated. This attachment to that which is good will make the evil that we are active in abhorring unable to get hold of our lives.

---

[53] Kenneth S. Wuest, *Wuest Word Studies: Volume One* (Grand Rapids, Michigan: Wm. B. Eerdmans Publishing Company, 1973), 213.

Develop good, godly habits that emulate loving good

Be kindly affectioned one to another with brotherly love; in honor preferring one another; not slothful in business; fervent in spirit; serving the Lord; rejoicing in hope; patient in tribulation; continuing instant in prayer; distributing to the necessity of saints; given to hospitality. Bless them which persecute you: bless, and curse not. Rejoice with them that do rejoice, and weep with them that weep. Be of the same mind one toward another. Mind not high things, but condescend to men of low estate. Be not wise in your own conceits. (Rom. 12:10–16)

Notice that this is a list of commands: be kindly affectioned; prefer one another; be fervent in spirit; be patient; be constant in prayer. Yes, we need to work to develop goodness in our lives. Kindness causes us to prefer others over ourselves. Acting in kindness is against anyone's nature, but especially a teen's natural behavior. Serving others, rejoicing in other's achievements, praying for others, giving to those in need, and sharing should be amplified in our lives and taught to those in our ministry or home.

Avoid the Dangerous Trap of Revenge

If it be possible, as much as lieth in you, live peaceably with all men. Dearly beloved, avenge not yourselves, but rather give place unto wrath: for it is written, Vengeance is mine; I will repay, saith the Lord. Therefore if thine enemy hunger, feed him; if he thirst, give him drink: for in so doing thou shalt heap coals of fire on his head. Be not overcome of evil, but overcome evil with good. (Rom. 12:17–21)

One man said it this way, "Revenge is a cruel word: manhood, some call it; but it is rather doghood. The manlier any man is, the milder and more merciful, as Julius Caesar, who, when he had Pompey's head presented to him, wept, and said, 'I seek not revenge, but victory.'"[54] Why would so much energy be put into the ruin of another? It sometimes might seem absurd to a person to see so much energy put into the tearing down of another, but we all seem to enjoy the toppling of a dynasty or a top-tier athlete, and the like. There is a built-in envy in our natural man that does not like for another human to gain notoriety above what we are able to achieve. Add to this natural tendency someone who is maligning and opposing us, and you have a very strong motive for revenge.

Revenge and hate are very popular rhetoric today in America. Everyone is supposed to have a cause to fight for, and those that have been slighted somehow by somebody should gain a following and march. However, this passage has been building toward our having a right mindset toward our fellow brethren in Christ. What is this mindset? Lay yourself and your ambitions at the foot of the Savior, realize that God is the giver of talents and gifts, work at developing an unfeigned love for others, strive to hate evil and love right, and then leave "getting back at someone" to God. God knows what has happened to you. Maybe He has a lesson for you to learn through the disappointment and hurt. Don't let the devil use outside circumstances that someone else is bringing into your life to gain an entrance into your heart.

Some think that speaking the truth is not kind. This is a worldly philosophy. The truth many times does hurt. We must be careful to speak kindly, but truthfully. Paul was a great example of not backing down from the truth, but also, not speaking it unkindly.

But he said, I am not mad, most noble Festus; but speak forth the words of truth and soberness. (Acts 26:25)

---

[54] Joseph S. Exell, *The Biblical Illustrator: Romans* (Grand Rapids, Michigan: Baker Book House, 1977), 544.

*Whereunto I am ordained a preacher, and an apostle, (I speak
the truth in Christ, and lie not;) a teacher of the Gentiles in
faith and verity. (I Tim. 2:7)*

The apostle Paul spoke the truth in love. He knew that he had to
present the gospel and knew that it might be offensive. There are times
when what you say may be offensive in its nature because the Word of
God is convicting. However, we need to be sure that our words are not
offensive because of our own carnal tendencies. Analyze your life to see
if your life clearly reveals the kindness that the Bible indicates should be
in a believer's life.

*But speaking the truth in love, may grow up into him in all
things, which is the head, even Christ: from whom the whole
body fitly joined together and compacted by that which
every joint supplieth, according to the effectual working in
the measure of every part, maketh increase of the body unto
the edifying of itself in love. (Eph. 4:15–16)*

Alexander Maclaren said, "Kindness does not require us to be blind
to facts or to live in fancies, but it does require us to cherish a habit of
goodwill, ready to show pity if sorrow appears, and slow to turn away
even if hostility appears."[55]

As we guide young people into spiritual maturity, don't forget the
godly grace of kindness. No, it is not compromise to be nice to someone.
It is evidence of the Spirit-filled life. We should teach a young person the
guidelines and right perspective so that compromise on biblical issues is
not developed. However, Christ told the disciples the world would see a
difference in their lives, and He seemed to indicate that the world might
even want their brand of Christianity. When? When they showed love
one toward another.

[55] https://www.christianquotes.info/quotes-by-author/alexander-maclaren-quotes/. Accessed on
July 23, 2018.

Chapter 12

L - Laziness

W"*ork*" is a sore subject with some people! The book of Proverbs has much valuable teaching on the issue of work from which we can glean life-changing truths. Work is an important part of all our lives. We will all deal with it because God has created us to work. It is imperative for all of us who deal with youth to present a biblical understanding of work. It is not uncommon for men to work today without really working. This may sound silly, but we have unionized and regulated the workplace to the point that there is little efficiency and no real satisfaction in a job well done. Some workers are tempted to do the least amount of work because it is acceptable. A biblical worker has a different calling and answers ultimately to God.

God puts His heart into His work. He doesn't finish things just to get them done. He commands us to do the same, *"And whatsoever ye do, do it heartily, as to the Lord, and not unto men;" (Col. 3:23).* His energy and creativity are without measure. This overflows into everything He does. Drudgery and bare minimums have no part in His work. Whatever He makes is not only useful but also beautiful and fascinating.[56]

These thoughts are vital in helping a young person understand that God is concerned with their work ethic. Let's contemplate the deep fulfillment that can be found in work.

---

[56] Bob Schultz. *Created for Work: Practical Insights for Young Men* (Eugene, Oregon: Great Expectations Book Co., 2006), 11.

<u>The Biblical Foundation for Work</u>

We see in the book of Genesis that God designed us to work. Our bodies are specifically fitted to be active and to be involved in taking dominion over the physical world that is around us. All of us know that work is necessary, although most people will avoid it all costs. Adam and Eve even worked before the curse of sin removed them from the Garden of Eden (Gen. 2:15), so we see that work is *not* a curse from God.

> Multiply. Fill the earth. Subdue it. Man was to range over all zones and inhabit all zones. The sea was to be his home as well as the land. The habitat of each beast or bird or fish was of narrow limit.

> Man was endowed with wisdom to adapt himself to all climates, protect himself from all dangers and surpass all barriers. There was given to him the spirit of intervention and exploration. He would climb mountains, descend into caves, navigate oceans, bridge rivers, cut canals through isthmuses. To subdue the earth was a vast commission which called out all of his reserve powers. Upon this point we cannot do better than quote the great Baptist scholar, Dr. Conant: "If we look at the earth, as prepared for the occupancy of man, we find little that is made ready for use but boundless material which his own labor and skill can fit for it."[57]

Certain aspects of the sweat and toil that are involved in work are a part of the curse of sin (Gen. 3:17–19), but we find many places in Scripture that work is a good, profitable thing in which we should be involved.

---

[57] B. H. Carroll. *An Interpretation of the English Bible: Genesis to Ruth* (Grand Rapids, Michigan: Baker Book House, 1948), page 63.

A Picture of Work

Go to the ant, thou sluggard; consider her ways, and be wise:
Which having no guide, overseer, or ruler, provideth her meat
in the summer, and gathereth her food in the harvest. How
long wilt thou sleep, O sluggard? when wilt thou arise out
of thy sleep? Yet a little sleep, a little slumber, a little folding
of the hands to sleep: So shall thy poverty come as one that
travelleth, and thy want as an armed man. (Prov. 6:6–11)

The natural illustration that Solomon gives to demonstrate the value of work is the ant. The ant is designed to be busy about its job, and it does so meticulously. Of course, the obvious lesson is that we are also created to be workers. The ants speak loudly to us, "Don't let us outwork you." Do they? It is interesting to study all the differing types of ants. A brief search of the internet will supply you a multitude of species of ants. Some estimate that there are well over 10,000 different species. Each ant has his job and function, and they can work to accomplish amazing feats in comparison to their body mass. So the lesson for us to carry to our young people is to not shy away from hard work. Work is good for all of us. Laziness will leave a young person handicapped in accomplishing the will of the Lord with the rest of his life.

Power in Work

Even a child is known by his doings, whether his work be
pure, and whether it be right" (Prov. 20:11).

The way we handle work will shape our reputation with others. This verse is normally used to talk about the general importance of guarding your testimony, but the phraseology points to the fact that even a child, within a little bit of time, will determine their reputation. "Even a child is known by his doings, whether his work be pure." Others do judge us by the quality and purity of our work in this life, and Christians ought to be hard workers! It is interesting that this verse indicates that a child is known by his work. You are cheating your children by not teaching them how to work and how to work hard.

WORK WHILE YOU WORK

This poem, which children memorized from McGuffey's Primer in the nineteenth and early twentieth centuries, is a good one for those modern souls who turn on the TV while they're doing their homework or spend more time at the coffee machine than at their desk. On the other hand, it's also a good one for those who can't bring themselves to venture onto a beach or into a movie theater without taking their beepers with them.

> Work while you work,
> Play while you play;
> One thing each time,
> That is the way
> All that you do,
> Do with your might;
> Things done by halves
> Are not done right.[58]

Profit in Work

Wealth gotten by vanity shall be diminished: but he that gathereth by labor shall increase. (Proverbs 13:11)

In all labor there is profit: but the talk of the lips tendeth only to penury. (Proverbs 14:23)

---

[58] William Bennett, *The Book of Virtues: A Treasury of Great Moral Stories* (New York, New York: Simon & Schuster, 1993), 355.

It is easy to talk about work, but the actual doing of work is another thing. Work is a very rewarding pursuit, and every work project has a reward attached to it, whether it is money gained, experience learned, or spiritual rewards added to our life. Don't shortcut the teaching of work to young people. It is vital to the building of youth that they understand the profit in work. God established work in the garden of Eden, and one can see a satisfaction in the life of Adam. He had fulfillment in his life because of the purpose of work. This can be accomplished physically in a young person's life. They can see how that good, old-fashioned, hard work will bring lasting rewards and satisfaction. The world even recognizes hard work and seems to acknowledge it. However, hard work should become second nature to a born-again, Spirit-filled Christian.

We have seen through Scripture that God has designed us to be workers. God also shows us in Scripture that we receive benefits from being hard workers. Most people speak of work as if it is a terrible thing. Given the choice, many people would readily accept the opportunity to stay at home all day and do nothing. However, this is a gross misconception that is widely accepted concerning work. In truth, work is a life-sustaining element. It gives us purpose and a reason for existence. Without any purpose for living, most people die in a short time.

The soul of the sluggard desireth, and hath nothing: but the soul of the diligent shall be made fat" (Prov. 13:4). This verse describes our soul as being fat when we work. Literally this verse tells us that our entire being will be satisfied and content when we are diligent in our work.

> Diligence brings its own reward in the world (Chap. xxii.
> 29); much more in religion. It will not be content with
> desiring, without the reality of possession. The "exercise
> of godliness" tends to health and profit. (I Timothy 4:8.)
> Useful habits are formed; dormant energy is excited. The

conflict of faith, and the violence of prayer, ensure success. (Matthew 11:12.) [59]

One must spiritually work to succeed as well.

Christians need to be careful about the "life of faith" approach, whereby we expect to lay around the house all day doing nothing and then expect God to provide us with our daily needs. This is not true faith, and it is certainly not inspired by God. God has given us the ability to work so that we can provide for our families and our physical needs.

Dangers of Avoiding Work

We have seen that God puts an emphasis on working hard. The opposite of a hard worker is a lazy person. Sadly, there are many people in our world that have lost the sense of value that God attaches to work. It is even sadder to see God's people who are too lazy to work. Consider the grave consequences of the life of the sluggard. The dictionary defines *slothful* as "inactive, sluggish, lazy or idle." In the Hebrew, there is the idea of being indolent or to lean idly. There seems to be no lack of the slothful in our day and age. In the job force, in the youth group, or in the church congregation, the diligent worker seems to be fading into ancient history. Slothfulness is not a trait of a strong country, a rising economy, or of a vibrant church. We will take a few passages from the book of Proverbs to see what some of the characteristics of the lazy man are. The slothful man is a very horrible testimony of Christ. [60]

1. He Will Suffer Hunger

Slothfulness casteth into a deep sleep; and an idle soul shall suffer hunger" *(Prov. 19:15)*. The lazy man goes hungry and lives in want. Don't be

---

[59] https://faculty.gordon.edu/hu/bi/ted_hildebrandt/otesources/20-proverbs/text/books/bridges-proverb-scommentary/bridges-proverbs.pdf. Accessed on September 4, 2018.

[60] Scott Hanks, *The Men in Proverbs* (Lawrence, Kansas: Mercy & Truth Publishers, 1992), 25–26.

surprised to see the slothful man in a poor estate and wanting the very necessities of life. It is to be expected because he will not work. There is a correlation between the slothful man and the activity in which they endeavor. The word *idle* is used to describe the inattention that is devoted to profitability. The idle soul is always wanting and yet has no energy to change what easily could be changed.

2. <u>He Will Be Reduced to Begging from Others</u>

The sluggard will not plow by reason of the cold; therefore shall he beg in harvest, and have nothing" (Prov. 20:4). It is a humiliating thing to have to beg from others, but the lazy man finds himself in this situation constantly. Perhaps it even gets comfortable after a while, and it is easier to beg from someone else than it is to work for himself. The lazy man, though, always has an excuse for why he does not have a harvest. It is cold; it is raining; it is too dangerous; it is too muddy. Be careful of creating in the youth an atmosphere of accepting excuses for not finishing a task.

The sluggard always has his excuses ready to shift off any work which requires exertion. He will not plough by reason of the cold; although the season (our autumn) offered no hindrance, where the heart was in the work. And does not the most trifling difficulty hinder where the heart is cold in the service of God? Let the professor ask himself—Have his prayers during his whole life cost him exercise answering to one hour's ploughing? What has he given to God but the shadow of duties when the world has had his full glow and energy?[61]

3. <u>His Vineyard Will Be Broken Down</u>

I went by the field of the slothful, and by the vineyard of the man void of understanding; And, lo, it was all grown over with thorns, and nettles had covered the face thereof, and

---

[61] https://faculty.gordon.edu/hu/bi/ted_hildebrandt/otesources/20-proverbs/text/books/bridges-proverb-scommentary/bridges-proverbs.pdf. Accessed on September 4, 2018.

the stone wall thereof was broken down. Then I saw, and considered it well: I looked upon it, and received instruction. Yet a little sleep, a little slumber, a little folding of the hands to sleep: So shall thy poverty come as one that travelleth; and thy want as an armed man. (Prov. 24:30–34)

The slothful man doesn't have time to maintain his property, home, vehicle, or even his own body because he is too busy sleeping and snoozing (or watching television, playing video games, surfing the internet, lounging in the easy chair, etc.). What a great picture of the lazy man! This reminds us of the passage in the New Testament where Christ tells the listener that if a person is not faithful in the least, he will not be given the greater responsibility. This means that we should take diligence with the small duties that we have in our youth. From the diligence with the small duties, one can learn vital lessons that garner greater significance later in life.

4. He Will Waste What He Does Have

The slothful man roasteth not that which he took in hunting: but the substance of a diligent man is precious. (Prov. 12:27)

He also that is slothful in his work is brother to him that is a great waster. (Prov. 18:9)

When a slothful man does get something, he doesn't appreciate it, and he wastes it without conscience. Many times it is squandered because the person didn't work very hard for it. As pastors, youth pastors, and parents, please be mindful of always giving the "handout" without the work necessary to obtain. Yes, there are some things that authority should provide; that is called responsibility. However, we need to be careful of supplying "dainties," which will never be appreciated unless earned with the sweat of the brow.

As you can see, the Bible does not portray a pretty picture for the lazy man. As a parent or a youth pastor looking to influence your young people, I implore you to stress the biblical concept of God-honoring work. Laziness is a vice that will destroy a young person's spiritual life. They will not only feel the effects in their physical and educational spheres, but spiritually they will never see the happiness and joy that God desires in their life. In our crowded cities and country of affluence, finding opportunities as a family unit to work is rare. Because of this, we as parents must manufacture tasks. We must find ways of giving our young people the joy of accomplishment, of seeing the fruits of their own labors, and of gaining confidence in themselves.

The Jewish nation insisted that each child be taught a trade as well as a profession, to use his hands as well as his mind. Jesus said, *"My Father worketh hitherto, and I work" (John 5:17)*. In following His perfect example, we will all be at work. Paul told the Thessalonians, *"If any would not work, neither should he eat" (II Thess. 3:10)*. If we as parents apply this precept in the training of our young people, we will see that they learn to work.

A young person who does not learn to work will never be a success in life. The parent's attitude toward work will many times be the attitude of the child. As a parent, do I find every excuse for shirking my responsibility, whether working at home, or even a day's work at the church building? Let us first strive to do what our hands find to do with a song in our hearts, and our young people will follow the example set for them.

But it is not always possible to find happiness in our work as children or as adults. Some things just must be done. The habit of seeing a job through to its completion is extremely valuable to a young person. This is a real challenge to parents. Can I be patient and firm in seeing that he finishes a job when it is so much easier to do it myself and it takes half the time? We must, of course, plan tasks suitable to the young person's level of maturity but must also allow them to learn. Patiently allowing them to do a job will reap great rewards in the future.

Hopefully this study on both what the Bible has to say about laziness and about hard work will challenge the pastor, youth pastor, and parent to make sure that young people under their tutelage will develop the characteristics of a hard worker. God rewards hard work, and we must make sure that a young man or woman understands that laziness is never rewarded in this life or in eternity.

Hear the famous words of Benjamin Franklin: "Work while it is called today, for you know not how much you may be hindered tomorrow. One today is worth two tomorrows; never leave that till tomorrow which you can do today."

MR. MEANT-TO
Anonymous

Mr. Meant-To has a comrade,
And his name is Didn't-Do;
Have you ever chanced to meet them?
Did they ever call on you?

These two fellows live together
In the house of Never-Win,
And I'm told that it is haunted
By the ghost of Might-Have-Been.[62]

---

[62] Bennett, 364.

Chapter 13

M - Music, Media, and Protecting the Mind

Music

In the area of music, we are going to examine the concept of worship. Our music, especially our church music, is an extension of our worship to the Lord. *Worship* is a word that has been "hijacked" by the liberal evangelicals; however, this word is found in Scripture many times. It is something that we need to make sure that our young people understand and are not afraid to study the biblical aspects of worship. There is a humorous story about a little boy who went to church and later that evening the boy and his father knelt together to pray. When it was the little boy's turn, he prayed the following, "Dear God, we had a great time at church today, but I wish You had been there." This silly story reminds us that our attendance in church service can be without the presence of God. Therefore, an understanding of worship and the music that is involved in our worship is an important study.

A Quick Study of the word *worship* in the Bible:

> *For thou shalt worship no other god: for the LORD, whose name is Jealous, is a jealous God. (Exod. 34:14)*

And it shall be, if thou do at all forget the LORD thy God, and walk after other gods, and serve them, and worship them, I testify against you this day that ye shall surely perish. (Deut. 8:19.

Take heed to yourselves, that your heart be not deceived, and ye turn aside, and serve other gods, and worship them. (Deut. 11:16)

Give unto the LORD the glory due unto his name: bring an offering, and come before him: worship the LORD in the beauty of holiness. (I Chron. 16:29)

Give unto the LORD the glory due unto his name; worship the LORD in the beauty of holiness. (Ps. 29:2)

So shall the king greatly desire thy beauty: for he is thy Lord; and worship thou him. (Ps. 45:11)

All the earth shall worship thee, and shall sing unto thee; they shall sing to thy name. (Ps. 66:4)

All nations whom thou hast made shall come and worship before thee, O Lord; and shall glorify thy name. (Ps. 86:9)

O come, let us worship and bow down: let us kneel before the LORD our maker. (Ps. 95:6)

O worship the LORD in the beauty of holiness: fear before him, all the earth. (Ps. 96:9)

Confounded be all they that serve graven images, that boast themselves of idols: worship him, all ye gods. (Ps. 97:7)

Exalt the LORD our God, and worship at his holy hill; for the LORD our God is holy. (Ps. 99:9)

I will worship toward thy holy temple, and praise thy name for thy lovingkindness and for thy truth: for thou hast magnified thy word above all thy name. (Ps. 138:2)

And saith unto him, All these things will I give thee, if thou wilt fall down and worship me. Then saith Jesus unto him, Get thee hence, Satan: for it is written, Thou shalt worship the Lord thy God, and him only shalt thou serve. (Matt. 4:9–10)

Our fathers worshipped in this mountain; and ye say, that in Jerusalem is the place where men ought to worship. Jesus saith unto her, Woman, believe me, the hour cometh, when ye shall neither in this mountain, nor yet at Jerusalem, worship the Father. Ye worship ye know not what: we know what we worship: for salvation is of the Jews. But the hour cometh, and now is, when the true worshippers shall worship the Father in spirit and in truth: for the Father seeketh such to worship him. God is a Spirit: and they that worship him must worship him in spirit and in truth. (John 4:20–24)

And I John saw these things, and heard them. And when I had heard and seen, I fell down to worship before the feet of the angel which shewed me these things. Then saith he unto me, See thou do it not: for I am thy fellowservant, and of thy brethren the prophets, and of them which keep the sayings of this book: worship God. (Rev. 22:8–9)

There are a few lessons that we can glean from the occurrences of worship in Scripture for which we should be teaching our teenagers.

1. Worship is supposed to be designated for God and God alone. He is worthy of our worship. This is clearly presented to us in the biblical account of the temptation of Christ. Satan was prodding Christ to bow down and was offering Him substantial compensation if He would do this. This is still happening today. The devil is still promising young people and churches great rewards and benefits if they will just sacrifice a little of their worship that should be appropriated to God and direct it to themselves. The devil may promise great numbers of people to follow; he may promise popularity (or "thumbs up" on social media); or he may promise financial remunerations. However, our answer should mirror Christ's—only the true God deserves our worship.

2. Satan desires to be worshipped and to take away worship that is only for God. It was the design of Lucifer, Son of the Morning, to lead in the worship of God, according to Isaiah 14. He became obsessed with his own worship and elevation. Since that time, Satan has been in the business of stealing that which belongs to the Lord. This is seen today in much of that which is called "worship" in congregations and gatherings. It is no more worship to God than calling a cat a dog. We must be careful in our musical tastes that we do not bypass God and give the devil the worship instead. Dr. Sorenson in his book, *Broad Is the Way* says, "The world's music is likewise spiritual. It synchronizes with the old sinful human nature called the flesh."[63] We must understand there is a wrong type of spirit or spirituality. We do not want to adapt that spirit.

3. God's Word must be followed regarding worship. Christ addressed this in the Gospel of John; worship must be in spirit and in truth. Where do we find truth? Truth is always tied to the words of God

---

[63] David Sorenson, *Broad is the Way: Fundamentalists Merging into the Evangelical Mainstream* (Duluth, MN: Northstar Ministries, 2014, 186.

and the Word of God, which is Christ. Christ must be lifted up and praised. Man's ideas when it comes to worship are not acceptable. This is similar to King Saul coming to Samuel and asking him to bless his work and present an offering. However, Samuel told King Saul that God was more impressed with obedience. Those who say that God does not care about how we worship have not read Scripture clearly, "Obedience is better than sacrifice." God's Word must be followed to have God's presence with us.

4. Not all who claim to be worshiping the Lord are truly worshiping. Christ said this in the Gospels when He proclaimed that all that say, Lord, Lord, are not heading to heaven. We who are biblical Baptists say this about other religions and cults that claim to be heading to heaven but are seeking that way through another way other than Christ. In a similar vein of thought, there are some who claim that their music style is worshiping God. We can be just as guilty of distorting true worship. A claim may be made but that does not mean it is true. I can say that my Honda is a Ferrari over 100 times, but it does not make my Honda magically change into another car.

5. An attitude of humility and lowliness is essential to worship. The word *worship* indicates a "bowing." The word itself is the concept of humility. We must come before the Lord in lowliness. There are a couple of thoughts that come to mind in the modern worship movement that shows a lack of humility. Having a "Top 40" does not seem to exude the concept of lowliness. It seems that popularity is more important. Also, the personality syndrome that seems to be heavily part of modern worship does not seem to promote an attitude of humility. We must be careful with our young people that we do not give them substitute "rock stars." It should be our desire to have the Lord ultimately glorified.

6. Worship is never seen as evangelistic in the Scriptures. To claim that we are trying to get folks to come and see our Lord through our worship is not a scriptural context. In fact, music is never seen as a soul-winning endeavor. Our worship is to glorify Christ first and foremost. To use the world's tactics and say that we are being evangelical is hypocritical and showing a lack of sound biblical doctrine.

Our worship and music should direct us to think good, godly thoughts. There is a well-known hymn which reflects this concept. That hymn is "My Jesus, I Love Thee." The spiritual insight in the words of "My Jesus, I Love Thee" is even more remarkable when you consider that it was written by a teenager, William R. Featherston, while growing up in Montreal, Canada. He found Christ at the age of sixteen, and his heart overflowed with gratitude and love to Christ for saving him, so he penned these words. Several years later, a well-known American Baptist pastor, Dr. A. J. Gordon, discovered the hymn in an English hymnbook. The hymn had a different melody that did not seem to fit well with the words, and Dr. Gordon decided to compose another melody for it. Think of the words as you read them below. May we learn to teach our young men and ladies the proper meaning of worship and music so that they may write a new song from a new heart?

MY JESUS, I LOVE THEE
By William R. Fetherston

My Jesus, I love Thee, I know Thou art mine;
For Thee all the follies of sin I resign;
My gracious Redeemer, my Savior art Thou;
If every I loved Thee, my Jesus, 'tis now.

I love Thee, because Thou hast first loved me,
And purchased my pardon on Calvary's tree;
I love Thee for wearing the thorns on Thy brow;
If ever I loved Thee, my Jesus, 'tis now.[64]

---

[64] Kenneth Osbeck, *Amazing Grace: 366 Inspiring Hymn Stories for Daily Devotions* (Grand Rapids, MI: Kregel Publications, 1990), 56.

Now, let's consider the first occurrence of the word *worship* in Scripture. It involves a father and his teenage son. It is in the story of Abraham coming to the mountain to sacrifice Isaac. This story can help us in understanding what worship is in both a public and private fashion. *And Abraham said unto his young men, Abide ye here with the ass; and I and the lad will go yonder and worship, and come again to you" (Gen. 22:5).*

First, sacrifice is almost always part of true worship. Very rarely can you find the idea of worship in the Bible without it being attached somehow to giving. Giving is an important part of worshiping the Lord. There is some interesting verbiage to consider as we reflect our worship to the Lord. Isaac is called Abraham's only son, showing us that our worship should be wholly dedicated to the Lord and should be something that requires all. The text also reveals the strong love that Abraham had for Isaac. This shows us that our worship should not be a "side" thing. Something that is easy to give up is not something that is worth much. This is not indicating that our worship and music should be drudgery, but it surely will cost our giving up our worldly tendencies and our fleshly desires.

Second, separation is necessary from the things of the World. We find this reference in Genesis 22:3–6:

> *And Abraham rose up early in the morning, and saddled his ass, and took two of his young men with him, and Isaac his son, and clave the wood for the burnt offering, and rose up, and went unto the place of which God had told him. Then on the third day Abraham lifted up his eyes, and saw the place afar off. And Abraham said unto his young men, Abide ye here with the ass; and I and the lad will go yonder and worship, and come again to you. And Abraham took the wood of the burnt offering, and laid it upon Isaac his son; and he took the fire in his hand, and a knife; and they went both of them together.*

Abraham was required to travel away from others, and it took effort to get away. In our lives today, worship will take effort. It is important as parents of teenagers that we have a family worship time. Our family worship should include our young people. These times will help them understand more about the God we serve. We cannot expect our children to truly love the Lord if the only worship and instruction in serving our Lord is heard from the pulpit. As clearly pointed out in Deuteronomy 11:19, teaching our children by the way and when they lie down and when they rise up is imperative to reinforce the truths taught in a good, solid, Bible-believing church.

It is interesting to note that Abraham was moving away from the everyday to worship the Lord. This separation is essential to developing a right spirit of separation. The claim of modern evangelicals and neo-independent Baptist that they are trying to reach the world by being like them is having the opposite effect. They are forsaking a very clear Bible principle of separation. Obedience to God's design of worship is essential for God's acceptance of our praise. Consider the story of Cain and Abel where this truth is clearly displayed. Cain's sacrifice was not accepted because he thought his way of worship was better than what God required.

Sacredness is apparent in the conversation and the demeanor of the individuals. This is referenced in Genesis 22:7–10

> *And Isaac spake unto Abraham his father, and said, My father: and he said, Here am I, my son. And he said, Behold the fire and the wood: but where is the lamb for a burnt offering? And Abraham said, My son, God will provide himself a lamb for a burnt offering: so they went both of them together. And they came to the place which God had told him of; and Abraham built an altar there, and laid the wood in order, and bound Isaac his son, and laid him on the altar upon the wood. And Abraham stretched forth his hand, and took the knife to slay his son.*

There is a sacredness and seriousness that is purveyed in the text. It is not a comedy hour. The conversation is about the offering and the provision of the Lord. It is a time of reflection on what God can do. There is a contemplative state that is lacking today in our worship. We have so much noise and activity that we cannot stop and think on the sacredness of our worship to the Lord.

Submission is required for the Lord to visit. Genesis 22:11–17:

> *And the angel of the LORD called unto him out of heaven, and said, Abraham, Abraham: and he said, Here am I. And he said, Lay not thine hand upon the lad, neither do thou any thing unto him: for now I know that thou fearest God, seeing thou hast not withheld thy son, thine only son from me. And Abraham lifted up his eyes, and looked, and behold behind him a ram caught in a thicket by his horns: and Abraham went and took the ram, and offered him up for a burnt offering in the stead of his son. And Abraham called the name of that place Jehovahjireh: as it is said to this day, In the mount of the LORD it shall be seen. And the angel of the LORD called unto Abraham out of heaven the second time, and said, By myself have I sworn, saith the LORD, for because thou hast done this thing, and hast not withheld thy son, thine only son: that in blessing I will bless thee, and in multiplying I will multiply thy seed as the stars of the heaven, and as the sand which is upon the sea shore; and thy seed shall possess the gate of his enemies.*

Without this, there can be no true worship of the Lord. Not to be submitted to the Lord's way of doing things is a mockery in worship. Notice that Abraham is stretching his hand in obedience, and you see his teenage son submitting to the will of his father. They were both willing to obey their Lord because the Lord meant so much to them. When we bow in submission to the will of the Lord, we will experience His presence and His blessing.

There is much more that can be discussed in worship and music, but we must lead our young people into further study of this topic to see them asking for the Holy Spirit to guide them into all truth. Mike Foster, in his book *A Spiritual Song,* gives seven tips to consider regarding our music.

1. Music should be used to worship God. What wonderful opportunity to bow our knees to the Lord and worship Him together.

2. Music should be used for instructional purposes. This is seen in Colossians 3:16 where the term *teaching* is used when referencing our church music. Songs that exemplify and expound sound doctrine can teach us how to live a life that pleases God.

3. Music should bring praise to the Lord. There is no better way praise the Lord than to lift up our voices in song! We should be ever looking for opportunities to be able to "Praise the Lord for His goodness and for His wonderful works unto the children of men."

4. Music should promote unity in the Church. As a Christian works and walks in this ungodly world, they can sometimes pick up the baggage of division and strife and bring that to church. Unification of the church cannot happen unless these things are confessed as sin and then they are removed from our hearts.

5. Music is a testimony of a changed heart to believers and unbelievers. This is clearly taught in Psalm 42 where the Psalmist cries out that we have a "new song in our heart." The old songs testify to carnality, but the new song reveals a transformation from inside to outside. This is wonderful way to show this change—whether it be of salvation or sanctification.

6. Music should honor and bring glory the Lord. When people hear music sung or played, it should point to Christ. He is the one who saved them, and the singer should uplift His name. No one else should get the glory; it is not about the performer.

7. Music should reflect Christ. Christ's attributes should be seen in our music. If we are filled with the Spirit and His music is being sung with His help, it should be a reflection of Christ. Revelation 4 clearly states that we are created for His pleasure. Our goal should be to please God in everything we do, not just honor and glorify Him. When we reflect God's Son in our music, then that is pleasing to Him. His standard has then become our standard.[65]

Media

The internet has taken over as the fastest-growing media in today's world. The "surface" web consists of approximately 2.5 billion documents and has a rate of growth of 7.3 million pages per day.

Email was one of the most widespread ways of communication in society. There are now many other technological communication forums, such as Twitter, Facebook, Instagram, WhatsApp, Snapchat, and there are hundreds more. Because of the ever-changing face of technology, it is imperative to develop some guidelines to help with youth. These guidelines are essential as they will be engrossed in an ever-increasing technological world.

Studies show that the average consumer is exposed to up to 10,000 brand messages a day. And as marketers are presented with more and more channels to reach their customers, that number is growing rapidly. Consumers switch between screens up to twenty-one times an hour

---

[65] Mike Foster, *The Spiritual Song: The Missing Element in Church Music* (Troy, OH: TBT Publications, 2011), 21.

according to a British study, which correlates with Microsoft's claim that the average person's attention span is now just eight seconds.[66]

Globally, a staggering 269 billion emails are sent each day, and there are currently just over 3.7 billion email users worldwide. The findings revealed in Radicati Group's February 2017 study mark a continual growth in the number of emails sent per day from 2015's figure of 205 billion emails per day. For scale, if 205 billion emails is the daily mail count, this means almost 2.4 million emails are sent every second and a mind-blowing 74 trillion emails per year.[67]

Some 73 percent of adult cell owners use the text messaging function on their phone at least occasionally (nearly identical to the 72 percent of cell owners who did so at a similar point in 2010). Text messaging users send or receive an average of 41.5 messages per day, with the median user sending or receiving ten texts daily. Young adults stand far above all other demographic groups when it comes to their usage of text messaging. Fully 95 percent of eighteen- to twenty-five-year-olds use the text messaging feature on their phones, and these users send or receive an average of 87.7 text messages on a normal day.[68]

These statistics help the reader see that the amount of information that is being pushed onto the consumer is staggering. Our young people are part of this information age, and they are being bombarded with this overload and being told that this is the norm. We must be aware of the purpose of this onslaught of information. Normally, it is not to help our young people become stronger Christians and to help them grow in the Lord. The media has a purpose of indoctrination and manipulating thought. Some may only want to do this in purchases, but others have a more sinister design.

---

[66] www.ama.org/partners/content/Pages/why-customers-attention-scarcest-resources-2017.aspx. Accessed on October 15, 2018.

[67] www.templafy.com/blog/how-many-emails-are-sent-every-day-top-email-statistics-your-business-needs-to-know. Accessed on October 15, 2018.

[68] http://www.pewinternet.org/2011/09/19/how-americans-use-text-messaging. Accessed on October 15, 2018.

There are six areas where media and the internet can affect a young person. We must be mindful of these areas and establish some guidelines to help with this dangerous world of influence.

1. <u>Pornography</u>

Because of technology, there is easy access to pornography. The accessibility of it through the internet has removed the shame that once surrounded purchasing pornographic magazines and materials. It used to be dirty old men sneaking around adult bookstores who were looking over their shoulders, but now that has all changed. The wicked bookstores have sneaked into your homes. No longer do our young people have to creep into a sleazy, seedy building with a fake ID to get material that is only for "adult" consumption. Access to pornography has changed with the invention of the laptop, home computers, mobile tablets, and smart phones. Pastors and parents both need to be aware that allowing unguarded access in the home to the internet is dangerous for anyone, especially a young impressionable mind.

Pornography that is legally restricted to adults can be accessed by children through the internet. A few clicks of a mouse and any child, of any age, can poison his mind, and those impressions will not be erased. The devil is sly, and he has his mignons that have touted the "first amendment" rights so that it is now a perceived "right" to allow "smut" to be available to all. Unless parents have boundaries in the home and technical help through filtering devices, they are allowing an open-door policy to all sorts of perversion to the very hearts of those they love so much. Pastors, parents, brothers, sisters, and friends must all be willing to warn of the poisonous snakes that are ready to strike. We must lovingly protect young people from this kind of evil that will prey upon their sinful nature by feeding it before they have the intellectual or spiritual maturity to deny their lusts.

The internet is home to a multitude of images that would be against the law to sell even in adult bookstores. When God shared with Ezekiel the phrases *great abominations, greater abominations,* and again, *greater abominations,* He was emphasizing the fact that His people seemingly had no limits—the unrestrained, unlimited, uncontrolled involvement is the most wicked of abominations. In the New Testament, there is an old English word that is used for this unbridled sin, *lasciviousness.* Lasciviousness simply is sin without restraint, sin without boundaries, or sin without limits. Lasciviousness is an attitude of life that believes in no authority or absolutes. It is the attitude of mind that says, "Nobody— absolutely no one—is going to tell me what to do, not even God!" Lasciviousness breaks the heart of God. Men who promote this unrestrained lifestyle deny God, hate God, and have hardened their hearts against God.[69]

Here are some verses to consider on this topic for discussion with your teenager.

> *Turn away mine eyes from beholding vanity; and quicken thou me in thy way. (Ps. 119:37)*

> *But I say unto you, That whosoever looketh on a woman to lust after her hath committed adultery with her already in his heart." (Matt. 5:28)*

> *Flee fornication. Every sin that a man doeth is without the body; but he that committeth fornication sinneth against his own body. What? know ye not that your body is the temple of the Holy Ghost which is in you, which ye have of God, and ye are not your own? For ye are bought with a price: therefore glorify God in your body, and in your spirit, which are God's. (I Cor. 6:18–20) There hath no temptation taken you but such as is common to man: but God is faithful, who will not suffer you to be tempted above that ye are able; but will with the temptation*

---

[69] Rand Hummel (*The Dark Side of the Internet* (BJU Press: Greenville, SC, 2005), 75–76.

also make a way to escape, that ye may be able to bear it.
(I Cor. 10:13)

This I say therefore, and testify in the Lord, that ye hence-
forth walk not as other Gentiles walk, in the vanity of their
mind, Having the understanding darkened, being alien-
ated from the life of God through the ignorance that is in
them, because of the blindness of their heart: who being past
feeling have given themselves over unto lasciviousness, to work
all uncleanness with greediness. But ye have not so learned
Christ; if so be that ye have heard him, and have been taught
by him, as the truth is in Jesus: that ye put off concerning the
former conversation the old man, which is corrupt according
to the deceitful lusts; and be renewed in the spirit of your
mind. (Eph. 4:17–23)

2. <u>Romance Novels</u>

While Satan uses visual images to attract men, he uses the idea of fairy tale relationships to lead women astray. This is seen in the hugely popular romance novel industry. These books are not geared toward the male reader but rather to females. Consider some of the wicked ladies found in the Bible: Lot's wife, Lot's daughters, Potiphar's wife, Delilah, Gomer, Jezebel, and Herodius. There are a few others that we could list, but as your mind reviews their stories and their wicked conniving, it is apparent that there is a definite danger in inappropriate chatter. Inappropriateness is often found in the pages of romance novels. We must teach our young people to be cautious of frivolity that leads to dangerous relationships.

3. <u>Availability of Violent Entertainment</u>

Ezekiel 8:17 mentions that the house of Judah was filled with violence. *"Then he said unto me, Hast thou seen this, O son of man? Is it* *a light thing to the house of Judah that they commit the abominations which they commit here? for they have filled the land with **violence**, and have returned to provoke me to anger: and, lo, they put the branch to their nose.* " When violent behavior, and by that we mean behavior which shows absolutely no regard for human life, becomes our daily entertainment, we are not far off from returning to the mentality of ancient pagan cultures, such as the wicked Roman culture of the time of Christ and the apostle Paul. Almost every type and form of violence can be found online. There is the serious violence of bomb-making tutorials to the praise of joining terrorist groups worldwide. Then there are the foolish, silly violent videos which glorify gore and horror.

The computer games, such as *Doom* and *Duke Nukem,* were highly publicized by the Paducah, Kentucky (December 1997), and Littleton, Colorado (April 1999), high school killings. The boys involved in the shootings not only played those games but also used the internet to gain information on how to make bombs. Both the graphic violence and incredibly wicked content of games like these have helped to desensitize teens and kids into thinking violence is just another way of having fun. For example, in the game *Postal 2,* players "go postal" and get points for killing innocent bystanders and police. God hates violence, and it is evident when you look at Scripture that He always has hated it. When God was grieved because of the wickedness of man, it was the violence on the earth that prompted the destruction of the world with the flood.[70]

> *The earth also was corrupt before God, and the earth was filled with **violence**. And God looked upon the earth, and, behold, it was corrupt; for all flesh had corrupted his way upon the earth. And God said unto Noah, the end of all flesh is come before me; for the earth is filled*

---

[70] Ibid., 135.

with **violence** *through them; and, behold, I will destroy them with the earth. (Gen. 6:11–13)*

After reading the text above, how can we as Christians not take a closer look at that which we present as innocent fun to our young people through violent video games? Those who view graphic violence as fun or entertaining are like the people of Ezekiel's day who were provoking God to anger. Never forget the clear warning of Scripture in Hebrews 10:31 *"It is a fearful thing to fall into the hands of the living God."*

4. Undocumented and Unrestrained Forum for False News and Reports

There was a recent report by Robert Epstein who talks about the way in which Google and other media giants manipulate people's thinking about news and events in this world. His study was expansive, and he was trying to show that it was possible through manipulation to control elections and the reputation of candidates.[71] We have seen this trend increase over the last decade enormously. Former President Donald Trump was relentless in calling down "fake news" to the anger of the media. The media has maligned good men and women because they do not want their political views to prevail. As parents and pastors, we must help our young people come up with restrictions and guidelines to give them a fair and balanced report that does not just include Fox News, CNN, or any other mainline news outlet.

There are great communication advantages of having Facetime, Facebook, Twitter, Instagram, and other media tools that can help one keep in touch when separated from close family and friends; however, with the push of a button, doubt and discredit can be made to someone's good reputation.

---

[71] https://www.breitbart.com/tech/2018/05/03/robert-epstein/. Accessed on October 15, 2018.

A woman once repeated a nasty piece of gossip about a friend. The news travelled, and soon everyone had heard the nasty news. The friend was deeply hurt, not only by the untruths that were being spread but also by the betrayal of her friend.

The woman who had first passed on the gossip was also wounded, wracked with guilt over the pain she had caused her dear friend. The offender approached her grandfather, a man she had always seen as very wise, and asked what she could do to set things right.

"Buy a chicken, and have it killed. Then on your way home, pluck its feathers and drop them along the road. When you have done this come and see me again."

The woman was somewhat perplexed by this advice, but she followed it anyway. The next day she returned to her grandfather. This time he told her to go and collect all the feathers she had dropped on the road the day before and bring them to him.

"But that's impossible" she said. "They'll have all blown away!"

"Exactly" said her grandfather, "it's easy to drop them, but it's impossible to get them back. It's the same with gossip. It doesn't take much to spread a rumor, but once you do, you can never undo the hurt. But perhaps you can ask forgiveness."[72]

---

[72] https://storiesforpreaching.com/category/sermonillustrations/gossip/. Accessed on October 15, 2018.

Consider the following verses in Scripture when it comes to the tongue and how not to be quick to judgment.

Trust in the LORD with all thine heart; and lean not unto thine own understanding. In all thy ways acknowledge him, and he shall direct thy paths. Be not wise in thine own eyes: fear the LORD, and depart from evil. (Prov. 3:5–7)

Also, that the soul be without knowledge, it is not good; and he that hasteth with his feet sinneth. (Prov. 19:2)

The thoughts of the diligent tend only to plenteousness; but of every one that is hasty only to want. (Prov. 21:5)

Be careful for nothing; but in every thing by prayer and supplication with thanksgiving let your requests be made known unto God. And the peace of God, which passeth all understanding, shall keep your hearts and minds through Christ Jesus. Finally, brethren, whatsoever things are true, whatsoever things are honest, whatsoever things are just, whatsoever things are pure, whatsoever things are lovely, whatsoever things are of good report; if there be any virtue, and if there be any praise, think on these things. Those things, which ye have both learned, and received, and heard, and seen in me, do: and the God of peace shall be with you. (Phil. 4:6–9)

Who is a wise man and endued with knowledge among you? let him shew out of a good conversation his works with meekness of wisdom. But if ye have bitter envying and strife in your hearts, glory not, and lie not against the truth. This wisdom descendeth not from above, but is earthly, sensual, devilish. For where envying and strife is, there is confusion and every evil work. But the wisdom that is from above is first pure, then peaceable, gentle, and easy to be intreated, full of mercy and good fruits, without partiality, and without hypocrisy. And the fruit of righteousness is sown in peace of them that make peace. (James 3:13–18)

All these verses tell us to be guided not by our own wisdom but by the Spirit of God. We need to be careful of the tendency that seems to rise up in our evil hearts to tear down and malign someone that may have more than us or may have succeeded. Another person's success does not give us free reign on the internet to tear down all that they have done. We also should not be hasty in our responses. Many commit horrible word atrocities through the ease of instant communication that could have been avoided if the response would have been prayed over or if the person had allowed it to simmer for a day or so. Be careful of haste.

5. Internet Relationships

This know also, that in the last days perilous times shall come. For men shall be lovers of their own selves, covetous, boasters, proud, blasphemers, disobedient to parents, unthankful, unholy, without natural affection, trucebreakers, false accusers, incontinent, fierce, despisers of those that are good, traitors, heady, highminded, lovers of pleasures more than lovers of God; having a form of godliness, but denying the power thereof: from such turn away. For of this sort are they which creep into houses, and lead captive silly women laden with sins, led away with divers lusts. (II Tim. 3:1–6)

Now what seems like a generation or two ago, the first rage of online connection began. It was introduced in July of 2003 and was known as "Myspace." Tom Anderson is an alumnus of UC Berkeley and UCLA, and his purpose for creating this social media network was to provide a place "where people could post music, chat, and spread the word about what's hot."[73]

Does that line up with a biblical philosophy? Consider a few Scripture texts which give principles from God's viewpoint.

No servant can serve two masters: for either he will hate the one, and love the other; or else he will hold to the one, and despise the other. Ye cannot serve God and mammon. (Luke 16:13)

If ye were of the world, the world would love his own: but because ye are not of the world, but I have chosen you out of the world, therefore the world hateth you. (John 15:19)

I have given them thy word; and the world hath hated them, because they are not of the world, even as I am not of the world. I pray not that thou shouldest take them out of the world, but that thou shouldest keep them from the evil. (John 17:14–15)

Jesus answered, "My kingdom is not of this world: if my kingdom were of this world, then would my servants fight, that I should not be delivered to the Jews: but now is my kingdom not from hence." (John 18:36)

We must be careful to teach our teens as they enter the technology world that the Bible's principles must rule there as much as it should in every other aspect of life. Let's take a few minutes and think about e-mail and chatrooms. A *U.S. News & World Report* article states, "Five girls sit side by side riveted to their screens. 'We're emailing each other,' one blurts out. Never mind that they could just talk; chatting in cyberspace is far

---

[73] Hummel, 125.

better."[74] So, what's wrong with chat rooms or secret friendship societies? Here's a list of just a few items to be considered regarding these types of relationships.

- You don't know who you're talking to.

- You don't know when you're being lied to.

- You meet people you would never hang out with in real life.

- You say things you would never say in person.

- You can get pulled into conversations without even realizing where you are headed.

- You waste tons of time.

6. Internet Addiction

This aspect of the internet and media has been studied more in the last few years. With the introduction of the internet, there was so much excitement, and no one wanted to "pour cold water" on this amazing new technology; however, now that the internet has been around a few years, you can find a plethora of articles that ask parents to exercise caution when it comes to media and internet usage. Even the great Bill Gates and Steve Jobs limited their children's use of internet and phone usage according to an article published in Business Insider in January of 2018.

> In 2007, Gates, the former CEO of Microsoft, implemented a cap on screen time when his daughter started developing an unhealthy attachment to a video game. He

---

[74] Ibid., 125.

also didn't let his kids get cell phones until they turned 14. (Today, the average age for a child getting their first phone is 10.)

Jobs, who was the CEO of Apple until his death in 2012, revealed in a 2011 New York Times interview that he prohibited his kids from using the newly-released iPad. "We limit how much technology our kids use at home," Jobs told reporter Nick Bilton.[75]

If these tech giants who have created this internet-crazy world would not let their children have too much screen time, why would we let our young people run headlong into something, which has so much unknown danger. There is now, more than ever, a need for strict separation from the world, yet it seems that less and less is practiced among those who claim to be Bible-believing people. We are in a desperate battle for the minds and hearts of our young people. Pastors and parents who do not get serious about this raging battlefront will surely regret it.

Here are a few of the specific types of internet addiction which rank as the most problematic for a young person.

1. Cyber-sexual addiction—This can be online pornography or adult fantasy chatrooms.

2. Cyber-relational addiction—This is virtual adultery, the online friends become more meaningful than real life relationships.

3. Compulsive surfing and data collection—This is a desire to always be looking up something for an endless supply of data.

---

[75] https://www.businessinsider.com/screen-time-limits-bill-gates-steve-jobs-red-flag-2017–10. Accessed on October 15, 2018.

4. Game addiction—This is online video gaming with others around the nation and around the world. Addicted individuals tend to be late, forget other responsibilities, and spend hours gaming.

5. Social Media addiction—This is when the phone can never be left unattended or the person is always checking some status or uploading some new item.

Consider the following article published by the CRC on Internet addictions for teenagers:

<u>Symptoms of an Internet Addiction:</u>

The core components of teen Internet addiction are similar to those of any other addiction or compulsion. Young people who struggle with teen Internet addiction are likely to meet many if not all of the following criteria:

- Obsession—Spending most offline time thinking about past online experiences and planning for future online sessions

- Frustration, anxiety, and/or irritability when not able to go online

- Abandoning friends and other hobbies in order to focus on online activities

- Continuing to spend time online even after negative repercussions (such as school problems, deteriorating relationships, and even health problems)

The following are among the specific signs that could indicate the presence of teen Internet addiction:

- Most non-school hours are spent on the computer or playing video games

- Falling asleep in school

- Falling behind with assignments

- Worsening grades

- Lying about computer or video game use

- Choosing to use the computer or play video games rather than see friends

- Dropping out of other social groups (clubs or sports)

- Being irritable when not playing a video game or being on the computer[76]

Ephesians 5:11–16; I Corinthians 9:24–27; 10:31; and II Corinthians 8:10; 10:5 are verses that help us in seeing that addictions are real; and as Christians, we must put safeguards in place so that we do not come under the power of any of them. Sin is very expensive. The price tag for online sin is out of sight. This "helpful tool" not only destroys homes and innocent victims, but it also addicts with unbelievable power.

---

[76] https://www.crchealth.com/troubled-teenagers/internet-addiction-teenagers/. Accessed on October 15, 2018.

Helps for strengthening the life in Music and Media

1. Protect Your Mind

In the following verses, we see that not all art forms are godly. The world today claims that there is no right or wrong in something that is considered "art." Yet, according to God, that belief is false.

> *And the tables were the work of God, and the writing was the writing of God, graven upon the tables. And when Joshua heard the noise of the people as they shouted, he said unto Moses, There is a noise of war in the camp. And he said, It is not the voice of them that shout for mastery, neither is it the voice of them that cry for being overcome: but the noise of them that sing do I hear. And it came to pass, as soon as he came nigh unto the camp, that he saw the calf, and the dancing: and Moses' anger waxed hot, and he cast the tables out of his hands, and brake them beneath the mount. And he took the calf which they had made, and burnt it in the fire, and ground it to powder, and strawed it upon the water, and made the children of Israel drink of it. (Exod. 32:16–20)*

> *For Herod feared John, knowing that he was a just man and an holy, and observed him; and when he heard him, he did many things, and heard him gladly. And when a convenient day was come, that Herod on his birthday made a supper to his lords, high captains, and chief estates of Galilee; And when the daughter of the said Herodias came in, and danced, and pleased Herod and them that sat with him, the king said unto the damsel, Ask of me whatsoever thou wilt, and I will give it thee. And he sware unto her, Whatsoever thou shalt ask of me, I will give it thee, unto the half of my kingdom. (Mark 6:20–23)*

It is evident that these stories are examples to us of worldly art that is wrong and repulsive to God.

However, as we focus our thoughts on protecting the minds of our youth in a culture that has surrounded us with entertainment of all types, let's understand that not all arts, entertainment, music, and drama are wrong. God has made us to enjoy the talents and creativity that He has put in us and revealed through others in developing those talents. The Psalms, the book of Job, the Song of Solomon are some of the most prominent examples of biblical poetry, and they are beautiful pictures of prose and poetry. The Bible also has other instances of the "arts" throughout its covers. For instance, drama is first mentioned in the Bible when Ezekiel is instructed to "act out" a drama, depicting the siege of Jerusalem (Ezek. 4). We find many other musical listings.

- David was a skillful musician and songwriter (I Sam. 16:18).

- Solomon wrote over 1,000 songs (I Kings 4:32).

- Kenaniah was a great vocalist and song leader (I Chron. 15:22).

- Bezalel was cited as a gifted visual artist (Exod. 35:30–33).

We need to express to our young people that we are not against creativity and those things that are beautiful in God's creation. We can learn to enjoy God's creation. Creativity is a gift from God. There is nothing wrong with drama, poetry, music, and other forms of the arts, but we must make sure that we have a biblical understanding of these items.

There is a well-known story in the annals of American history concerning the use of media to affect the mind. It happened the day before Halloween, on October 30, 1938, when millions of Americans tuned in to a radio program that featured plays by Orson Welles. The performance that evening was an adaptation of the science fiction novel *The War of the Worlds* which is about a Martian invasion of the earth. Welles made an important change: under his direction, the play was written and performed so it would sound like an actual news broadcast. It was supposed to heighten the dramatic effect. It did. Thousands of people across the United States went into a panic, thinking that the country was actually being overrun by Martians.

In the *New York Tribune,* Dorothy Thompson wrote: "Mr. Orson Welles and the Mercury Theater of the Air have made one of the most fascinating and important demonstrations of all time. They have proved that a few effective voices, accompanied by sound effects, can convince masses of people of a totally unreasonable, completely fantastic proposition as to create a nation-wide panic."[77] Entertainment is powerful! Our choices of what we watch, listen, and view regarding media does shape our lives. There is no immunity from it.

Socrates once said, "When the soul hears music, it drops its best guard." That description also can be true of almost any media that we allow into our lives. This is why it is important to teach our young people the importance of protecting the mind in a biblical fashion. In II Corinthians 5:10, the Bible is clear that believers are to take every thought captive. This includes the music and media that we are allowing into our lives. America is consumed with media and the internet. It is around us all. We must be on guard.

> As has been the case since the Center began surveying about the use of different social media in 2012, Facebook remains the primary platform for most Americans. Roughly two-thirds of U.S. adults (68%) now report that they are Facebook users, and roughly three-quarters of those users access Facebook on a daily basis. With the exception of those 65 and older, a majority of Americans across a wide range of demographic groups now use Facebook.

---

[77] https://mapeel.blogspot.com/2011/10/orson-welless-war-of-worlds-first-hand.html. Accessed on October 22, 2018.

But the social media story extends well beyond Facebook. The video-sharing site YouTube—which contains many social elements, even if it is not a traditional social media platform—is now used by nearly three-quarters of U.S. adults and 94% of 18 to 24 year olds. And the typical (median) American reports that they use three of the eight major platforms that the Center measured in this survey."

Overall, 59% of U.S. adults say cable connections are their primary means of watching TV, while 28% cite streaming services and 9% say they use digital antennas. A generation ago, television was far and away the dominant news source for Americans, but now, the Internet substantially outpaces TV as a regular news source for adults younger than 50.

Additionally, 37% of the younger adults who prefer watching the news over reading it cite the web, not television, as their platform of choice. Social media is also a rising source of news: Two-thirds of adults—including 78% of those under 50—get at least some news from social media sites.[78]

You can try to wish things were like they used to be. They won't be. So, what are we to do? We can't stop the use of media. We can't leave our homes, or even stay in them, and be totally free of it. How can our homes survive our media intake? Let's teach young people to protect their minds.

---

[78] http://www.pewresearch.org/fact-tank/2017/09/13/about-6-in-10-young-adults-in-u-s-primarily-use-online-streaming-to-watch-tv. Accessed on October 22, 2018.

2. <u>Free Your Mind</u>

All things are lawful unto me, but all things are not expedient: all things are lawful for me, but I will not be brought under the power of any. (I Cor. 6:12).

All things are lawful for me, but all things are not expedient: all things are lawful for me, but all things edify not. (I Cor. 10:23).

Whether therefore ye eat, or drink, or whatsoever ye do, do all to the glory of God. (I Cor. 10:31).

As God's children, we are given great freedom. We are free from the chains of sin and death! We are given freedom to have fun and be entertained, but are we being responsible in our choices? Is the music that you are listening to building you up or tearing you down? Do the movies and TV shows you are watching glorify God? Do they send a good message? Have you set standards for yourself, or do you accept anything that comes out of Hollywood? We must free our minds—to God and to His leading in our lives. With so much noise that seems to be all around us, we need to make sure that we are not becoming slaves to the technology.

Practice learning the difference between what is necessary and what is entertainment. What if, at least one day a week, your home became technology free; or there was a ban on social media for a certain number of days. What if, for some period of time, the radio was silenced, or you lived without the internet or cell phone? What if, when you normally would have watched a movie, you played a game as a family? Over time, you'd rediscover how our lives have been filled with nonessential things to the point where we let them crowd out what really matters.

Try it. Try giving up entertainment in the name of focusing on what is really necessary. This needs to be championed by the adults that are in a teenager's life. It is imperative that they see adults who are not addicted to the devices that are around them.

3. Surrender Your Mind

> *I beseech you therefore, brethren, by the mercies of God, that ye present your bodies a **living sacrifice**, holy, acceptable unto God, which is your reasonable service. And be **not conformed** to this world: but be ye **transformed** by the renewing of your mind, that ye may prove what is that good, and acceptable, and perfect, will of God. (Rom. 12:1–2)*

As Christians, we must be willing to offer God the best that we have, not just what is left after we fill the desires of our carnal hearts. Too many young people say that they will surrender to the Lord when they are older, but they forget this passage demands surrender in the present tense. We are not to conform but be transformed. God wants your body, heart, and your mind, not to limit what you can do as a Christian, but to transform your life. In this area of music and media, God desires us to surrender our minds to His will, and then He can transform our thinking. What does that look like? According to the text in Romans 12, a young person needs to surrender their will and their wants. This includes the music, media, and technological aspects of our lives.

In the text in Romans 12:1, this surrender includes the sacrifice of our physical bodies.

> But observe the pregnant collocation here of "the body" with "the reason." "Give over your bodies"; not now your spirit, your intelligence, your sentiments, your aspirations, but "your bodies," to your Lord. Is this an anticlimax? Have we retreated from the higher to the lower, in coming from the contemplation of sovereign grace and the eternal

glory to that of the physical frame of man? No more than the Lord Jesus did when He walked down from the hill of Transfiguration to the crowd below, and to the sins and miseries it presented. He came from the scene of glory to serve man in its abiding inner light. And even He, in the days of His flesh, served men, ordinarily, only through His sacred body: walking to them with His feet; touching them with His hands; meeting their eyes with His; speaking with His lips the words that were spirit and life. As with Him so with us, it is only through the body, practically, that we can "serve our generation by the will of God." Not without the body but through it the spirit must tell on the embodied spirits around us. We look, we speak, we hear, we write, we do, we travel, by means of these material servants of the will, our living limbs. Without the body, where should we be, as to other men? And therefore, without the surrender of the body, where are we, as to other men, from the point of view of the will of God?[79]

In this text, we also see that surrender means a restriction of the world's influence. This is found in verse 2 where we are not to let the world conform us. This is so important when we are talking about music and media. The world continually pressures the young person to conform. This pressure must be overcome by surrendering their will to an Almighty God.

Several great truths are self-evident if serious consideration is given to the challenge of the text. First, evil is contagious and aggressive. Like a fatal disease it will invade every cell of our being if we consent to let it have its course.

---

[79] Jimmy Swaggart, *The Expositors Study Bible King James Version* (Baton Rouge, LA: Jimmy Swaggart Ministries, 2005), 326.

Second, spiritual progress is to be made despite handicaps. The world about us will not congratulate us because of our utter devotion to God. Third, the Christian life is not be thought of as "business as usual."

The world about us is active and aggressive. It insists on conformity. It resents and opposes nonconformity. Jesus was referring to this danger in the parable of the soils as he described the fate of the seed that fell among the thorns, "And that which fell among thorns are they, which, when they have heard, go forth, and are choked with the cares and riches and pleasures of this life, and bring no fruit to perfection." (Luke 8:14)[80]

4. Defend Your Mind

The sacrifice of the wicked is abomination: how much more, when he bringeth it with a wicked mind? (Prov. 21:27)

Thou wilt keep him in perfect peace, whose mind is stayed on thee: because he trusteth in thee. (Isa. 26:3.

But when his heart was lifted up, and his mind hardened in pride, he was deposed from his kingly throne, and they took his glory from him. (Dan. 5:20)

Jesus said unto him, Thou shalt love the Lord thy God with all thy heart, and with all thy soul, and with all thy mind. (Matt. 22:37)

---

[80] https://timelesstruths.wordpress.com/2010/12/01/i-know-you-are-hurting. Accessed on October 22, 2018.

These were more noble than those in Thessalonica, in that they received the word with all readiness of mind, and searched the scriptures daily, whether those things were so. (Acts 17:11)

Finally, brethren, whatsoever things are true, whatsoever things are honest, whatsoever things are just, whatsoever things are pure, whatsoever things are lovely, whatsoever things are of good report; if there be any virtue, and if there be any praise, think on these things. Those things, which ye have both learned, and received, and heard, and seen in me, do: and the God of peace shall be with you. (Phil. 4:8–9)

Take the verses listed above and underline them in your Bible. Better yet, make a wallpaper for your phone and laptop. Keep the Word of God in front of you more than you are keeping the ever-creeping devilish media in front of you. When the message of media comes and it is challenging your Christian principles or ethics, fight back with the protection of God's Word. The Word of God is powerful, and it is alive. Through the power of the Word of God, we can overcome the massive onslaught that this current age of media seems to be inflicting on the lives of adults and young people.

Learn to exercise discernment. Please take some time to come up with some protections for the young person in your home and in your church. Consider some texts in Scripture and find some good books and other resources that will help you to ponder the path of your feet. You want to promote truth in your home and in your church. The book of Proverbs tells us to *"Buy the truth and sell it not; also wisdom, and instruction, and understanding" (Prov. 23:23)*. Don't settle for the media to train your young people. Let the godly influence of Scripture, good parents, and a good church be the basis for the truth that your young people will build their life.

There is a great song that we have sung for years in churches written by the blind author, Fanny Crosby. The words are a great reminder of what we should be meditating upon as we go through this life. This gospel song by Fanny Crosby first appeared with William Kirkpatrick's tune in the hymnal *Songs of Redeeming Love* published in 1882. This is one of 8,000 hymns composed by the blind American poetess. You can sense the scriptural context as you read through the verses and chorus of the song.

> Redeemed—how I love to proclaim it!
> Redeemed by the blood of the Lamb;
> Redeemed thru His infinite mercy—
> His child, and forever, I am.
> I think of my blessed Redeemer.
> I think of Him all the day long;
> I sing, for I cannot be silent;
> His love is the theme of my song.

> Chorus:
> Redeemed, redeemed,
> Redeemed by the blood of the Lamb;
> redeemed, redeemed,
> His child, and forever, I am.[81]

Additional Resources for Personal Study

Sermonaudio.com

Dr. Dan Sweatt, *5 Principles to Measure Music* ~ 1/6/2004 & 1/7/2004 ~ Preached at BJU

CCM Is a Spiritual Failure ~ 3/3/2004 ~ Preached at BJU

Pastor Mark Montgomery, *Godly Christian Music* ~ 6/28/16 ~ Preached at Mt. Zion Camp

---

[81] Osbeck, 92.

Pastor Archie Parrish, *Technology: A Biblical Perspective* ~ 3/2/2017—preached at Fairhaven Baptist Church

Pastor Archie Parrish, *Technology: The Biblical Practice* ~ 3/9/2017—preached at Fairhaven Baptist Church

Books

Tim Fisher, *The Battle for Christian Music*

Tim Fisher, *Harmony at Home*

Dan Lucarini, *Why I left the Contemporary Christian Music Movement: Confessions of a Former Worship Leader*

Mike Foster, *The Spiritual Song: The Missing Element in Church Music*

Kent Brandenburg, *Sound Music or Sounding Brass: The Issue of Biblically Godly Music*

Dana F. Everson, *Sound Roots: Steps to Building a Biblical Philosophy of Music*

Lindsay Terry, *A Complete Manual for the Ministry of Church*

Frank Garlock & Kurt Woetzel, *Music in the Balance*

Erich McCandless, *The Lord's Song*

John Dyer, *From the Garden to the City*

Tim Challies, *The Next Story*

Tony Reinke, *12 Ways Your Phone Is Changing You*

Rand Humell, *The Dark Side of the Internet*

YouTube.com

David Cloud, *The Foreign Spirit of Contemporary Worship Music*

David Cloud, *Music for Good or Evil*

Jeremiah Mitchell, FairhavenClasses Channel: *Church Music Materials & Methods*

Jeremiah Mitchell, Fairhavenmedia Channel: *Standards and Separation: Music Standards*

Chapter 14

N - The Need for Wisdom

Get wisdom, get understanding: forget it not; neither decline from the words of my mouth. Forsake her not, and she shall preserve thee: love her, and she shall keep thee. Wisdom is the principal thing; therefore get wisdom: and with all thy getting get understanding. Exalt her, and she shall promote thee: she shall bring thee to honor, when thou dost embrace her. She shall give to thine head an ornament of grace: a crown of glory shall she deliver to thee. Hear, O my son, and receive my sayings; and the years of thy life shall be many. I have taught thee in the way of wisdom; I have led thee in right paths. (Prov. 4:5–11)

The *New York Times* reported in 1994 that the Quaker Oats Company was purchasing Snapple drinks. Many can remember the popularity of Snapple drinks because at the time they were the beverage leader for fruit drinks and iced teas. Ultimately, the purchase of Snapple turned out to be a total debacle for the Quaker Oats Company and for numerous executives within the company. Quaker Oats Company paid $1.7 billion to buy Snapple. A few years later they sold the Snapple side of the company for only $300 million—a loss of a mere $1.4 billion![82] Needless to say, it wasn't long thereafter that the chairman and chief executive who had promoted the acquisition of Snapple resigned.

---

[82] https://www.nytimes.com/1997/03/28/business/quaker-to-sell-snapple-for-300-million.html. Accessed on August 17, 2018.

As Christians, the choices we make can have negative spiritual consequences if we are not careful of the paths that we choose. It is important in dealing with teenagers that we present the proper path to godly wisdom. Without godly wisdom, a young person will be at the will and whim of every person, theorem, philosophy, and wind of doctrine. It's imperative that parents and spiritual leaders start the process early to instill godly wisdom in a young person's life. Take the time to read and study Proverbs 4:5–9 and then consider the following information that helps in understanding the book of Proverbs.

What is wisdom and the importance of wisdom? Proverbs 2:10–11 tells us that wisdom protects our paths. This chapter deals much with our walk. Proverbs 3:5–6 also tells us that wisdom directs our paths. Proverbs 3 deals more with some specific things to do and the blessing enjoined when we follow wisdom's way. We then come to the text listed above in verses 10–12. This chapter concludes this pathway discussion telling us that wisdom perfects our path. So, what is wisdom?

The Characteristics of Wisdom

I wisdom dwell with prudence, and find out knowledge of witty inventions. (Prov. 8:12)

The fear of the Lord is to hate evil: pride, and arrogancy, and the evil way, and the froward mouth, do I hate. (Prov. 8:13)

We might say it as "the mouth of perversions do I hate."[83] This is something that is quite real today. How often do we hear vile speech in our society? Wisdom flows from the character of God, and that character has been revealed in Christ. Evil, pride, arrogance, and an evil way are hateful to Him. If we belong to Him, we will hate these things also.

---

[83] J. Vernon McGee, *Through the Bible with J. Vernon McGee* (Nashville, Tennessee: Nelson Publishers, 1991), 85.

Counsel is mine, and sound wisdom: I am understanding; I have strength. (Prov. 8:14)

My fruit is better than gold, yea, than fine gold; and my revenue than choice silver. (Prov. 8:19)

These are not stocks or bonds or real estate but wonderful spiritual gifts that He bestows. A wise person has an inner strength of spirit, and God will bless their lives and their efforts. "*That I may cause those that love me to inherit substance; and I will fill their treasures*" *(Prov. 8:21)*.

Wisdom is found in a relationship with Jesus Christ.

When there were no depths, I was brought forth; when there were no fountains abounding with water. Before the mountains were settled, before the hills was I brought forth: while as yet he had not made the earth, nor the fields, nor the highest part of the dust of the world. When he prepared the heavens, I was there: when he set a compass upon the face of the depth. (Prov. 8:24–27)

A saved person can rest and grow in the knowledge of Jesus Christ. We are living amid great unbelief in our day, but let the skeptic be skeptical. Our relationship is a personal relationship with the Lord Jesus Christ, and He is the Word. "The Word was with God, and the Word was God" (John 1:1). What a tremendous statement!

All things were made by him; and without him was not any thing made that was made. (John 1:3)

When he established the clouds above: when he strengthened the fountains of the deep: When he gave to the sea his decree, that the waters should not pass his commandment: when he appointed the foundations of the earth. (Prov. 8:28–29)

Have you ever stood by the seashore and wondered why the water doesn't spill over? Why does it stay where it is? The Word says, *"He gave to the sea his decree, that the waters should not pass his commandment."* God has made a law that keeps the sea right where it is.

Without the Lord Jesus was *"not anything made that was made"* because *"All things were made by Him."* He is the firstborn of all creation. He is superior to all. Why? Because by Him the Father brought all things into being, for He is the uncreated God, and He was "rejoicing always before Him." These wonderful delights and joys come to us through the amazing grace of God. How wonderful all of this is! This is the power that is available through the wisdom of Jesus Christ. This wisdom is able to establish, give strength, bless our efforts, and establish safe boundaries to live by. *"Now therefore hearken unto me, O ye children: for blessed are they that keep my ways. Hear instruction, and be wise, and refuse it not" (Prov. 8:32–33).*

Wisdom is Christ, and there must be a love for Him. So then, we come back to our question of how we get wisdom. Proverbs 2:7 says, *"He layeth up sound wisdom for the righteous: he is a buckler to them that walk uprightly,"* and James 1:5 says, *"If any of you lack wisdom, let him ask of God."* God is the author of wisdom; Christ personifies wisdom; and the Holy Spirit who indwells us teaches us wisdom. Therefore, it is important to develop a relationship with Christ as early as possible. When a parent or authority decides to go their own way and forsake God's Word, they are choosing folly. When a young person decides to float through life without a love and desire for God, Christ, and the Holy Spirit, they are choosing folly. God's wisdom is gained through a knowledge and deep love for Jesus Christ.

Spurgeon tells the story of an American vessel that was attacked by a wounded whale. The huge monster ran out for the length of a mile from the ship and then turned around with the whole force of its being and struck the ship, and making it leak at every timber. It quickly began to sink. The sailors dispensed the lifeboats, filled them as quickly as they could with the necessaries of life, and began to pull away from the sinking ship. Just then two strong men could be seen leaping into the water from the safety of a lifeboat and swam toward the doomed vessel. They leapt on board, disappeared for a moment, and then came up holding something in their hands. Just as they sprang into the sea, down went the vessel, and they were carried round in the vortex; but they were observed to be swimming, not as if struggling to get away, but as if looking for something, which at last they both seized and carried to the boats.

What was this treasure? What could have been of such importance that they would risk their lives to save? It was the ship's compass, which had been left behind, without which they could not have found their way out of those lonely southern seas into the high-road of commerce.[84] That compass was life to them, and the gospel of the living God is the same to us. You and I must venture all for the gospel; this infallible Word of God must be guarded to the death. Men may tell us what they please and say what they will, but we will risk everything sooner than give up those eternal principles by which we have been saved.

Wisdom in Choosing Between Paths

1. Do Not Take the Path of Darkness (Prov 4:14–17, 19)

The Way of the Fraudulent. If you cannot be rich without doing right and being honest, then be content to be poor. Notice the following verses and see to what the path of the crooked and fraudulent leads. This path is self-centered and devious and is only out to gain treasures for the coffers of evil.

> *My son, if sinners entice thee, consent thou not. If they say, Come with us, let us lay wait for blood, let us lurk privily for the innocent without cause: let us swallow them up alive as the grave; and whole, as those that go down into the pit: my son, walk not thou in the way with them; refrain thy foot*

---

[84] https://en.wikipedia.org/wiki/Sultana_(steamboat). Accessed on July 31, 2018.

from their path: for their feet run to evil, and make haste to shed blood. Surely in vain the net is spread in the sight of any bird. And they lay wait for their own blood; they lurk privily for their own lives. So are the ways of every one that is greedy of gain; which taketh away the life of the owners thereof. (Prov. 1:10–12; 15–19)

The Way of the Extravagant. Spending money you do not possess is the path of the foolish. Let this be one of your maxims, *"Owe no man anything."* Learn to be wise with the use of the money that God gives you.

The rich ruleth over the poor, and the borrower is servant to the lender. (Prov. 22:7)

Honor the LORD with thy substance, and with the firstfruits of all thine increase: So shall thy barns be filled with plenty, and thy presses shall burst out with new wine. (Prov. 3:9–10.

The Way of the Insolent (Disrespecter, Scorner, New Thinker)

When wisdom entereth into thine heart, and knowledge is pleasant unto thy soul; Discretion shall preserve thee, understanding shall keep thee: To deliver thee from the way of the evil man, from the man that speaketh froward things; Who leave the paths of uprightness, to walk in the ways of darkness; Who rejoice to do evil, and delight in the frowardness of the wicked; Whose ways are crooked, and they froward in their paths. (Prov. 2:10–15)

Surely he scorneth the scorners: but he giveth grace unto the lowly. (Prov. 3:34)

*Put away from thee a froward mouth, and perverse lips put
far from thee. Let thine eyes look right on, and let thine eyelids look straight before thee. Ponder the path of thy feet, and
let all thy ways be established. Turn not to the right hand nor
to the left: remove thy foot from evil. (Prov. 4:24–27)*

a. **A Scorner Is Void of Wisdom.** *"A scorner seeketh wisdom, and
findeth it not: but knowledge is easy unto him that understan-
deth" (Prov. 14:6).* A scorner is one who chooses the wicked,
froward path. The interesting point of this verse is that the
scorner comes to the place that he would like to get wisdom,
but he cannot obtain it because he is unteachable. He is only
trying to gain this for his own evil ways, and God is the giver
of wisdom and sees through his wicked intentions.

b. **A Scorner Hates Those That Try to Help Him**. *"Reprove not
a scorner, lest he hate thee: rebuke a wise man, and he will love
thee" (Prov. 9:8).*

*A wise son heareth his father's instruction: but a scorner
heareth not rebuke. (Prov. 13:1)*

*A scorner loveth not one that reproveth him: neither will
he go unto the wise. (Prov. 15:12)*

c. **A Scorner Is Hard to Deal With** But the proud spirit does not
easily bend. He has never heard his father's instruction with defer-
ence. Soon therefore he takes "the scorner's seat." (Ps. i. 1) When
rebuke becomes necessary, he hears it not (Chap. xv. 12); turns
from it to his own course at the extreme point from wisdom (Chap.
xii. 1; xv. 5), on the brink of ruin (Chap. xv. 10; xxix. 1); carrying
about him a fearful mark of reprobation! (1 Sam. ii. 25) Let me

remember—If I am reluctant to hear the faithful rebuke of men, I am prepared to resist the rebuke of God. And how soon may this stubborn revolt bring his long-suffering to an end (2 Chron. xxxvi. 16), and my soul to destruction! (Jer. v. 3. Zeph. iii. 2) 'From hardness of heart, and contempt of thy word and commandment, Good Lord, deliver me.[85]

d. **A Scorner is Filled with Himself.** *"Proud and haughty scorner is his name, who dealeth in proud wrath" (Prov. 21:24).*

e. **A Scorner Can't Be Reconciled–Cast Him Out!** *"Cast out the scorner, and contention shall go out; yea, strife and reproach shall cease" (Prov. 22:10).* Oh, the hard path that the scorner chooses. This insolent, rebellious attitude needs to be cast out. There comes a point that the spiritual safety of others around him or her needs to be considered. We should always be in the business of restoration and love, but the Bible is clear about the person that chooses to stay in the path of the scorner— steer clear and avoid them!

2. <u>Take the Path of Light (Prov. 4:18–27)</u>

But the path of the just is as the shining light, that shineth more and more unto the perfect day. The way of the wicked is as darkness: they know not at what they stumble. My son, attend to my words; incline thine ear unto my sayings. Let them not depart from thine eyes; keep them in the midst of thine heart. For they are life unto those that find them, and health to all their flesh. Keep thy heart with all diligence; for out of it are the issues of life. (Prov. 4:18–23)

---

[85] https://faculty.gordon.edu/hu/bi/ted_hildebrandt/otesources/20-proverbs/text/books/bridges-proverbscommentary/bridges-proverbs.pdf. Accessed on September 4, 2018.

Notice how much comparison there is from a pathway of light and a pathway of darkness (Prov. 1:27–28; 2:12–13,17–18; 4:19).

A Path of Listening, *"My Son, attend unto my words." (Proverbs 4:20.* Whatever enters my ears will affect my mind, my heart, and my decisions, so I'd better be careful what and to whom I am listening. The Psalmist in Psalm 1 tells the reader that if you listen to the wrong crowd, they will affect you. How? You will congregate, start walking, and eventually you will enjoy their company so much that you are sitting with the ungodly. When God speaks, we must be able to hear God's voice. John 10 speaks of the sheep hearing the Shepherd's voice and then obeying what He says.[86]

A Path of Guarding, *"Keep thy heart with all diligence." (Proverbs 4:23).* We need to be careful what we allow in our heart. For what comes into the heart can soften or harden it. Whatever the heart loves, the ears will hear, and the eyes will see. If we allow pollution into our heart, disease can spread throughout our whole being. It will not be long before wrongful appetites and desires will become open sins and public shame.

Consider some other passages about the heart. The Bible warns us to avoid a double heart (Ps. 12:2), a hard heart (Prov. 28:14), a proud heart (Prov. 21:4), an unbelieving heart (Heb. 3:12), a cold heart (Matt. 24:12), and an unclean heart (Ps. 51:10). Therefore the Psalmist cried out to the Lord to *"Search me, O God, and know my heart"* (Ps. 139:23).[87]

A Path of Right Speaking, *"Put away from thee a froward mouth and perverse lips put far from thee." (Proverbs 4:24).* Whatever is in the heart will eventually come out of the lips (Matt. 12:33–34). A person with a regenerated heart should have speech that's gracious and *"seasoned with salt"* (Col. 4:6). The ancient Romans in the area of public speaking had a saying, *"Cum grano salis"*—"Take it with a grain of salt." However,

---

[86] Warren Wiersbe, *The Wiersbe Bible Commentary* (Colorado Springs, CO: David C. Cook, 2007), 1065.

[87] ibid., 1065.

Christians are supposed to insert salt into their speech. The idea is that a Christian's words are pure and honest.

Proverbs has a lot to say about human speech. The word *mouth* is used over fifty times and the word *lips* over forty times just in the book of Proverbs. Solomon gives stern advice on what to avoid with the tongue. He warns about perverse lips (Prov. 4:24), lying lips (Prov. 12:22), flattering lips (Prov. 20:19), deceptive lips (Prov. 24:28), and undisciplined lips (Prov. 10:19). *"He that keepeth his mouth keepeth his life: but he that openeth wide his lips shall have destruction" (Prov. 13:3).* It is imperative that we as pastors and parents help our young people choose a path of wise words. This will help them avoid many sorrows that evil words can bring.[88]

A Path of Right Viewing, *"Let thine eyes look right on, and let thine eyelids look straight before thee." (Proverbs 4:25).* Our eyes many times are the gate to either good results or bad results. Abraham was the friend of God because he walked by faith and *"looked for a city . . . whose builder and maker is God" (Heb. 11:10).* Lot was a friend of the world because he chose to live by sight and moved his family toward the wicked city of Sodom (Gen. 13:10, 12). Everybody has a choice in which direction they will look. The direction that we are looking helps to determine our values, actions, and plans. The wise man will imitate David who said, *"I will set no wicked thing before mine eyes" (Ps. 101:3),* and who prayed, *"Turn away mine eyes from beholding vanity" (Ps. 119:37).* Instead of looking to this world, focus and look unto Jesus as instructed in Hebrews 12:2.

A Path of Contemplating, *"Ponder the path of thy feet, and let all thy ways be established. Turn not to the right hand nor the left: remove thy foot from evil." (Proverbs 4:26–27).* The Hebrew word for *ponder* has the meaning "to weigh" or "to make level." It is a relative of the word *scales* (Prov. 16:11). There is an interesting tale of the great philosopher Socrates. He gave a final speech before committing suicide. He said, "The

---

[88] Ibid.,1065.

unexamined life is not worth living." In II Corinthians 13:5, the apostle Paul wrote, "Examine yourselves." We would be wise to heed both Socrates and the apostle Paul's advice. We need to teach our youth at an early age to consider the path that they are taking. There are always choices, and we need to help our youth learn to be wise in their choices. They sometimes take wrong paths because they have not paused to think about the end of that pathway. The wise youth will foresee the end of the path; they will pause to consider and not just be carried by the crowd down a path that is popular at the moment. *"All the ways of a man are clean in his own eyes; but the Lord weigheth the spirits" (Prov. 16:2).* We have seen this before in Proverbs 14:12, *"There is a way which seemeth right unto a man, but the end thereof are the ways of death."*

There are even a great many Christians who think that their walk is perfect before God. The whole issue is wrapped up in this one verse of Scripture: *"But if we walk in the light, as he is in the light, we have fellowship one with another, and the blood of Jesus Christ his Son cleanseth us from all sin" (I John 1:7).* We need to hold up the mirror of the Word of God to our lives, and it will reveal that things are not quite right, that we don't measure up to God's standard. You may measure up to the standard of the chamber of commerce, and they may make you Man of the Year; your club may reward you and give you a plaque; your church may pat you on the back; and your neighbors may say that you are a great guy. But my friend, when you see yourself in the light of the Word of God, then you see that you have a need and that there are spots on your life. You will see that you have come short of the glory of God. Your way may be clean in your own eyes, but it is not clean in God's eyes. *"If we say that we have fellowship with Him, and walk in darkness, we lie, and do not the truth" (I John 1:6).*[89]

What path will you choose? As a counselor that leads the youth in their paths of life, let's make sure that we are showing the true meaning of wisdom. Wisdom is found in a deep-rooted knowledge of Jesus Christ. From that vantage point, we can build a godly teenager who can understand what pathways are out there. They will know that there are many choices throughout life. Some are not so harmful, but other choices appear pleasant at first, but the end thereof are the ways of destruction.

A FENCE or an AMBULANCE
Joseph Malins

'Twas a dangerous cliff, as they freely confessed,
Though to walk near its crest was so pleasant;
But over its terrible edge there had slipped
A duke and full many a peasant.
So the people said something would have to be done,
But their projects did not at all tally;
Some said, "Put a fence around the edge of the cliff,"
Some, "An ambulance down in the valley."

But the cry for the ambulance carried the day,
For it spread through the neighboring city;
A fence may be useful or not, it is true,
But each heart became brimful of pity
For those who slipped over that dangerous cliff;
And the dwellers in highway and alley
Gave pounds or gave pence, not to put up a fence,
But an ambulance down in the valley.

---

[89] McGee, 55.

"For the cliff is all right, if you're careful," they said,
"And, if folks even slip and are dropping,
It isn't the slipping that hurts them so much,
As the shock down below when they're stopping."
So day after day, as these mishaps occurred,
Quick forth would these rescuers sally
To pick up the victims who fell off the cliff,
With their ambulance down in the valley.

Then an old sage remarked: "It's a marvel to me
That people give far more attention to repairing results
Than to stopping the cause,
When they'd much better aim at prevention.
Let us stop at its source all this mischief," cried he,
"Come, neighbors and friends, let us rally;
If the cliff we will fence we might almost dispense
With the ambulance down in the valley.

"Oh, he's a fanatic," the others rejoined,
"Dispense with the ambulance? Never!
He's dispense with all charities, too, if he could;
No! No! We'll support them forever.
Aren't we picking up folks just as fast as they fall?
And shall this man dictate to us? Shall he?
Why should people of sense stop to put up a fence,
While the ambulance works in the valley?"

But a sensible few, who are practical took,
Will not bear with such nonsense much longer;
They believe that prevention is better than cure,
And their party will soon be the stronger.
Encourage them then, with your purse, voice, and pen,
And while other philanthropists dally,

They will scorn all pretense and put up a stout fence
On the cliff that hangs over the valley.

Better guide well the young than reclaim them when old,
For the voice of true wisdom is calling,
"To rescue the fallen is good, but 'tis best
To prevent other people from falling."
Better close up the source of temptation and crime
Than deliver from dungeon or galley;
Better put a strong fence round the top of the cliff
Than an ambulance down in the valley.[90]

---

[90] Hazel Felleman, *The Best Loved Poems of the American People* (Garden City, NY: Doubleday & Company, Inc., 1936), 273.

Chapter 15

O - Obedience—The Pathway of Blessing

The Bible clearly outlines that obedience is a vital part of the Christian's walk with the Lord. Without a proper understanding of obedience, a Christian young person will fail in his youth, but he will also develop bad habits for the remaining life here on this earth.[91] Obedience is the starting point of true holiness. In I Peter 1:22 we read, *"Seeing ye have purified your souls in obeying the truth."* Complete acceptance of God's truth was not merely a matter of intellectual assent or strong emotion. It was subjecting one's life to the dominion of the truth of God. The Christian life is, first and foremost, characterized by obedience.[92]

What Is Obedience?

Let's define obedience both in the aspect of dictionary definition and then a biblical definition.

Webster's 1828 dictionary definitions:
OBEY, verb transitive [Latin obedio; Gr.]

---

[91] David Sorenson, *Obedience: The Key to Christian Living* (Pekin, IL: Faith Baptist Church, 1977), 3–4.

[92] Andrew Murray, *The Blessings of Obedience* (New Kensington, PA: Whitaker House, 1984), 17.

1. To comply with the commands, orders or instructions of a superior, or with the requirements of law, moral, political or municipal; to do that which is commanded or required, or to forbear doing that which is prohibited.

   "Children, obey your parents in the Lord." Eph. 6:1

   "Servants, obey in all things your masters." Col. 3:20

   "He who has learned to obey will know how to command."

2. To submit to the government of; to be ruled by.

   All Israel obeyed (Song of Solomon 1; I Chronicles 29; Daniel 7:27)

3. To submit to the direction or control of. Seamen say, the ship will not obey the helm.

   Let not sin therefore reign in your mortal body, that ye should obey it in the lusts thereof. (Romans 6:12; James 3:3)

4. To yield to the impulse, power or operation of; as, to obey stimulus.

   Relentless time, destroying power, whom stone and brass obey.

The Biblical Concept of Obedience

Not every one that saith unto me, Lord, Lord, shall enter into the kingdom of heaven; but he that doeth the will of my Father which is in heaven. (Matt. 7:21)

And why call ye me, Lord, Lord, and do not the things which I say?

(Luke 6:46)

If ye love me, keep my commandments. (John 14:15)

Then Peter and the other apostles answered and said, We ought to obey God rather than men. (Acts 5:29)

Know ye not, that to whom ye yield yourselves servants to obey, his servants ye are to whom ye obey; whether of sin unto death, or of obedience unto righteousness? (Rom. 6:16)

Children, obey your parents in the Lord: for this is right. Honor thy father and mother; (which is the first commandment with promise;) That it may be well with thee, and thou mayest live long on the earth. And, ye fathers, provoke not your children to wrath: but bring them up in the nurture and admonition of the Lord. Servants, be obedient to them that are your masters according to the flesh, with fear and trembling, in singleness of your heart, as unto Christ; not with eyeservice, as menpleasers; but as the servants of Christ, doing the will of God from the heart; with good will doing service, as to the Lord, and not to men: knowing that whatsoever good thing any man doeth, the same shall he receive of the Lord, whether he be bond or free. And, ye masters, do the same things unto them, forbearing threatening: knowing that your Master also is in heaven; neither is there respect of persons with him. (Eph. 6:1–9)

Remember them which have the rule over you, who have spoken unto you the word of God: whose faith follow, considering the end of their conversation. (Heb. 13:7)

Obey them that have the rule over you, and submit yourselves: for they watch for your souls, as they that must give account, that they may do it with joy, and not with grief: for that is unprofitable for you. (Heb. 13:17)

But be ye doers of the word, and not hearers only, deceiving your own selves. (James 1:22.

As obedient children, not fashioning yourselves according to the former lusts in your ignorance. (I Pet. 1:14)

For this is the love of God, that we keep his commandments: and his commandments are not grievous. (I John 5:3)

Looking at both the dictionary definition and some of the biblical references, we can draw some important conclusions about obedience in a young person's life.

Obedience can be defined as "following commands from someone superior to another." Examples of authority figures are parents, teachers, coaches, and babysitters. The pastor falls into a unique category because families are members of a church. The pastor should not undermine parental authority, but his job is to help parents lead in their home. This leading and guiding occurs through preaching and teaching. Because God ordained this, we shouldn't have to worry about teenagers pitting their pastor against the parent. This would be the same as a young person pitting one parent against the other. Both have authority, and the teenager is wrong in pitting authority to get an advantage in his way of doing things or in getting away with sin.

There is authority beyond parental authority. Adults have God-given authority as well as employers, spiritual leaders, and governmental authority. It is not right to rebel against authority. It is imperative to lead our young people in good relationships with the authority that is around us. There are ways and times to resist authority when they are leading against God's Word or are out of the boundaries set for them by God. However, this must be approached with much caution, prayer, and fasting. Breaking down authority will have grave consequences for a younger generation.

Submission or surrender is a very important aspect of obedience. The devil will tell a young person that they are weak by surrendering or submitting to authority. The devil will tell them that they should do their own thing and go their own way. In reality, when someone does not submit to God and their God given authority, they are submitting to the flesh and the devil. This is still yielding or submitting. It is surrendering to that which is wrong. Surrender is the first step in the direction one will go.

Obedience to God is an expression of love for Him. This is revealed in passages found in the books of John, Peter, and I John. All these texts indicate that our love for God will be expressed by our doing what He says. We cannot say that we love God and then do our own desires, which will be contrary to the Lord.

LOVE CONSTRAINING TO OBEDIENCE
By William Cowper

No strength of nature can suffice
To serve the Lord aright:
And what she has she misapplies,
For want of clearer light.

How long beneath the law I lay
In bondage and distress;
I toil'd the precept to obey,
But toil'd without success.

Then, to abstain from outward sin
Was more than I could do;
Now, if I feel its power within,
I feel I hate it too.

Then all my servile works were done
A righteousness to raise;
Now, freely chosen in the Son,
I freely choose His ways.

"What shall I do," was then the word,
"That I may worthier grow?"
"What shall I render to the Lord?"
Is my inquiry now.

To see the law by Christ fulfill'd
And hear His pardoning voice,
Changes a slave into a child,
And duty into choice.[93]

How Do I Obey?

There are seven areas of obeying that seem to be clearly taught in Scripture. We will consider these seven in the next few paragraphs.

1. Obedience in Salvation

It is clearly taught in Scripture that salvation happens by faith. It is a step of obedience that must be taken by the unbeliever. Romans 10:13 says, "Call on the name of the Lord." This calling is a command; it is something that is required of the unbeliever. Without this confession of

---

[93] http://hymnbook.igracemusic.com/hymns/love-constraining-to-obedience. Accessed on September 20, 2018.

faith, there will be no salvation. As we consider what obedience means in the life of a young person, salvation is the starting point. A right understanding of his standing in God's eyes regarding sin, separation from God, and need for salvation is a primary starting point.

The Bible shows a young person that his righteousness is not impressive to God:

> *But we are all as an unclean thing, and all our righteousnesses are as filthy rags; and we all do fade as a leaf; and our iniquities, like the wind, have taken us away. (Isa. 64:6)*

> *As it is written, there is none righteous, no, not one: there is none that understandeth, there is none that seeketh after God. They are all gone out of the way, they are together become unprofitable; there is none that doeth good, no, not one. Their throat is an open sepulchre; with their tongues they have used deceit; the poison of asps is under their lips: whose mouth is full of cursing and bitterness: their feet are swift to shed blood: destruction and misery are in their ways: and the way of peace have they not known: there is no fear of God before their eyes (Rom. 3:10–18)*

Man is sinful, and so is a young person. Until he knows and understands that he was born in sin and that sin has ruined his relationship with the Lord, he will never be able to start down the road of blessing that comes with obedience. This sin is a rebellion that has been inbred since Adam and has been passed down to every generation since. Sin is a violation of God's law. It is a shortcoming of God's standard; it is a rebellion against God. According to Romans 6:23, this sin of disobedience will result in death. It must be resolved by calling upon the name of the Lord, confessing this sin of disobedience, and accepting God's free gift of salvation.

2. <u>Obedience in Church Attendance</u>

When a baby is born, he is brought home where he is then reared in a good, loving environment. This home will help the child to mature, to learn about love, to learn how to function outside of the home, and to understand obedience. Even so, a new believer is a spiritual "baby." The apostles Paul and Peter both reference the new believer as a "new-born babe."

> *And I, brethren, could not speak unto you as unto spiritual, but as unto carnal, even as unto babes in Christ. I have fed you with milk, and not with meat: for hitherto ye were not able to bear it, neither yet now are ye able. (I Cor. 3:1–2)*

> *As newborn babes, desire the sincere milk of the word that ye may grow thereby. (I Pet. 2:2)*

These verses show us that the new believer is a "babe in Christ." God in His wisdom made a "home" for that new believer. It is in the local, independent body of believers called the church. The book of Hebrews instructs the believer to get there and be a part of that group of believers. *"And let us consider one another to provoke unto love and to good works: Not forsaking the assembling of ourselves together, as the manner of some is; but exhorting one another: and so much the more, as ye see the day approaching"* (Heb. 10:24–25).

It is vital that we teach our young people the importance of the local church. It has become popular to demonize the local church, its ministries, and its outreach to the youth. Many claim that the church is usurping the authority of the family. If this is true, the fault is with the families themselves, not the church, because families make up the church. The leadership of the church and the membership work together to help young people *"grow in grace and in the knowledge of our Lord and Savior Jesus Christ"* (II Pet. 3:18).

3. <u>**Obedience in Strengthening the Christian Life**</u>

The Bible gives clear instructions about the reading and studying of His Word and in building up our Christian life. Consider the following:

> *And Jesus increased in wisdom and stature, and in favor with God and man. (Luke 2:52)*

> *But all that heard him were amazed, and said; is not this he that destroyed them which called on this name in Jerusalem, and came hither for that intent, that he might bring them bound unto the chief priests? But Saul increased the more in strength, and confounded the Jews which dwelt at Damascus, proving that this is very Christ. (Acts 9:21–22)*

> *For this cause we also, since the day we heard it, do not cease to pray for you, and to desire that ye might be filled with the knowledge of his will in all wisdom and spiritual under-standing; That ye might walk worthy of the Lord unto all pleasing, being fruitful in every good work, and increasing in the knowledge of God. (Col. 1:9–10)*

> *Whereby are given unto us exceeding great and precious prom-ises: that by these ye might be partakers of the divine nature, having escaped the corruption that is in the world through lust. And beside this, giving all diligence, add to your faith virtue; and to virtue knowledge; And to knowledge temper-ance; and to temperance patience; and to patience godli-ness; And to godliness brotherly kindness; and to brotherly kindness charity. For if these things be in you, and abound, they make you that ye shall neither be barren nor unfruitful in the knowledge of our Lord Jesus Christ. (II Pet. 1:4–8)*

These are not all the verses that can be found in the Bible on this subject, but these verses give a clear understanding that God wants the believer to grow. It is not a large leap of intellect to understand that growing requires proper food and exercise. For the believer, this comes through a disciplined regiment of studying God's Word and praying. A personal relationship with Jesus Christ is vital for the spiritual growth of a young person. As a member of God's family, it is living in disobedience to not read the Bible and pray properly. It should be a normal occurrence for the young person to get in God's Word and learn some things on his own. He needs to be obedient in reading the Bible so that he will come to the realization that God is not just the God of his parents and pastor, but God is his God as well.

4. Obedience in Public Statement of Faith

The Bible is clear that God expects a person to confess Him before men and not to be ashamed of the fact that he now belongs to Him.

> *For I am not ashamed of the gospel of Christ: for it is the power of God unto salvation to every one that believeth; to the Jew first, and also to the Greek. (Rom. 1:16.*

> *That if thou shalt confess with thy mouth the Lord Jesus, and shalt believe in thine heart that God hath raised him from the dead, thou shalt be saved. For with the heart man believeth unto righteousness; and with the mouth confession is made unto salvation. For the scripture saith, "Whosoever believeth on him shall not be ashamed. (Rom. 10:9–11)*

When a young lady gets engaged to her fiancé, there is usually no hesitation about making it public. In a sense, accepting Christ is similar in many respects to being married to Christ, and it should be made known publicly. This is first done through baptism. Scriptural baptism is a manifestation for the believer of what has transpired in his life. It is also a public testimony to others that something has changed in the new convert's life. It is also done through openly speaking about Christ to others (more on that aspect later).

5. <u>**Obedience in Separation from the World and Ungodly Influences**</u>

> *Be ye not unequally yoked together with unbelievers: for what fellowship hath righteousness with unrighteousness? and what communion hath light with darkness? And what concord hath Christ with Belial? or what part hath he that believeth with an infidel? And what agreement hath the temple of God with idols? for ye are the temple of the living God; as God hath said, I will dwell in them, and walk in them; and I will be their God, and they shall be my people. Wherefore come out from among them, and be ye separate, saith the Lord, and touch not the unclean thing; and I will receive you, And will be a Father unto you, and ye shall be my sons and daughters, saith the Lord Almighty. (II Cor. 6:14–18)*

> *If any man teach otherwise, and consent not to wholesome words, even the words of our Lord Jesus Christ, and to the doctrine which is according to godliness; He is proud, knowing nothing, but doting about questions and strifes of words, whereof cometh envy, strife, railings, evil surmisings, perverse disputings of men of corrupt minds, and destitute of the truth, supposing that gain is godliness: from such withdraw thyself. (I Tim. 6:3–5)*

These verses teach two important ideas for separation when it comes to a young person. The first is separation from the world. A good parent does not want his son chumming with those friends who will influence him to become a delinquent. They want him to separate from those ungodly influences. In the same way, God desires that for His children. God's nature is holy. He is completely apart from sin. He knows no sin. He is not capable of sinning. God actively hates sin and vents His wrath in punishment against sin.

The second idea presented in the book of I Timothy is that there will be those that will try to tear down good doctrine. This will happen in church and in youth groups. Godly authority will take note of this and help a young person to steer clear of those that will be divisive within the church. These types of young people and adults need to be avoided.

6. Obedience in Stewardship

"*The earth is the Lord's, and the fullness thereof; the world, and they that dwell therein*" *(Ps. 24:1).* This passage gives us the foundational principle for a Christian's stewardship. All that we have belongs to God. This is again verified in the New Testament:

> *What? Know ye not that your body is the temple of the Holy Ghost which is in you, which ye have of God, and ye are not your own? For ye are bought with a price: therefore glorify God in your body, and in your spirit, which are God's. (I Cor. 6:19–20)*

A steward is one who manages another's estate. In the Bible, a steward is someone whom God has given of His treasure. A steward is a manager or caretaker over the property which God has given to him. God expects His stewards to properly handle and to be obedient in his dealings with His property. Read the story of the talents in Matthew 25:14–30. This passage teaches great biblical principles regarding stewardship. God gives differing gifts or talents to individuals. He expects us to be careful and wise with that which has been given to us.

This means that every young person has been given some gift or talent by God. He may not believe it, even though that gift or talent may not be very well developed at this stage in his life. It is important for those that work with youth to understand this and to help nurture those gifts and talents. A one-talent youth or a five-talent youth is still responsible equally to take what they are given and use those talents to further Christ's kingdom. They are not to be used for personal gain or to be hidden and not multiplied.

7. <u>Obedience in Soul Winning</u>

Before Christ went back to heaven, He told His disciples that they should be witnesses. A witness is one who has seen and experienced first-hand what has transpired. A witness in a court is brought into the court-room to bear an eyewitness testimony concerning the case that is on trial. A Christian witness is one who has a first-hand experience or a first-hand account concerning the Christ, the Savior of the world. We are told in the Gospel of Mark what we are to witness about—we are to share the gospel, the good news that Jesus came to save sinners! This is soul winning. It is imperative that we teach our young people at an early age to be obedient to this command of sharing Christ with others. How can this be accomplished? Here are a few ideas.

1. Plan a time of soul winning for the teens. This could be once a month on their special youth day. There should be teaching times set up to help them understand how to share Christ with other young people.

2. Organize special days such as youth friend days or a special teen night designed to bring in an unsaved young person.

3. Set apart a special day where parents and young people go soul winning together.

4. Train the teens to be involved in outreach ministries in the church. This will develop a burden for the lost in the community.

5. Encourage parents to take their young people on a short mission's trip to a foreign field or to help a small church plant. This will again help them develop a godly burden to reach the world for Christ.

Why is Obedience Important?

Obedience is important because it is commanded in Scripture. Previously listed were numerous Scriptures that clearly show that God is concerned with obedience. There is a well-known story in the Old Testament about the life of King Saul. He was told to utterly destroy the Amalekites. King Saul had a different idea of what "utterly" meant.

And Samuel came to Saul: and Saul said unto him, Blessed be thou of the LORD: I have performed the commandment of the LORD. And Samuel said, What meaneth then this bleating of the sheep in mine ears, and the lowing of the oxen which I hear? And Samuel said, Hath the LORD as great delight in burnt offerings and sacrifices, as in obeying the voice of the LORD? Behold, to obey is better than sacrifice, and to hearken than the fat of rams. For rebellion is as the sin of witchcraft, and stubbornness is as iniquity and idolatry. Because thou hast rejected the word of the LORD, he hath also rejected thee from being king. (I Sam. 15:13–14, 22–23)

Obedience is a very important attribute for a believer. It is not a light thing to let a command of the Lord go undone. Obedience is also important because it reveals if we truly love the Lord. Love is shown by actions. Words are cheap, but actions reveal what the real heart is like.

<u>LOVE AND ACTIONS</u>

"I love Thee, I love Thee
and that Thou doest know;
But how much I love Thee,
my actions will show."[94]

<u>When Do I Stop Obeying?</u>

This may seem like a silly question, but many children and young people dream of the day that they will be "adults" so that they *don't have to obey anyone*! This, however, is not reality. The Bible clearly defines other types of authority besides parental authority. One example is governmental authority. The Bible tells us in Romans 13 that we are to be subject to those higher powers. In Hebrews 13, we are told as believers that there are pastors given to a church, who watch over the souls of its members. We see also in Romans 12 and in Ephesians 5 that there is a submissiveness that is to be common among all Christians. The "ladder-climbing" and "step-on" attitudes that permeate the world is to not be evident in a believer's life. Christian love is that which makes the world see that God has saved and made believers different according to John 13.

In *Discipleship Journal,* author Elaine Creasman writes:

> Pursuit of "good things" can hinder obedience. It has been said that "the good is the enemy of the best." I think of times my husband has asked me to do one thing for him during the day. When he gets home from work, I tell him all the good things I have done. But the question he always has for me is, "What about the thing I asked you to do?"

---

[94] https://hymnary.org/text/i_love_thee_i_love_thee_i_love_thee_my. Accessed on September 20, 2018.

Many times I have answered, "I forgot," or "I didn't have time." Or I've dismissed his request as trivial.

God asks that same question of us: "What about the thing I asked you to do? . . ."

I'm sure Abraham could have thought of a lot of good things to do instead of taking Isaac to be sacrificed. But I see no excuses in Genesis 22. God commanded; Abraham obeyed.[95]

What Are the Dangers of Disobeying?

In *General Patton's Principles for Life and Leadership,* General George S. Patton, Jr., says:

Picking the right leader is the most important task of any commander. I line up the candidates and say, "Men, I want a trench dug behind warehouse ten. Make this trench eight feet long, three feet wide and six inches deep."

While the candidates are checking their tools out at the warehouse, I watch them from a distance. They puzzle over why I want such a shallow trench. They argue over whether six inches is deep enough for a gun emplacement. Some complain that such a trench should be dug with power equipment. Others gripe that it is too hot or too cold to dig. If the men are above the rank of lieutenant, there will be complaints that they should not be doing such lowly labor. Finally, one man will order, "What

---

[95] Craig Brian Larson, *750 Engaging Illustrations for Preachers, Teachers, and Writers* (Grand Rapids, MI: Baker Books, 1993), 492.

difference does it make what [he] wants to do with this trench! Let's get it dug and get out of here."

That man will get the promotion. Pick the man who can get the job done!

God, too, is looking for people to whom He can give authority and responsibility. He gives people jobs and watches to see how they respond. Most of all, God is looking for obedience and faithfulness.[96]

Looking at King Saul in I Samuel 15, let's consider the dangers of disobedience. He was a man that seemed the perfect fit for the throne, yet he had trouble following orders. It appears that King Saul got to the place where he thought that he no longer needed to obey God. A young person is growing and maturing in the Lord. As those that are in authority, we must help them to understand that they will never outgrow the need to be a submissive and obedient servant of the Lord. There are three dangers of disobedience that can be learned from the life of King Saul.

1. Self-Deception

"And Samuel came to Saul: and Saul said unto him, 'Blessed be thou of the LORD: I have performed the commandment of the LORD'" (I Sam. 15:13).

Recent experiments have been made in which people were fitted with special prismatic glasses. These devices greatly distorted the vision so that straight lines appeared to be curved, and sharp outlines seemed fringed with color. Within just a few days, however, the unnatural shapes, tinted edges, and inverted landscapes gradually disappeared, and the world began to be normal again, even though they still wore their optical fittings. The brain was finally able to overcome the false data that came through

---

[96] Ibid, 487.

the prismatic lenses.[97] This adaptability in the physical realm is indeed a blessing; however, in the area of the spiritual, this can be a dangerous trait when it comes to sin. In fact, man is a sinner whose deepest imaginations are evil, and his thought life produces a world of illusions. He thinks of himself as pure when in reality he is guilty before God. In this context, we find that disobedience leads to self-deception so that you believe you are right with the Lord when you are in rebellion against the Lord.

2. Making Excuses

"And Saul said, 'They have brought them from the Amalekites: for the people spared the best of the sheep and of the oxen, to sacrifice unto the LORD thy God; and the rest we have utterly destroyed'" (I Sam. 15:15). Does this sound familiar? It is not just young people who come up with the excuses that "others made me do it" or "the devil made me do it." How often these phrases have been used to justify one's disobedience. There is one reason that a young person or any believer disobeys—their own sinful nature. Until we stop pointing the finger at everyone else and accept responsibility for our own actions, there can never be true growth and maturity in the child of God.

3. Warped Priorities

It is like the story of the mother who shouted up the stairs for her son to come for dinner. No response. So, she shouted again. No response. She shouted a third time with anger in her voice, and the son came running down the stairs. When asked why he did not respond, he said, "I didn't hear you the first two times." It was not that he did not hear; he just did not obey.

Saul's issue in this story is that he did not obey God's first command in battle. The sacrifices had been appointed by divine authority; therefore,

---

[97] http://gbcnq.com/devotional/spiritual-warfare-righteous-thinking-2/. Accessed on September 20, 2018.

they were to be duly performed. However, the outward observance was considered of greater importance to Saul than the inward sentiment or the spiritual feeling. There was a perversion of worship, which was displeasing to God. Obedience is the true test of a religious profession.

Let me finish this discussion with an illustration from history that can demonstrate the importance about the little things of obedience.

The first attempt to dig the Panama Canal across the Isthmus of Panama was made by a French company. Men and machinery tackled the mountains and jungles. Eventually, the project was abandoned; however, it was not because of the mountains but because of the mosquitoes. Yellow fever contracted from mosquitoes killed thousands. Finally, American doctors found ways to protect people against the mosquitoes. When the mosquitoes were finally under control, the mountains soon succumbed.

There is a vast difference between the size of a mountain and the size of a mosquito, yet the small mosquitoes did more damage. More men perished from the bite of the mosquitoes than from danger in the mountains.[98] No one succeeds in the big opportunities of life who has not been faithful in the small obligations. *"He that is faithful in that which is least is faithful also in much: and he that is unjust in the least is unjust also in much" (Luke 16:10).*

Let's make sure that we are teaching our young people to be obedient in all things. God will not bless any young person's life if they have rebellion like Saul. They will be heading down the wrong path. If we yield ourselves to the searching of God's Spirit, we may find that we never gave obedience its proper place in our life which resulted in the failure of both prayer and work. We may see that the deeper blessings of God's grace and the full enjoyment of God's love and nearness have been beyond our reach simply because we never made obedience what God meant it to be. It is the starting point and the goal of our Christian life.[99]

---

[98] https://en.wikipedia.org/wiki/History_of_the_Panama_Canal. Accessed on September 20, 2018.

[99] Andrew Murray, *The Blessings of Obedience* (New Kensington, Pennsylvania: Whitaker House, 1984), 18.

May God help us to teach our young people the value of obedience. Without this attribute, much heartache and trouble will follow the young person. With obedience, both their life and the lives of those they meet will be spiritually uplifted.

Chapter 16

P - Patience

"In every field of knowledge, half of what is true today will one day be updated with better information, and it turns out that we actually know when that day will come for many academic pursuits." This is what author Sam Arbesman calls "the half-life of facts." In medical school, they tell you that half of what you are about to learn won't be true when you graduate—they just don't know which half. The premise is that for every domain, silo, discipline, and school of knowledge, the facts contained within are slowly being overturned, augmented, replaced, and refined. In medicine, for example, the rate of that overturning is high enough that if you never really complete your education. Medical school, in other words, never ends.[100] For instance, in physics, about half of all research findings will be disconfirmed within thirteen years. In psychology, it's every seven years. In other words, if you graduated with a degree in psychology seven years ago, half of the information in your textbooks is now inaccurate.[101]

By contrast, the Bible is the very "words of God." The fact is that there have been millions of people all over the world who have found this claim to be credible for thousands of years. This alone is one of the amazing proofs that the truths that matter most are not nullified by the passing of

---

[100] www.google.com/search?q=In+every+field+of+knowledge%2C+half+of+what+is+true+to-day+will+one+day+be+updated+with+better+information%2C+and+it+turns+ou t+that+we+actually+know+when+that+day+willcome+for+many+academic+pur-suits.&ie=utf-8&oe=utf-8&client=firefox-b-1-ab. Accessed on September 24, 2018.

[101] https://youarenotsosmart.com/2017/07/18/yanss-099-the-half-life-of-facts/. Accessed on September 24, 2018.

time. There is no half-life to the truth that God in His love for mankind sent His Son, Jesus into this world to die for the sins of all man.

These truths are grounded in God's unfailing nature and will never be overturned.

The grass withereth, the flower fadeth: but the word of our God shall stand for ever. (Isa. 40:8)

For verily I say unto you, Till heaven and earth pass, one jot or one tittle shall in no wise pass from the law, till all be fulfilled. (Matt. 5:18)

With these thoughts about the certainty of the Word of God, we want to help our young people in the area of patience. We must turn them to the never-changing principles of God's Word to achieve this. One of the passages that can help a young person in this area is James 5. James 5 is a little different than the previous chapters. James has been quite terse with his audience, but in verse 7, his tone softens even to the point of being warm and sympathetic: *"Be patient therefore, brethren, unto the coming of the Lord. Behold, the husbandman waiteth for the precious fruit of the earth, and hath long patience for it, until he receive the early and latter rain."* The surrounding section is something of a conclusion made in light of the *"coming of the Lord."* It is as if James is saying that there is a reckoning day coming for your tormentors and a day of glory coming for the tormented.

We live in an impatient world where time is money, and people want everything yesterday. The computer age has introduced number-crunching and data management, drastically cutting the number of people-hours to do every job, and suggesting that everything ought to be done in an instant. Stories about waiting for the vacuum tubes to warm up on a television or radio sound like ancient history to our children. We all have grown accustomed to time-saving appliances, instant information from the internet, instant cash from the ATM, and even instant shopping from Amazon. Why should I have to wait for anything or anyone—even God?

This is what the fifth chapter of James is dealing with, waiting on God and His perfect will. It could even be that we must wait for His return as His children.

The Exhortation

Patience is a very important aspect of the believer's life. It is something that must be nurtured in a young person's life. It does not come naturally to the old man. The word suggests the self-restraint that enables one to bear an insult or injury without a hasty retaliation.[102] This type of patience is described as an attribute of God according to Exodus 34:6, Romans 2:4, and I Peter 3:20. So for a Christian young person to be like Christ, he must work to put this trait into his daily life.

In the book of Galatians, we find in chapter 5 that one of the fruits of the Spirit is longsuffering. This word for longsuffering has a root which gives us the idea of forbearance or patience.[103] The Spirit of God helps us to adjust the inner man so that we can patiently learn to endure hardness as a good soldier of Jesus Christ. Clear evidence of the Spirit of God is the manifestation of patience in the life of the Christian.

As fruit of the Spirit, biblical patience is the ability to endure, to wait for God's pathway and His working to a righteous end. When the word *longsuffering* is used, it suggests active commitment rather than passive waiting. This type of patience when applied to anger means delayed anger or being long-tempered, which is the opposite of short-tempered. The bomb is there, but the fuse is long. Perhaps no explosion will come.[104]

Speaking of patience in the believer, Dr. David Burton writes, "Keep still. When trouble is brewing, keep still. When slander is getting on its

---

[102] Jerry Bridges, *The Practice of Godliness* (Colorado Springs, Colorado: NavPress, 1983), 204–208.

[103] https://biblehub.com/greek/3115.htm. Accessed on September 25, 2018.

[104] Wiersbe, 882–883.

legs, keep still. When your feelings are hurt, keep still till you recover from your excitement at any rate."[105]

James 5 teaches us that we are to be longsuffering in reference to hardships. He does not say that we are to be patient as in waiting listlessly, doing nothing. Patience and procrastination are not the same. Many excuse their laziness with a false definition of patience. James is saying that we must "be patient" in not seeking retaliation or harboring resentment.

This is an important point to help young people understand as they progress through their teen years. In my own ministry, I have talked with older folks who in their youth became disenchanted or bitter toward someone because they were never taught to be longsuffering. This lack of godliness made them miss so many blessings in life because they held a grudge ultimately against God for what occurred in their life. Patience and longsuffering are tied to an understanding of the providence of God. If God is in control, He allows circumstances, hardships, and even individuals into my life to teach me important lessons.

The Example

Before considering the illustrations from the text in James 5, let's consider the author of the book of James. This James is believed to have been one of the principal leaders of the church in Jerusalem. Their church congregation knew of persecution because they faced it continuously. James had learned, though, that difficulties and trials taught patience and steadfastness. He does not indicate to the reader to go into a pretend world that ignores the trial. Instead, he asks the reader to develop a strong faith that works to see God in the trial and to see God's goodness.[106]

The illustration that James offers first is that of a farmer. He patiently waits for his land to produce precious crops. He does not simply sit; he is

---

[105] David Burton, *Pennsylvania School Journal: Volume 55* (London, England: Forgotten Books, 2012), 492.

[106] Ruth Peters, *Bible Illustrations: A Treasury of Bible Illustrations (Book Two)*, (Chattanooga, Tennessee: AMG Publishers, 1998), 347.

not lazy. Instead, he prepares the soil, sows seed, and keeps his fields free of grass and weeds. But for the germination of the seed and the growth of the plants, he must trust the providential care of God. Patience, therefore, suggests the attitude of watchful and constant expectancy. Consider the following text in relation to patience:

Patience Reduces Pain

As the lid is made to open and shut, to save the eye; so patience is set to keep the soul, and save the heart whole to cheer the body again. Therefore, if you mark when you can go by an offence and take a little wrong, and suffer trouble quietly, you have a kind of peace and joy in your heart, as if you had gotten a victory; and the more your patience is, still the less your pain is. For as a light burden, borne at the arm's end, weigheth heavier by much than a burden of treble weight if it be borne upon the shoulders, which are made to bear; so if a man set impatience to bear a cross, which is not fit to bear, it will grumble and murmur, and start and shrink, and let the burden fall upon his head; like a broken staff which promiseth to help him over the water, and leaveth him in the ditch. But if you put it to patience, and set her to bear it which is appointed to bear, she is like the hearty spies that came from Canaan, and said, "It is nothing to overcome them"; so patience saith, "It is nothing to bear, it is nothing to fast, it is nothing to watch, it is nothing to labour, it is nothing to be envied, it is nothing to be backbited, it is nothing to be imprisoned; "In all these things we are more than conquerors." (*Henry Smith*)[107]

---

[107] Joseph S. Exell, *The Biblical Illustrator: St. James* (Grand Rapids, Michigan: Baker book House, 1973), 457.

"Take, my brethren, the prophets, who have spoken in the name of the Lord, for an example of suffering affliction, and of patience" (James 5:10). Here he gives an illustration of patience as that of the prophets. They were examples to us in their suffering and in their patience. Can you think of the prophets of old that suffered for their testimony? At the time of the writing of this book, there were many Old Testament men that had patiently endured such as Daniel, Jeremiah Amos, Hosea, and many more. Consider the patience they must have had.

> Many of the prophets had to endure great trials and sufferings, not only at the hands of professed believers. Jeremiah was arrested as a traitor and even thrown into an abandoned well to die. God fed Jeremiah and protected him throughout that terrible siege of Jerusalem, even though at times it looked as though the prophet was going to be killed. Both Ezekiel and Daniel had their share of hardships, but the Lord delivered them. And even those who were not delivered, who died for the faith, received that special reward for those who are true to Him.[108]

James 5:11 gives us the third example—Job. *"Behold, we count them happy which endure. Ye have heard of the patience of Job, and have seen the end of the Lord; that the Lord is very pitiful, and of tender mercy."* We can read the book of Job and get a different portrayal of patience than we sometimes see. Job was not always quiet, but his faith in God was constant. His faith in friends was not always there, and his faith in circumstances waivered, but his longsuffering toward God was there.

The conclusion James draws as expressed in verse 8 is to *"stablish your hearts."* This suggests mustering courage or strengthening your inner being because of the imminent coming of the Lord. God is still on the throne, and we should patiently wait for His return when He, the righteous Judge, will make all things right.

---

[108] Wiersbe, 883.

So, let's consider a couple of instances in modern vernacular to illustrate the patience that needs to be taught and exemplified to young people. Obviously, these are fictional scenarios, and we are only giving three examples. Hopefully, they will help parents and pastoral authority to find that young people today need patience in the situations that they face.

1. A young person should have patience in waiting for the right mate. The world teaches "do what feels right." The world teaches "dream and achieve." Neither of these approaches are biblical approaches to finding the right mate for life. We need to teach our young people that waiting on the Lord and having the patience to wait for the right spouse is God's best and perfect will. Cheating the system by letting fleshly lusts run ahead of God's way is not evidence of the Spirit-filled life. It is evidence of the sinful nature taking control. How sad to see a young person forsake the will of God in not being patient for the working of God's perfect will.

2. A young person should learn patience in family trials. Suppose a young man or woman in your church has experienced a divorce in their home. They may say that it is not fair, and they may turn to hate to one of the parents. This is an area where authority can help a young person biblically. Teach them that the Bible demands of Christians to be longsuffering. They need to be patient with the working of God's will in their life. God still cares for that young person even though the circumstances seem to say the contrary. God is not a dictator; He does not force His will on anyone. The parents that have chosen this wrong path have gone against God's way, but that teenager can still be in the loving care of their heavenly Father. Teach the young person to patiently wait on the Lord and let the Lord give them a right spirit.

3. A young person should learn patience when someone has wronged them. This is a great opportunity for parents and pastoral authority

to help the young person look through the Word of God and see how patiently waiting on the Lord will give great reward. In Genesis, you see this displayed with Joseph's life when being deceived by his brothers. In Exodus, you see the working of God in Moses's life and how God had to teach him valuable lessons on the back side of the desert. Many other examples can be shown to the young person with the ultimate example in Christ's earthly life. The patience that Christ exhibited is amazing. Consider His patient kindness and forgiveness on the cross. These examples should be able to help a young person see that "just because someone did me wrong" is no justification for an unrighteous retaliation.

The End Result

Doubtless, early Christians hoped that Jesus would come back soon to deliver them from the trying conditions in which they lived. They were not all confident that He would return immediately, and they became impatient—even with others who were closely associated with them. James concludes in verse 9, *"the judge standeth before the door."* God is there ready to help and intercede. Wait on the Lord; He is in control.

Because God is in control, there is victory in patience. It is always comforting to feel that others have previously experienced what we have to go through. In James 5:10–11, James reminds his readers that the prophets and the people of God never could have done their work and borne witness had they not patiently endured. James reminds them that Jesus said that one who endured to the end was blessed and would be saved. Then he reminds them of the victory won by Job because of his patience. We generally speak of the patience of Job. Job was anything but passive. But Job, despite the barrage of questions that tore at his heart, never lost faith in God. He said, *"Though he slay me, yet will I trust him."*

The very greatness of Job lies in the fact that he endured and was patient in suffering.

Finally, moving away from the book of James, consider the great text in Hebrews:

> *And what shall I more say? for the time would fail me to tell of Gedeon, and of Barak, and of Samson, and of Jephthae; of David also, and Samuel, and of the prophets: Who through faith subdued kingdoms, wrought righteousness, obtained promises, stopped the mouths of lions, Quenched the violence of fire, escaped the edge of the sword, out of weakness were made strong, waxed valiant in fight, turned to flight the armies of the aliens. (Heb. 11:32–34)*

> *And these all, having obtained a good report through faith, received not the promise: God having provided some better thing for us, that they without us should not be made perfect. (Heb. 11:39–40)*

This text in Hebrews 11 says that these great men of faith died without receiving the promises. This implies that they endured or had patience in the perfect plan of God. The temporal circumstances did not change their faith in an Almighty, all-knowing God.[109]

The fruit of the Spirit is not about getting what you want in life whenever you want it. The fruit of the Spirit is not some magic potion as the charismatics or the prosperity gospel folks lead their people to believe. The fruit of the Spirit allows you to live content without what you want, accept what you get, and hold onto God's promises anyway. It is not about instantaneous results. Patience lives toward the ultimate reward: "Well done, thou good and faithful servant."

---

[109] Ibid., 838.

Fanny Crosby wrote the following words:

> Wait on the Lord, wait cheerfully,
> And He will thy youth renew;
> Wait on the Lord obediently,
> Whatever He bids thee do.
> Wait on the Lord, for whom hast thou,
> On earth or in heaven but He?
> Over thy soul a watch He keeps,
> Whatever thy path may be.[110]

Have you ever seen a blacksmith work with a piece of iron? He holds it in the fire to soften it and make it pliable. That is what God does in our lives. He permits the testing of your faith by temptations and trials to soften us. He wants you to acquire patience, to acquire pliability. If you and I are constantly out of the fire of affliction, we become stiff and useless. God wants to reshape us according to His image, for in the fall of Adam, we lost our divine shape or divine image.[111]

---

[110] http://www.hymntime.com/tch/htm/w/a/i/waitlord.htm. Accessed on September 20, 2018.

[111] Ruth Peters, *Bible Illustrations: Illustrations of Bible Truths (Book One)* (Chattanooga, Tennessee: AMG Publishers, 1998), 77.

Chapter 17

Q - Quit You Like Men

"Watch ye, stand fast in the faith, quit you like men*, be strong"*

(I Cor. 16:13; emphasis added).

The words *quit you like men* occurs nowhere else in the New Testament. But it occurs in the Old Testament in Joshua 1:6–7, 9,18; I Chronicles 28:20; II Chronicles 32:7; Nehemiah 2:1; and in eighteen other places. It occurs also in the classic authors. It means "to render one manly or brave; to show oneself a man; that is, not to be a coward, or timid, or alarmed at enemies, but to be bold and brave." We have similar phrases in common use: "Be a man," or "show yourself a man"; that is, not to be cowardly.[112]

> Act the manly, firm, and resolved part: behave strenuously, in opposition to the bad men who would divide and corrupt you, those who would split you into factions or seduce you from the faith: be not terrified nor inveigled by them; but show yourselves men in Christ, by your steadiness, by your sound judgment and firm resolution." Note, Christians should be manly and firm in all their

---

[112] Albert Barnes, *Barnes' Notes on the New Testament: I Corinthians* (Grand Rapids, Michigan: Baker Books, 2005), 332.

189

contests with their enemies, in defending their faith, and in maintaining their integrity.[113]

I am afraid that sometime in the late twentieth century or so, a lot of evangelical readers mistook the message and thought it meant, "quit being men." Paul is commending all those characteristics that we think of as masculine rather than feminine even though it is not politically correct these days to say that. Paul is including in that command attributes like courage, strength, boldness, stoutheartedness, heroism, daring, gallantry, or gusto. Be a man. The church has begun to look weak and effeminate—frightened, and sissified, like a bunch of fops and milk sops. We are supposed to be soldiers. We are told relentlessly that we must be always agreeable no matter what—seeker sensitive, gender neutral, effervescent, sentimental, and delicate in everything we say and do. Those sound like rules for figure skaters, not warriors. We are warriors in the army of Christ.

Consider the following written by a well-respected pediatric physician in America:

> But today that natural, healthy boyhood is under attack. It is threatened not only by an educational establishment that devalues masculinity and boyishness, and not only by widely remarked social changes including widespread divorce and the rise of single-parent households that deprive boys of the responsible fathers they need, but by a noxious popular culture that is as degrading to boys as it is dangerous to girls.

> We remember when boys used to go trout fishing, sitting under a tree while daydreaming about the future, and now we fear that our boys are cutting themselves off from us with iPods, earbuds, and computer porn. When we grew

---

[113] Matthew Henry, *Matthew Henry's Commentary on the Whole Bible: Volume 6* (Peabody, Massachusetts: Hendrickson Publishers, 1991), 486.

up in the '60s, '70s, and even in the '80s for the most part, it was safe for boys to flip on the TV, because the networks still upheld a general moral consensus; but now we grimace as our boys are inundated with cheap, nasty dialogue and graphic images that reflect cheap, nasty values and an impoverished imagination. Even when they watch a football game we feel a gnawing in our stomach because commercials will educate them about Viagra, erectile dysfunction, and most certainly about voluptuous older women. Outwardly we go about our work but inwardly we hold our breath. During the past decade, psychologists have written about the emotional troubles our boys endure. Educators have sounded alarms because elementary school and high school boys are performing much more poorly than girls. Their SAT scores are too low—fewer are graduating from high school and college. In my own profession of medicine, medical school applications from young men have dropped.[114]

Be strong—be firm, fixed, steadfast; compare to Ephesians 6:10, *"Be strong in the Lord, and in the power of his might."* Let's consider some characteristics that we should instill into our young men for them to learn to be strong as godly men.

Work Hard

"The Work Is What Counts"
By Theodore Roosevelt

(Delivered in his September 8, 1902, speech to the brotherhood of locomotive firemen in Chattanooga, Tennessee.)

---

[114] Meeker, 7–8.

Your work is hard. Do you suppose that I mention that because I pity you? NO; not a bit. I don't pity any man who does hard work worth doing. I admire him. I pity the creature who doesn't work, at whichever end of the social scale he may regard himself at being. The law of worthy work well done is the law of successful American life. I believe in play, too—play, and play hard while you play; but don't make the mistake of thinking that play is the main thing. The work is what counts, and if a man does his work well and it is worth doing, then it matters but little in which line that work is done; the man is a good American citizen. If he does his work in slipshod fashion, then no matter what kind of work it is, he is a poor American citizen.[115]

The Bible has much to say about hard work. Consider the following verses:

And the LORD God took the man, and put him into the garden of Eden to dress it and to keep it. (Gen. 2:15)

He also that is slothful in his work is brother to him that is a great waster. (Prov. 18:9)

Commit thy works unto the LORD, and thy thoughts shall be established. (Prov. 16:3)

Whether therefore ye eat, or drink, or whatsoever ye do, do all to the glory of God. (I Cor. 10:31)

---

[115] William J. Bennett, *The Book of Man: Readings on the Path to Manhood* (Nashville, Tennessee: Thomas Nelson Publishers, 2011), 104.

Let him that stole steal no more: but rather let him labor, working with his hands the thing which is good, that he may have to give to him that needeth. (Eph. 4:28)

Servants, obey in all things [your] masters according to the flesh; not with eyeservice, as menpleasers; but in singleness of heart, fearing God: And whatsoever ye do, do it heartily, as to the Lord, and not unto men. (Col. 3:22–23)

For even when we were with you, this we commanded you, that if any would not work, neither should he eat. (II Thess. 3:10)

Obviously, the Bible cares how a man works. This should be a manly trait; a man is a hard worker. As we desire to make godly men, help your young men to learn to enjoy the work that God has for them. If your church has work to be done, have your boys there to help. Make sweat a normal part of their life. A lazy demeanor will ruin the ability of a young man to develop into a godly man. Study the Bible and show your young people that God desires all to have a work to do in this life on earth. Even Christ was able to finish His work. He came focused on His task at hand and had a mind to accomplish that task.

Keep the World at Arm's Length

There are a couple of ways that young men can be helped in keeping the world at arm's length. Two ideas come to mind: teaching a young man not to live for this physical world and not to live for this present world. Both areas are hard to keep in check. Teaching young men to do this will help them in understanding that this world is temporal, and its pull is hard to shake and can be addicting.

1. <u>Living for the Physical</u>

> *And one of the company said unto him, Master, speak to my brother, that he divide the inheritance with me. And he said unto him, Man, who made me a judge or a divider over you? And he said unto them, Take heed, and beware of covetousness: for a man's life consisteth not in the abundance of the things which he possesseth. (Luke 12:13–15)*

Christ instructs to take heed and beware of covetousness. *Take heed* literally means "to look out." *Beware* means "to guard or defend, to protect and keep safe."[116] It demands extreme caution in the presence of danger. Covetousness gives the idea of a thirst for having more. Othello in his writings described greed in AD 166, "the green-eyed monster which doth mock the meat it feeds on."[117] As young men learn to work, they will find that they can make money and plenty of it. As American culture becomes more pagan, the work ethic is slipping rapidly into slothfulness and laziness. A parent that teaches their young man the value of hard work will find a line of endless employers who want their young man to work because he will do just that—*work*. This will provide many more opportunities to gather this world's goods. Teach young men the temptation of covetousness. This physical world can grab the heart and make a young man forsake the best that God has for him for the temporary good that "mammon" can bring into a life.

2. <u>Living for the Present</u>

Eve was tempted through sight. Lot was tempted through sight. David was tempted through sight. Guard your eyes (Gen. 19:17; Prov. 23:31–33. 4:23–25). The temporal is visible and earthly. The eternal is invisible and

---

[116] http://webstersdictionary1828.com/Dictionary/beware. Accessed on September 10, 2018.

[117] https://www.merriam-webster.com/words-at-play/top-10-phrases-from-shakespeare. Accessed on September 10, 2018.

heavenly. This can be hard to present to a young person, so we must be vigilant to have a young man in the Word of God. Through the power of the Word of God, a young man can gain a vision of the eternal. A parent's or pastor's words may not always be able to grab the heart, but God's words do not return void.

<u>No Whining</u>

Several team members came to a boss with a frustrated complaint. One of their co-workers never stopped complaining, and they meant never. He complained about every task, about every sentence someone said, about the weather, the food, and even the toilet paper in the men's room. What they were concerned about was how his whining and naysaying were big "de-motivators" for everyone else. By the end of the day, they were all beginning to see the glass as half empty too. It was like a virus that was attacking their emotions.[118]

Whiners are martyrs who feel they are doing most of the work and getting no acknowledgment for their efforts. They have a black cloud over their heads, and every time they open their mouths, the cloud shoots out a thunderstorm of dank, messy rain. We must teach our young men to bear the burden of hard work and carry the load with a tongue that is in check. This is not always easy. A young man will have days that are not always sunny, days that are not filled with bonus pay, and days that are not overly cheerful. This does not change the no-whining rule. The apostle Paul gave us a great challenge in the books of Philippians and I Timothy.

> *Not that I speak in respect of want: for I have learned, in whatsoever state I am, therewith to be content. I know both how to be abased, and I know how to abound: every where and in all things I am instructed both to be full and to be hungry, both to abound and to suffer need. (Phil. 4:11–12)*

---

[118] https://www.huffingtonpost.com/rabbi-alan-lurie/stop-complaining_b_255132.html. Accessed on September 10, 2018.

But godliness with contentment is great gain. For we brought nothing into this world, and it is certain we can carry nothing out. And having food and raiment let us be therewith content. (I Tim. 6:6–8)

What is interesting in the passage in Philippians is that the apostle Paul says that he *learned* to be content. This means that contentment needs to be taught and that it can be learned. With that in mind, a parent or youth pastor needs to help young people learn this trait. The following list may help give some thoughts for contentment.

1. Teach young men to give sacrificially to God. (Luke 6:38; Acts 20:35; II Cor. 9)

2. Teach young men to work on the church facilities. (Ps. 84; I Cor. 3)

3. Teach young men that money will not bring happiness. (I Tim. 6)

4. Teach young men that trials will come in the Christian life. (John 16:33; James 1; I Pet. 5)

5. Teach young men that God will give strength for all He asks us to do. (Luke 10; II Cor. 9; Phil. 4)

Watch Out for Women

We now come to a section that most avoid with young men. We have left the teaching of our young men regarding what a godly woman is to the world, to the locker room, to Hollywood, or to the academics. This has created a mess in our Christian families and in our churches. Purity is a vital area for a godly man. It has become even more difficult in this technological age, which has pornography available for the youngest of men to view with no accountability. It is ever more necessary to start teaching our young men at an early age to be vigilant against the "strange woman." We must give them godly, biblical principles that can establish purity in their hearts.

1. <u>Beware of the Strange Woman</u>

When wisdom entereth into thine heart, and knowledge is pleasant unto thy soul; Discretion shall preserve thee, understanding shall keep thee: To deliver thee from the way of the evil man, from the man that speaketh froward things; Who leave the paths of uprightness, to walk in the ways of darkness; Who rejoice to do evil, and delight in the frowardness of the wicked; Whose ways are crooked, and they froward in their paths: To deliver thee from the strange woman, even from the stranger which flattereth with her words; Which forsaketh the guide of her youth, and forgetteth the covenant of her God. For her house inclineth unto death, and her paths unto the dead. None that go unto her return again, neither take they hold of the paths of life. (Prov. 2:10–19)

For the lips of a strange woman drop as an honeycomb, and her mouth is smoother than oil: But her end is bitter as wormwood, sharp as a twoedged sword. Her feet go down to death; her steps take hold on hell. Lest thou shouldest ponder the path of life, her ways are moveable, that thou canst not know them. Hear me now therefore, O ye children, and depart not from the words of my mouth. Remove thy way far from her, and come not nigh the door of her house: Lest thou give thine honor unto others, and thy years unto the cruel. (Prov. 5:3–9)

The warnings against the strange woman are plentiful in the book of Proverbs. In this politically correct day, we are not "allowed" to teach that women will dress inappropriately in order to lead the "simple" man astray. This however must be addressed by the good dad, mother, and authority in a young man's life. He must know that all women have not been "created equal" when it comes to temptation. The Bible gives us warning signs to take heed in helping our young men to see when they might be taken advantage of. Notice a couple of ideas in these two passages.

1. The strange woman is a flatterer. This means that she will say whatever is necessary to fulfill her own desires and wants. Her desire is not for the betterment of the young man.

2. The strange woman is rebellious. She goes against her authority. This can be done through mocking or belittling the advice of *"her youth."*

3. Her pathway is leading away from life. This may not be obvious to a young man, but those that are in the place of guidance should be observing the direction of her walk.

4. The strange woman is not always easily detected. Her speech is smoother than oil. That means that a young man must rely heavily on his elders and the guidance of his God-given authority.

Matthew Henry comments the following regarding the strange woman.

"The caution itself is to abstain from fleshly lusts, from adultery, fornication, and all uncleanness. Some apply this figuratively, and by the adulterous woman here, understand idolatry, or false doctrine, tends to debauch men's minds and manners and arouse the sensual appetite, to which the preceding verses may as fitly as anything be applied. The primary scope of it is plainly to warn us again Seventh Commandment sins, which youth is so prone to, the temptations to which are so violent, the examples of which are so many, and which, where admitted, are so destructive to all the seeds of virtue in the soul that it is not strange that Solomon's cautions against it are so very pressing and so often repeated. Solomon here, as a faithful watchman, gives fair warning to all, as they regard their lives and comforts, to dread this sin, for it will certainly be their ruin."[119]

2. Search for the Virtuous Woman

A virtuous woman is a crown to her husband: but she that maketh ashamed is as rottenness in his bones. (Prov. 12:4)

Who can find a virtuous woman? for her price is far above rubies. The heart of her husband doth safely trust in her, so that he shall have no need of spoil. She will do him good and not evil all the days of her life. (Prov. 31:10–12)

Take time to teach young men the greatness of a virtuous woman. There is no substitute for a godly wife. The Bible says that her "price is far above rubies." This was not written as an afterthought. A godly wife and mother is a special gift from God that can satisfy a husband's needs in all areas. This needs to be explained to a young man. The devil has counterfeits in every area of life. He has his own "fruits" that he likes to substitute for God's harvest which can come in a believer's life when he obeys. Teach young men the difference in this area of purity. Notice some of the blessed traits of the virtuous woman.

---

[119] Matthew Henry, *Matthew Henry's Commentary on the Whole Bible: Volume 3* (Peabody, Massachusetts: Hendrickson Publishers, 1991), 668–669.

1. The virtuous woman meets the needs of her husband. (Prov. 31:11)

2. The virtuous woman has pure motives in her work at the home. (Prov. 31:12)

3. The virtuous woman is not afraid of hard work. (Prov. 31:13–15)

4. The virtuous woman is wise and frugal with her money. (Prov. 31:16)

5. The virtuous woman is charitable to others in need. (Prov. 31:20)

Matthew Henry has the following thoughts on the virtuous woman:

"She is a woman of strength (so the word is), though the weaker vessel, yet made strong by wisdom and grace, and the fear of God. It is the same word that is used in the character of good judges (Exodus 18:21), that they are able men, men qualified for the business to which they are called, men of truth, fearing God. So it follows, a virtuous woman is a woman of spirit, who has the command of her own spirit and knows how to manage other people's, one that is pious and industrious, and a help meet for a man. In opposition to this strength, we read of the weakness of the heart of an imperious whorish woman in Ezekiel 16:30. A virtuous woman is a woman of resolution, who, having espoused good principles, is firm and steady to them, and will not be frightened with winds and clouds from any part of her duty. The difficulty of meeting with such a one: Who can find her? This intimates that good women are very scarce, and many that seem to be so do not prove so; he that thought he had found a virtuous woman was deceived; Behold, it was Leah, and not the Rachel he expected. But he that designs to marry ought to seek diligently for such a one, to have this principally in his eye, in all his enquiries, and to take heed that he be not biased by beauty or gaiety. Wealth or parentage, dressing well; for all these may be and yet the woman not be virtuous, and there is many a woman truly virtuous who yet is not recommended by these advantages. The unspeakable worth of such a one, and the value which he that has such a wife ought to put upon her, showing it by his thankfulness to God and his kindness and respect to her, whom he must never think he can do too much for. Her price is far above rubies, and all the rich ornaments with which vain women adorn themselves. The more rare such good wives are the more they are to be valued."[120]

Want Strength

Listen to what Spurgeon himself said about that very same phenomenon in his era:

"It is very pretty, is it not, to read of Luther and his brave deeds. Of course, everybody admires Luther. Yes, yes. But you do not want anyone else to do the same thing today. When you go to the zoo you all admire the bears," "But how would you like a bear at home or a bear wandering loose in the street?" You tell me that would be unbearable. And no doubt you are right. So, "we admire a man who is firm in the faith, say, 400 years ago. The past ages are sort of a bear pit and the iron cage for him. But such

---

[120] Ibid., 801–802.

a man today is a nuisance and must be put down. Call him a narrow-minded bigot or give him a worse name if you can think of one and yet imagine if in those days passed, Luther, Zwingli, Calvin, and their compeers had said, 'The world is out of order, but if we try to set it right, we shall only make a great row and get ourselves into disgrace.' So let us go to our chambers and put on our night caps and sleep over the bad times. And perhaps when we wake up things will have gotten better. Such conduct on their part would have entailed on us a heritage of error. Age after age would have gone down into the infernal deeps and all the pestiferous bogs of error would have swallowed all. These men loved the faith and the name of Jesus too well to see them trampled on.[121]

What is the point of this long quote by C. H. Spurgeon? Don't be afraid of struggle or something that takes some grunt. We should read of the men of the past and understand that the reason we admire them is because they had the courage and fortitude to go "against the grain" of compromise. We are raising a sissy generation that thinks when anything is hard for someone, then something must be wrong. No, strength is born in adversity. Let's teach our young men to want the tough road, not the easy road.

HOW DO YOU TACKLE YOUR WORK?
Edgar A. Guest

How do you tackle your work each day?
Are you scared of the job you find?
Do you grapple the task that comes your way
With a confident, easy mind?

---

[121] http://www.thegracelifepulpit.com/Sermons.aspx?code=2013–07–28-PJ. Accessed on September 10, 2018.

Do you stand right up to the work ahead
Or fearfully pause to view it?
Do you start to toil with a sense of dread
Or feel that you're going to do it?

You can do as much as you think you can,
But you'll never accomplish more;
If you're afraid of yourself, young man,
There's little for you in store.
For failure comes from the inside first,
It's there if we only knew it,
And you can win, though you face the worst,
If you feel that you're going to do it.

Success! It's found in the soul of you,
And not in the realm of luck!
The world will furnish the work to do,
But you must provide the pluck.
You can do whatever you think you can,
It's all in the way you view it.
It's all in the start you make, young man:
You must feel that you're going to do it.

How do you tackle your work each day?
With confidence clear, or dread?
What to yourself do you stop and say
When a new task lies ahead?
What is the thought that is in your mind?
Is fear ever running through it?
If so, just tackle the next you find
By thinking you're going to do it.

1. <u>God Expects a Man to Grow Stronger in the Lord.</u>

Thou therefore, my son, be strong in the grace that is in Christ Jesus. And the things that thou hast heard of me among many witnesses, the same commit thou to faithful men, who shall be able to teach others also. Thou therefore endure hardness, as a good soldier of Jesus Christ. No man that warreth entangleth himself with the affairs of this life; that he may please him who hath chosen him to be a soldier. And if a man also strive for masteries, yet is he not crowned, except he strive lawfully. (II Tim. 2:1–5)

But sanctify the Lord God in your hearts: and be ready always to give an answer to every man that asketh you a reason of the hope that is in you with meekness and fear. (I Pet. 3:15)

For though we walk in the flesh, we do not war after the flesh; (For the weapons of our warfare are not carnal, but mighty through God to the pulling down of strong holds;) Casting down imaginations, and every high thing that exalteth itself against the knowledge of God, and bringing into captivity every thought to the obedience of Christ. (II Cor. 10:3–5)

2. <u>Exercise and Practice Are Essential to Physical Development</u>

<u>Athletes and musicians know they must exercise and practice to improve.</u>

Developing skills requires continual repetition: playing a song, throwing pitches, shooting baskets. Athletes run, lift weights, and practice hour after hour to grow strong and develop endurance.

<u>Children practice skills over and over to learn them.</u>

Children learning to walk try again and again. They are proud to learn a new word; then they use it until they drive you crazy! They want to do the same thing over and over: play the same tape recording, put the clothes on a doll, and so forth. Parents encourage children to repeat what they must learn: drill math facts, study spelling, read, or practice piano. They get tired, but we encourage them because that's how they learn. "Practice makes perfect"—or at least it promotes improvement.

3. Exercise and Practice Are Essential to Spiritual Growth

Those who are of full age, by reason of use have their senses exercised to discern both good and evil. Growth requires exercise as well as nourishment. (Heb. 5:14)

Exercise yourself toward godliness. (I Tim. 4:7)

Like children, athletes, and musicians, we must work again and again at applying Bible principles to become effective in the Lord's work.

Applications:

- To learn to teach, we must do it repeatedly—teach your children, have home studies, teach Bible classes, preach sermons—again and again.

- To learn to lead singing, practice songs at home, sing with your family, and lead during church meetings over and over.

- To understand the Bible, study it again and again, talk to others, drill yourself, and memorize it. Get in and dig.

- To learn to pray; do it over and over.

Kids may not be good at activities at first, but parents encourage them to do it over and over. Likewise, older members must encourage the newer ones to use their talents. They may not be skilled at first, but they learn by doing. We need to encourage those youthful teachers, preachers, and all of those that are striving in their service to the Lord to stay faithful at the task.

The world needs strong, Christian young men. Let's be in the business of teaching our young men to act like Biblical men.

Chapter 18

R - Rebellion: The Shame to a Mother

In 1844, a medical doctor named Ignas Phillip Semmelweis, who was assistant director at the Vienna Maternity Hospital, suggested to the doctors that the high rate of death of patients and new babies was because the doctors attending them were carrying infections from the diseased and dead people whom they had previously touched. Semmelweis ordered doctors to wash their hands with soap and water and rinse them in a strong chemical before examining their patients. He tried to get doctors to wear clean clothes, and he battled for clean wards. However, the majority of doctors disagreed with Semmelweis, and they deliberately disobeyed his orders. In the late nineteenth century, based on the work by Semmelweis, Joseph Lister began soaking surgery instruments, the operating table, his hands, and the patients with carbolic acid. The results were astonishing. What was previously considered to be a risky surgery now became routine. However, most doctors criticized his work.[122]

Today we know that Lister and Semmelweis were right; the majority of doctors in their day were wrong. Just because the majority believes one thing does not necessarily mean it is true. The majority is rarely the right group. Many times, rebels lead a group like lambs to a slaughter. This is the path of the backslider: following a rebel.

Backsliding on God, whether that of an individual or that of a nation, does not take place all at once; it is a gradual process. This spiritual malady usually begins with little departures from the truth of God's

---

[122] https://en.wikipedia.org/wiki/Ignaz_Semmelweis. Accessed on July 31, 2018.

Word—making little allowances here and there with truths upon which one once firmly stood. Backsliding begins with a rationalization of one's behavior (excuses for one's actions or beliefs which are usually superficial), and a relativistic approach to determining right and wrong (resorting to situational ethics, or what's right for you is okay, but not for me—there are no absolutes). Though Satan isn't beyond using blatant, in-your-face temptations to pull God's people away from the Lord, his usual method is to use temptations that appear harmless or almost imperceptible. However, as Song of Solomon 2:15a says, it is *"the little foxes that spoil the vine."*

Such has been the case with our nation. Once our country proudly proclaimed itself a "Christian nation." Nevertheless, as Dr. Tim LaHaye has said, "During the last 200 years, humanism (man's wisdom) has captivated the thinking of the Western world. After conquering Europe's colleges and universities, it spread to America, where it has developed a stranglehold on all public education."[123] Humanism seems so credible and logical to the man who does not understand God's wisdom that it is adopted readily by the masses—much to their own peril. Today's wave of crime and violence in our streets, promiscuity, divorce, shattered dreams, and broken hearts can be laid right at the door of secular humanism.

Simply defined, humanism is man's attempt to solve his problems independently of God. The bottom line is that, due to humanism, our nation has developed an "I'm okay, you're okay" philosophy of life. Since the religion of humanism is atheistic, morality is viewed as an irrelevant and outmoded idea in our society; and as a result, our nation is crumbling from within. For all practical purposes, the great, good, and moral nation we once knew is a dream of the past. Whether an individual or a nation has backslidden on God, only repentance and revival can turn the tide.

Just as the spiritual decline of Israel was gradual in the days of Jeremiah, so the spiritual decline in the life of a young person many times is a gradual slippery slope. Let's learn from Israel's mistakes and pray that God can teach us that work with youth to turn back rebellious hearts to

---

[123] Tim LaHaye, *The Battle for the Mind: A Subtle War* (Old Tappan, NJ: Fleming H. Revell Company, n.d.), 25–26.

the Lord. There is a rebel in each one of our hearts that doesn't want to obey, surrender, or submit to anybody—not even God. But being a rebel is foolish.

On October 22, 1999, professional parachutist Jan Davis was practicing the dangerous sport of BASE jumping—parachuting off fixed objects, such as high cliffs or towers. She was attempting to make a jump off the 3,200-foot granite cliff of El Capitan in Yosemite National Park. She knew BASE jumping had been outlawed due to the death of six others who had died doing the same thing that she was doing. Her own jump was meant as a protest to prove that BASE jumping was safe. She stood at the top of the mountain and leapt off as her husband and several others watched. Her parachute did not open properly, and Jan Davis fell for twenty seconds before she crashed to her death.[124] Jan Davis paid for her rebellion with her life. Does this sound foolish to you? Of course. But it's no more foolish that willful rebellion against God and the legitimate authorities that He has set up in the world. What will your rebellion cost you? I don't know. All I really know is that when you and I rebel, we all travel down the road to destruction.

Rebellion defined: REBEL,' v.i. [L. rebello, to make war again; re and bello.]

1. To revolt; to renounce the authority of the laws and government to which one owes allegiance. Subjects may rebel by an open renunciation of the authority of the government, without taking arms; but ordinarily, rebellion is accompanied by resistance in arms. Ye have built you an altar that ye might rebel this day against the Lord. (Joshua 22; Isaiah 1)

2. To rise in violent opposition against lawful authority.[125]

---

[124] https://www.cbsnews.com/news/parachutist-plunges-to-death/. Accessed on July 31, 2018.

[125] http://sorabji.com/1828/words/r/rebel.html. Accessed on July 31, 2018.

The Actions of a Rebel

Let's consider some actions of a rebel. The Bible gives us some clear indicators that help us identify rebellion in one's life.

1. **He Undermines Authority**

> *And it came to pass after this, that Absalom prepared him chariots and horses, and fifty men to run before him. And Absalom rose up early, and stood beside the way of the gate: and it was so, that when any man that had a controversy came to the king for judgment, then Absalom called unto him, and said, Of what city art thou? And he said, Thy servant is of one of the tribes of Israel. And Absalom said unto him, See, thy matters are good and right; but there is no man deputed of the king to hear thee. Absalom said moreover, Oh that I were made judge in the land, that every man which hath any suit or cause might come unto me, and I would do him justice! And it was so, that when any man came nigh to him to do him obeisance, he put forth his hand, and took him, and kissed him. And on this manner did Absalom to all Israel that came to the king for judgment: so Absalom stole the hearts of the men of Israel. (II Sam. 15:1–6)*

Our text is relating the story of Absalom who is standing by the gates. This means that he had taken a place of judgment or of offering counsel and advice. The gate is the place of concourse, of business, and of justice in Asian and Middle Eastern cities (see Judg. 19:15; Gen. 34:20; Deut. 16:18). J. Vernon McGee expresses the following on this gate, "Absalom stationed himself at the busiest gate of the city. Absalom was a bad boy, but a good politician."[126]

---

[126] J. Vernon McGee, *Thru the Bible with J. Vernon McGee* (Nashville, TN: Thomas Nelson Publishers), 221.

2. <u>He Honors Himself</u>

And they took Absalom, and cast him into a great pit in the wood, and laid a very great heap of stones upon him: and all Israel fled every one to his tent. Now Absalom in his lifetime had taken and reared up for himself a pillar, which is in the king's dale: for he said, I have no son to keep my name in remembrance: and he called the pillar after his own name: and it is called unto this day, Absalom's place. (II Sam. 18:17–18)

This is quite the young man. His picture, his social media presence, and his prominence are very evident. Rebellion has a strain of pride that runs all through the fiber of it. Matthew Henry comments on this passage "yet in this also providence crosses him, and a rude heap of stones shall be his monument, instead of this marble pillar. Thus, those that exalt themselves shall be abased. His care was to have his name kept in remembrance, and it is so, to his everlasting dishonor.[127]

3. <u>He Cares for Looks Alone</u>

"Having a form of godliness, but denying the power thereof: from such turn away" (II Tim. 3:5).

A rebel is more concerned with himself and his appearance than his inside spiritual decor and temperature. The passage in II Timothy 3 describes a host of characteristics which indicate this trait: heady, high-minded, proud, and boaster to name a few. The rebel is consumed with his image, his name, and his agenda. This is opposite of a humble born-again believer who is concerned with lifting up Christ in his life (see John 3:30).

---

[127] Matthew Henry, *Matthew Henry's Commentary on the Whole Bible: Volume 2* (Peabody, MA: Hendrickson Publishers, 1991), 421.

4. <u>He Leads Weak People</u>

"For of this sort are they which creep into houses, and lead captive silly women laden with sins, led away with divers lusts, Ever learning, and never able to come to the knowledge of the truth." (II Tim. 3:6–7)

In the midst of a great independent revival campaign in Waxahachie, Texas, a man that had just returned from serving five years in the State Penitentiary as a bootlegger sent for me. I had preached plainly against sin. My wife was frightened and urged me not to go. There had been many threats because of my preaching on the liquor traffic, but I knew God was in it.

I found the man in a wheelchair due to heart trouble. The doctor had told him that he probably wouldn't live but a few months.

He started to complain, telling how he had provided a car for the man who had run for the sheriff's office, had put $200 cash into his support, and then he said, "He was elected, and then he sent me to five years in hell in the penitentiary!"

I told him frankly, "I am glad to help you any way I can, and I will be glad to pray for you, but let's have it understood from the beginning: I am against the dirty liquor business and everybody who takes part in it, and I am for the law enforcement and the men in authority."

The man looked up to me and very pitifully said, "That is why I sent for you. There are many preachers in this town, but you can't tell what side they are on. You can't trust what they tell you. I have only a few months to live, and I have to get right with God. I want somebody true to God to tell me how." The man soon forgave those he hated and trusted the Lord and was wonderfully saved. Every week young people would go to his home to sing and pray with him until the day he died. He had wanted somebody who would speak plainly against sin, and he could trust such a man of God.

Oh, how can anybody trust any man of God who doesn't take a plain, sharp stand against sin and wickedness![128]

This may seem like an odd illustration to make this point to those working with a rebel. However, in my years of working with youth and in talking with both parents and pastors, there is a fear that starts to overwhelm the spiritual man or woman who needs to confront a rebel. The godly man must understand that the rebel's desire is not to be alone. There will be more tragedy and more carnage if the rebel is not called out. As those working with youth, we must pray that God gives us the boldness of a lion to stop the evil spread of rebellion.

5. He Is Purposefully Ignorant

A stag overpowered by heat came to a spring to drink. Seeing his own shadow reflected in the water, he greatly admired the size and variety of his horns, but felt angry with himself for having such slender and weak feet. While he was thus contemplating himself, a lion appeared at the pool and crouched to spring upon him. The stag immediately took to flight, and exerting his utmost speed, as long

---

[128] https://www.gospeltruth.net/soulwinnersfire/soulwinnersfire.htm. Accessed on July 31, 2018.

as the plain was smooth and open kept himself easily at a safe distance from the lion. But entering a wood he became entangled by his horns, and the lion quickly came up to him and caught him. When too late, he thus reproached himself: "Woe is me! How I have deceived myself! These feet which would have saved me I despised, and I gloried in these antlers which have proved my destruction."[129]

6. He Has Misplaced Priorities

Finally, as we have considered the characteristics of a rebel, we find that the rebel has misplaced priorities. In essence, the rebel will glory in the carnal—the nonessential qualities in their life. The rebel will discount the true riches of the kingdom. I have seen young men glory in their physical strength or mental intellect rather than in the true strength, which is internal and harder to see. I have seen young women glory in their outward beauty and worship the vanity of looks rather than that inward beauty which God desires to blossom inside the heart of a young lady.

The Consequences of a Rebel

Hear, O my people, and I will testify unto thee: O Israel, if thou wilt hearken unto me; There shall no strange god be in thee; neither shalt thou worship any strange god. I am the LORD thy God, which brought thee out of the land of Egypt: open thy mouth wide, and I will fill it. But my people would not hearken to my voice; and Israel would none of me. So I gave them up unto their own hearts' lust: and they walked in their own counsels. Oh that my people had hearkened unto me, and Israel had walked in my ways! I should soon have subdued their enemies, and turned my hand against their

---

[129] http://www.sacred-texts.com/cla/aesop/aes258.htm. Accessed on July 31, 2018.

adversaries. The haters of the LORD should have submitted themselves unto him: but their time should have endured for ever. He should have fed them also with the finest of the wheat: and with honey out of the rock should I have satisfied thee. (Ps. 81:8–16)

Notice in this passage that the blessings of God are cut off. Some is because of the closing of the ears to the voice of the Lord, but it also is because God *"gave them up."* This phrase is a scary phrase for those who work with young people. Rebellion can lead to a point that God "gives them up." I have had young people during their time of rebellion or later in their time of reaping who cast judgment on me or the church. They say they were given up on. I don't think I am the one doing this. According to the Scripture, there comes a point that God says that He has had enough rebellion, and God will "give them up."

> They walked in their own counsels, in the way of their heart and in the sight of their eye, both in their worships and in their conversation. 'I left them to do as they would, and then they did all that was ill;' they walked in their own counsels, and not according to the counsels of God and his advice. God therefore was not the author of their sin; He left them to the lusts of their own hearts and the counsels of their own heads; if they do not well, the blame must lie upon their own hearts and the blood upon their own heads.[130]

Later in Psalm 81, God reveals that although the claim of a rebel is that he was given up on, in the grace of God, He was there ready for the repentant sinner to turn. Victory could have been had. The rebellious young person is sacrificing victory for sure when he stubbornly refuses

---

[130] Matthew Henry, *Matthew Henry's Commentary on the Whole Bible: Volume 3* (Peabody, MA: Hendrickson Publishers, 1991), 449.

to heed the authority place in his life. He is heading toward defeat and despondency. Warn the young person that is in rebellion and pray for God's mercy to intervene.

How to Treat a Rebel

But now I have written unto you not to keep company, if any man that is called a brother be a fornicator, or covetous, or an idolater, or a railer, or a drunkard, or an extortioner; with such a one no not to eat. (I Cor. 5:11)

And if we know that he hear us, whatsoever we ask, we know that we have the petitions that we desired of him. If any man see his brother sin a sin which is not unto death, he shall ask, and he shall give him life for them that sin not unto death. There is a sin unto death: I do not say that he shall pray for it. (I John 5:15–16)

And if any man obey not our word by this epistle, note that man, and have no company with him, that he may be ashamed. Yet count him not as an enemy, but admonish him as a brother. (II Thess. 3:14–15)

1. Stay Away from Them

Recently, I heard about a terrible wreck. It seems that a man who had already been convicted four times for drunk driving decided to risk a fifth conviction and drove off in his car after having a few too many drinks. He ended up plowing into a family's van, killing several, and critically wounding several others. Of course, the drunk was not hurt but is now charged with more serious crimes, including vehicular homicide. I don't suppose this drunkard really intended on killing anybody when he started his car that night. But the fact is that his rebellion cost some people their lives. This fellow illustrates another important answer to the question, "What's wrong with being a rebel?" Answer: they always hurt others.

2. Warn Them

Let us suppose for a moment that later in life you may be saved. I think it is unlikely if you neglect salvation in your youth. The vast majority of all the people who are ever saved are saved when they are young. Far more than half of those saved are saved before they are fifteen years old. And the vast majority of all those who wait until they are grown before accepting Christ, never accept Him and die and go to hell. But suppose, for the sake of argument, that you may be later converted, born again, and that you miss going to hell. I am afraid you will not do it, but if you do, what then? Still you cannot escape a wasted life if you neglect your soul's salvation.

Go with me back to my boyhood in West Texas. An old farmer-ranchman was wonderfully converted when he was nearly sixty years old. His face was lined and weather-beaten with the Texas sun and wind. It was lined also with the marks of long years of sinning. But he was wonderfully saved. I recall with great joy how he used to stand in the little Methodist prayer meeting and, with tears running down his face, tell how gracious God had been to him to save an old sinner so long gone in sin. It was sweet to hear.

But that was not the end of his testimony. He never sat down before he pleaded with the people, pleaded with tears, that they should pray for his unconverted sons. One daughter he was able to win to Christ. His sons all remained unconcerned, unconverted. They never sought the Lord, they never repented, and they never trusted Christ.

Out in the cemetery lay the body of one boy who had died at fourteen, I believe, unconverted. He died before the father turned to God.

Another son of the old converted stockman stood in the last row at the Baptist church one Saturday night in a revival campaign when I went to plead with him to turn to Christ and be saved. "Roy, you ought to go," I said. "Roy, if you will go maybe others will turn to Christ and be saved. Think of your brothers. Think of your friends." But Roy shook his head and said emphatically that he was not going to go.

That happened on a Saturday night. One week later, on Saturday afternoon, Roy drove a bronco colt to a breaking cart to town, a little West Texas cow town. Some juggler friend sailed a Stetson hat under his belly and the colt plunged and ran away. Roy fell off the cart backward. A rider soon caught the colt, Roy got up and dusted his clothes and laughed at the joke with the others. But as he drove home, he fell off the cart unconscious from internal injuries; and the next day he died. I was at his funeral on Monday. The old cow-man came and stood beside the casket after the kindly Methodist preacher had brought a gospel message. The father patted the cold face and said, "Good-bye, Roy." Then he said it again, "Good-bye, Roy." He was loathe to leave. The tears rained down his face and his lips quivered. He brushed back a hair from the cold forehead with trembling fingers and said again, "Good-bye,

Roy." I knew what he meant. Everybody else there knew what he meant. He was saying, "Good-bye forever!"

Oh, yes, God in His mercy saved that old stockman. All the years of his neglect did not wipe out the great mercy of God, and at last he was saved, like a brand from the burning, after he was almost in hell. But, alas, when the father was saved he could not win his boys. His life's influence was wasted and gone!

I was at the funeral of another son of the same father. After a weekend of drunkenness, he was smitten with intestinal paralysis and was rushed to the hospital and died on the operating table. Later, as a young preacher, I went into the homes of the two remaining out of five sons. Now they were married men with grown children, yet they never would go to church. They were not interested in the gospel; they went on their way of blasphemy and rejection of Christ. God was merciful to save the old stockman, but, and I say this as reverently as I know how, even God Himself, being just and holy, could not undo all the wasted years and influence of the man who was saved in his old age.

I solemnly warn you today that you cannot escape the ruin of a wasted life, if you neglect this great salvation. Even if you should later be saved, you will have nothing but tears and heartache over the years that are wasted and gone, which can never be redeemed.[131]

---

[131] John R. Rice. *Neglect: The Shortest Way to Hell* (Murfreesboro, Tennessee: Sword of the Lord Publishers, 1954), 12.

I used a large excerpt from this sermon by John R. Rice to show to us in the twenty-first century that not much has changed when it comes to a rebel. Rebels have been around for a long time. They have certain characteristics which have been shown to us in Scripture, and we can go back in ancient history and in recent history and find examples to highlight for our young people.

As a pastor, youth pastor, or parent, please don't allow the spirit of rebellion to fester in a young person. It is damaging to their soul, and it will affect others. Find this spirit and ask for God's wisdom and guidance to root it out.

Chapter 19

S - The Battle of Self

What Others Have Said About Self

o   Burton: "Conquer thyself. Till thou hast done that thou art a slave; for it is almost as well for thee to be in subjection to another's appetite as thy own."

o   Milton: "He who reigns within himself, and rules passions, desires, and fears, is more than a king."

o   Seneca: "Most powerful is he who has himself in his power."

o   Walter Scott: "Sordid selfishness doth contract and narrow our benevolence, and cause us, like serpents, to enfold ourselves within ourselves, and to turn out our stings to all of the world besides."

o   Emerson: "The selfish man suffers more from his selfishness than he from whom that selfishness withholds some important benefit."[132]

The greatest hero is the man who is the master of himself. The greatest battle is the battle which is fought within unto victory. The greatest character is the character which is built on will power. The highest form

---

[132] Ibid., 778.

of education is an educated will, a will to be right, to do right. Test yourself at the point where you have the least suspicion of weakness. Be master of yourself.[133]

<u>What Does the Bible Says About Self</u>

The way of a fool is right in his own eyes: but he that hearkeneth unto counsel is wise. (Prov. 12:15)

There is a way which seemeth right unto a man, but the end thereof are the ways of death. (Prov. 14:12)

He that is slow to anger is better than the mighty; and he that ruleth his spirit than he that taketh a city. (Prov. 16:32)

Put a knife to thy throat, if thou be a man given to a appetite. (Prov. 23:2)

Thus saith the Lord; Cursed be the man that trusteth in man, and maketh flesh his arm, and whose heart departeth from the Lord. (Jer. 17:5)

And if thy right eye offend thee, pluck it out, and cast it from thee: for it is profitable for thee that one of thy members should perish, and not that thy whole body should be cast into hell. And if thy right hand offend thee, cut it off, and cast it from thee: for it is profitable for thee that one of thy members should perish, and not that thy whole body should be cast into hell. (Matt. 5:29–30)

---

[133] *The System Bible Study* (Chicago, Illinois: John Rudin & Company, Inc., 1971), 777.

Then said Jesus unto his disciples, If any man will come after me, let him deny himself, and take up his cross, and follow me. For whosoever will save his life shall lose it: and whosoever will lose his life for my ask shall find it. (Matt. 16:24–25)

But put ye on the Lord Jesus Christ, and make not provision for the flesh, to fulfil the lusts thereof. (Rom. 13:14)

Every man that striveth for the mastery is temperate in all things. Now they do it to obtain a corruptible crown, but we an incorruptible. But I keep under my body, and bring it into subjection: lest that by any means, when I have preached to others, I myself should be a castaway. (I Cor. 9:25, 27)

The Bible teaches to us that trusting in the arm of flesh, relying on our self-will, and building our self-esteem is not wise in God's eyes. Our view of self (flesh) is a foundation truth.

Creation	Evolution
Created being in the image of God so my being should reflect God's attributes	Survival of the fittest: we climb and develop a selfish take-all attitude.

Foundational Truth	
God's nature is a giving, caring nature. His nature is love. "God is love," the Bible says, and His love was expressed in giving to others.	Selective breeding and survival of the fittest is the way of man. (self-oriented and self-made)

With this concept in mind, we must then consider that the Bible's concept of our flesh or self is that it must be brought under submission

(I Cor. 9). Take, for example, the *"works of the flesh"* found in Galatians 5:19–21. All these things are a lack of self-control in some area. We must bring ourselves and our flesh into subjection. It is vital in the training of young people that our kids are taught to have self-control.

Think about the area of food preferences. What a grown person likes to eat or drink depends largely on what that person was trained to eat or drink as a child. In today's American culture, most do not realize that a child can be trained to like almost any sort of food or drink, whether it be good or bad. So, it is crucial that parents and other authority figures teach their children at an early age the importance of having the right kind of appetites. Our modern culture is reaping the fruit of teaching generations of young people that they can work when they want to work, play for as long as they want to play, and live life however they feel like living. We have sown generations of unrestraint, and we are reaping the fruits of undisciplined lives.

Let's consider a few ideas regarding the subduing of self.

The Defense of Self-Discipline

Everything in life requires some sort of discipline. Whether it is hitting a baseball, climbing a mountain, playing a musical instrument, or making good grades, it all comes down to a matter of discipline. Many people have ambitions that will never be realized, goals that will never be reached, and achievements that will never materialize simply because they have no discipline. If a young person wants to become a doctor or an important scientist, but he doesn't want to buckle down to years of hard study, he will never achieve those desires because of a lack of subduing himself. Many young people would like to achieve greatness in music but never will because they are not willing to commit to the long hours of practice required year after year. They may even possess the natural talent to play an instrument, but they will still fail if they are unwilling to dedicate the time and effort that is needed to master the instrument. Their dreams don't lie beyond their abilities but beyond their discipline. Pastors, youth pastors, and parents, be careful of touting the world's philosophy that "if you believe, you can achieve." That's a nice saying, but discipline must accompany the belief.

The Christian life is no different. The church is filled with people who have a desire to be mature Christians who possess a tremendous knowledge of God's Word, yet they are not willing to pay the price to achieve it. One time, a Christian told a pastor, "I'd give my life to know the Bible like you do." To which the pastor replied, "That's what it took."[134] The world is full of naturally brilliant people who will never be anything more than ordinary because they aren't willing to make the sacrifice necessary to become great. The church is full of people like that too. People who have gone to church, listened to countless sermons, but have never taken the time to personally get in the Word and do a Bible study will not venture out with steps of faith in the Christian life.

Consider the example of John Wesley. It is said that John Wesley traveled an average of twenty miles per day for forty years. He got up at four every morning. He preached 40,000 sermons. He produced 400 books and knew ten languages. At the age of eighty-three, he was annoyed because he couldn't write more than fifteen hours a day without hurting his eyes; and at the age of eighty-six, he was ashamed that he couldn't preach more than twice a day. He complained in his diary that there was an increasing tendency to lie in bed until half after five in the morning. [135]As we read about men like John Wesley, it should motivate us to do more with our lives for the cause of Christ. The person who learns the power of self-discipline is going to be the person who accomplishes great things in this life and for eternity for the Lord.

---

[134] http://fcob.net/am-site/media/sermon-93012-script.pdf. Accessed on September 4, 2018.

[135] https://www.christianitytoday.com/history/issues/issue-2/john-wesley-did-you-know.html. Accessed on September 4, 2018.

The Direction of Self-Discipline

Let's consider some direction for the discipline in our lives. There are three areas in which we should help our young people. First, we should teach our young people discipline in their faith. This may seem to be an oversimplification, but it is not. In over twenty-five years of working with young people, it still amazes me that the simple things, such as reading the Bible, praying, and studying the Bible, are so easily ignored. Folks want a special recipe that is a "secret sauce" to add to the formula of an everyday Christian life. This is not going to happen without discipline in building faith. Consider the following list from II Peter:

> *According as his divine power hath given unto us all things that pertain unto life and godliness, through the knowledge of him that hath called us to glory and virtue: Whereby are given unto us exceeding great and precious promises: that by these ye might be partakers of the divine nature, having escaped the corruption that is in the world through lust. And beside this, giving all diligence, add to your faith virtue; and to virtue knowledge; And to knowledge temperance; and to temperance patience; and to patience godliness; And to godliness brotherly kindness; and to brotherly kindness charity. For if these things be in you, and abound, they make you that ye shall neither be barren nor unfruitful in the knowledge of our Lord Jesus Christ. (II Pet. 1:3–8)*

What powerful verses! These verses are written to help us to understand that divine power has been given to us through the great promises in the Bible. We need to get into the Word of God and study it and meditate upon it so that we can add to our faith those things which will make us profitable and fruitful. This will take a regimented schedule of work and study.

The second area by which we must help our young people is having discipline in our families. This discipline should start at an early age and be consistent and loving. The world has a disdain for any discipline because the world follows their father the devil. Don't feel ashamed about having godly discipline in the home. The world tries to shame Christians for disciplining their children, yet it marvels at the results of a disciplined home. I have experienced this personally from folks in our church who have reared young people with discipline as well as in my home. The community calls frequently to ask if some of our young people are free to work because they know that we have discipline in our homes and teach our children the biblical value of hard work. Unfortunately, the community does not want to accept the biblical mandate enough to start practicing it in their own homes.

Do these symptoms characterize your children?

<u>They lack self-restraint.</u>

- Self-indulgent people rarely say "no" to themselves.

- They have a difficult time doing anything in moderation..

- They are driven by passion, whether it is anger, lust, gluttony, pride, covetousness, etc. They cannot delay gratification.

<u>They are self-absorbed.</u>

- Self-centeredness so rules self-indulgent people that they live as if the world revolves around them—life is interpreted by how it affects them.

- Those who are self-consumed push and lobby parents constantly to get what they want and persist even after being refused.

- Insist on their "rights" to personal decisions and living their "own life."[136]

The last area in which we should help our young people with discipline is in finances. There should be training to help a young person understand that money can be used for the furthering of God's kingdom and the betterment of society. Money also can be a detriment to oneself if not put in its proper place. Money management should start well before the teen years. This can be done by paying a small amount of money to young children to do odd jobs around the house. They could also earn additional money by completing tasks for others in the neighborhood or for members of their church family. Once they begin to earn some money, it is important to teach them about budgeting. Since the amount of money will be small, it will be simple to set up a budget with them, and this allows them to see the breakdown of tithing, savings, and other expenses.

Teaching godly principles from the Word of God will help a young person see that God is the giver of talents and treasure.

The Dangers of Self-Discipline

Discipline is a good thing and something that needs work, but there are some dangers that need to be addressed. Some people may get the idea that achieving discipline is the greatest thing we can strive for as a Christian, but it's not. A right relationship with God is the most important thing. Self-discipline by itself doesn't make us right with God. In Colossians 2, Paul rebukes the Christians in Colossi because some of them were laying down strict rules, "Don't touch this! Don't taste this! Don't handle this!" thinking that those rules would make them right with God, but they didn't. The Pharisees were a highly disciplined people, but their hearts

---

[136] Reb Bradley, Child Training Tips (Washington, D.C.: WND Books, 2014), 23–24.

weren't right. We always need to remember that discipline is only a servant to be used in our attempts to glorify God.

We need to be careful that discipline doesn't fill us with pride. There is a certain satisfaction in being able to control ourselves, but it's wrong when that satisfaction becomes self-satisfaction. Such a disciplined person gives himself the glory rather than God. Like the Pharisee who prayed, Father, *"I thank thee that I am not as other men are" (Luke 18:11–12)*.

There is a danger of overdoing self-discipline. One example would be monasticism. Another word for this lifestyle is called asceticism. Monks and other religious men of past centuries denied themselves anything that brought them pleasure. They didn't marry, didn't eat much, and didn't partake in other various and sundry laws which would make them appear to be extreme in their discipline of self-desires. What is the difference between asceticism and a healthy dose of self-discipline? Asceticism focuses on rules that are petty when it comes to the overall concept of spirituality with God. Spiritual discipline puts restrictions in place that will help us to be better Christians. For instance, one could live in the woods for months on end with little food or water, but the practice of setting aside twenty minutes every morning to study the Bible would be a better spiritual discipline.

Asceticism tends to despise the good things in life. It denies joys and pleasures which are really the gifts of God. This practice of absurd denials comes from a mistaken idea that everything in this world is evil. In contrast, a proper spiritual discipline uses those things that God has given us within proper boundaries to accomplish spiritual purposes.

Have you heard about the Chinese bamboo tree?[137] The Chinese plant the seed; they water and fertilize it, but the first year nothing happens. The second year they water and fertilize it and still nothing happens. The third and fourth years they water and fertilize it, and nothing happens. Then the fifth year, they water and fertilize it; and sometime during the course

---

[137] https://www.preachit.org/newsletters/article/327. Accessed on September 4, 2018.

of the fifth year, in a period of approximately six weeks, the Chinese bamboo trees grows roughly ninety feet.

The question is, "Did it grow ninety feet in six weeks, or did it grow ninety feet in five years?" The obvious answer is that it grew ninety feet in five years because had they not applied the water and fertilizer each year, there would have been no Chinese bamboo tree.

Let's teach our young people the Biblical concept of self and then help them to understand the Biblical instructions to be self-disciplined.

Chapter 20

T - Tips for Troubling Times

Once upon a time, people understood that in changing times, certain things should not change, that there must always be certain constants in culture. A short list of those changeless things includes morality, the need for adults to be contributing members of society, and constants regarding how the family should function, including how children should be brought up. Once upon a time, people understood that change would deteriorate into chaos unless change was organized around unchanging "still points" in the culture, and child rearing was one of those points. In fact, there is no evidence that in the Judeo-Christian world, the fundamental principles governing child rearing had appreciably changed since its founding by Abraham and Sarah. For thousands of years, the child-rearing "baton" was handed down, intact, from generation to generation. Children honored their parents by growing up and raising their children the same way their parents had raised them; and let there be no doubt: the "way" in question was based on biblical principles.[138]

This quote reminds us that "times have changed." The change, however, has not been for the better. The biblical foundations that have

---

[138] John Rosemond, Parenting by the Book: Biblical Wisdom for Raising Your Child (New York, New York: Howard Books, 2007), 15–16.

for centuries been a constant have now become a sandy foundation. This makes troubling times that much more difficult. It is imperative that we pause with our young people and focus back on what can solve problems.

> *And when the people saw that Moses delayed to come down out of the mount, the people gathered themselves together unto Aaron, and said unto him, Up, make us gods, which shall go before us; for as for this Moses, the man that brought us up out of the land of Egypt, we wot not what is become of him. And Aaron said unto them, Break off the golden earrings, which are in the ears of your wives, of your sons, and of your daughters, and bring them unto me. (Exod. 32:1–2.*

> *And he received them at their hand, and fashioned it with a graving tool, after he had made it a molten calf: and they said, These be thy gods, O Israel, which brought thee up out of the land of Egypt. And when Aaron saw it, he built an altar before it; and Aaron made proclamation, and said, Tomorrow is a feast to the LORD. (Exod. 32:4–5)*

> *And the LORD said unto Moses, Go, get thee down; for thy people, which thou broughtest out of the land of Egypt, have corrupted themselves. (Exod. 32:7)*

> *And Moses besought the LORD his God, and said, LORD, why doth thy wrath wax hot against thy people, which thou hast brought forth out of the land of Egypt with great power, and with a mighty hand. (Exod. 32:11)*

> *And he took the calf which they had made, and burnt it in the fire, and ground it to powder, and strawed it upon the water, and made the children of Israel drink of it. And Moses*

> *said unto Aaron, What did this people unto thee, that thou*
> *hast brought so great a sin upon them?" (Exod. 32:20, 21)*

Moses came face to face with a troubling time. He had been in the presence of Jehovah, getting direction for the people he was called to lead. While doing this, the people went away from the Lord and started to rebel against God. We find a few ideas in this passage and in other passages in Scripture that can help us when troubling times come into the home.

Find Godly Help to Assist

Don't underestimate the help that God brings into your life to assist in troubled times. Remember that the Bible tells us in Hebrews 13 that godly pastors watch for the souls of their sheep. Go to those in authority whom God has given you to get sound advice when troubling times strike. Great can be the help to a parent for clarity when the storms of life roll into a family. The Bible, the Holy Spirit, and your godly authority have been given to help guide and direct through the difficult times of parenting.

Don't get so emotionally involved that you justify or excuse the sin. Many times, the forest can't be seen for the trees. As parents, we may not be able to see the evil that is present in our young person. We can't believe that this young person who we fed, clothed, and have seen grow from an infant is now rebelling as a teenager. Yet, many times this actually does happen during a young person's life. The hymn writer put it appropriately, "Prone to wander, Lord, I feel it; prone to leave the God I love."[139] Don't forget to spend time with God. A key ingredient to success is God. In the text in Exodus 32, the passage says, "And Moses sought the Lord." This is easily said but sometimes forgotten to practice when the battle is raging. We will have decisions to make and the stress and pressure that seems to come on at this time will be overwhelming. This is the time to spend more, not less time, with your Savior. You will have to fight for this time, but a parent will never regret spending some extra time to gain the

---

[139] https://en.wikipedia.org/wiki/Come_Thou_Fount_of_Every_Blessing. Accessed on September 7, 2018.

peace, understanding, and guidance that only the Lord can give. Consider the following verses:

Wait on the LORD: be of good courage, and he shall strengthen thine heart: wait, I say, on the LORD. (Ps. 27:14)

Rest in the LORD, and wait patiently for him: fret not thyself because of him who prospereth in his way, because of the man who bringeth wicked devices to pass. (Ps. 37:7)

Wait on the LORD, and keep his way, and he shall exalt thee to inherit the land: when the wicked are cut off, thou shalt see it. (Ps. 37:34)

I wait for the LORD, my soul doth wait, and in his word do I hope. (Ps. 130:5)

But they that wait upon the LORD shall renew their strength; they shall mount up with wings as eagles; they shall run, and not be weary; and they shall walk, and not faint. (Isa. 40:31)

The Lord is the great heart specialist.[140] He is able to help the wounded heart and then give guidance and direction when none seems to be evident. Many times, this will only come when we spend the extra time that is necessary in the Lord's presence. In the Lord's presence, a troubled heart can find the comfort, strength, and direction from the Lord.

Show the Danger of Rebellion Against God

There are two examples in the Old Testament that stand out when it comes to dealing with rebellion and sin—Moses and Nathan. Remember

---

[140] J. Vernon McGee, Thru the Bible with J. Vernon McGee: Volume 2 (Nashville, Tennessee: Thomas Nelson Publishers, 1982), 721.

the story of Moses and the golden calves? Moses had interceded for the cause of the people, then came down and found the Israelites in open rebellion against God's commands. He ground up the idols, mixed them with water, and had the people drink it. He was not easy on the rebellion of the children of Israel. In the same way, leadership and parents should not be soft on rebellion. Samuel told King Saul that rebellion is as the sin of witchcraft. This analogy is not something to make light of with young people. Outright devil worship is not a common sight in America, but in reality, there's a whole lot of it going on in the hearts of a rebellious teen-agers. Be bold like Moses and root out the rebellion. Don't back down. The enemy is the devil, and the victim is the teen. Being hard on rebellion is saving that teen's life.

Nathan was also bold when he presented the consequences of David's sin.

> *And David's anger was greatly kindled against the man; and he said to Nathan, As the LORD liveth, the man that hath done this thing shall surely die: And he shall restore the lamb fourfold, because he did this thing, and because he had no pity. And Nathan said to David, Thou art the man. Thus saith the LORD God of Israel, I anointed thee king over Israel, and I delivered thee out of the hand of Saul; And I gave thee thy master's house, and thy master's wives into thy bosom, and gave thee the house of Israel and of Judah; and if that had been too little, I would moreover have given unto thee such and such things. Wherefore hast thou despised the commandment of the LORD, to do evil in his sight? thou hast killed Uriah the Hittite with the sword, and hast taken his wife to be thy wife, and hast slain him with the sword of the children of Ammon. Now therefore the sword shall never depart from thine house; because thou hast despised me, and hast taken the wife of Uriah the Hittite to be thy wife. Thus saith the LORD, Behold, I will raise up evil against thee out*

of thine own house, and I will take thy wives before thine eyes, and give them unto thy neighbour, and he shall lie with thy wives in the sight of this sun. For thou didst it secretly: but I will do this thing before all Israel, and before the sun. (II Sam. 12:5–12)

Don't be afraid to be hard on sin! Yes, intercede, but don't let the sin go unpunished. Look at the boldness that Nathan the prophet had. Make the sin apparent to your young person.

Teach a Young Person Never to Give Up

"If thou faint in the day of adversity, thy strength is small".
(Prov. 24:10).

Help them to understand that quitting is a bad thing. A pastor or parent can encourage a young person to stand again by showing examples in the Bible of failure, but those that failed got up. Help them understand that no one is perfect, but that through Christ we can have victory. Let's consider a couple of helps after the battle of Jericho. We remember that Joshua was discouraged and felt a huge weight of responsibility for leading his men into a battle at Ai. Thirty-six men were killed because of sin in the camp. Joshua then shows us how to get back up after defeat.

1. Begin with Humility

Joshua first began by humbling himself before God. This is found in Joshua 7:6. *"And Joshua rent his clothes, and fell to the earth upon his face before the ark of the LORD until the eventide, he and the elders of Israel, and put dust upon their heads."*

This is always a wonderful place to begin. No matter how smart or spiritual a Christian believes himself to be, no one can identify a problem or help a person like the Lord can. We must learn to go to God and bow before Him humbly and let Him deal with us. When we read of men used of God in the Bible, we see that they all came before God on differing occasions to have Him look at things in their lives and to give them direction on what to do. Begin with humility.

Young people should not stiffen at reproof or criticism, thinking that authority must be conspiring against them. No, godly authority was placed by God to help them to grow spiritually, and one way is dealing with sin and flaws. There is way too much self in the Christian realm today. It is self-image, self-recognition, self-love, self-importance, self-reliance, and self-will. Self needs to be set aside, and God must be bowed before. I am not saying that there can't be an overestimated opinion of leadership or authority, but most of those claiming this have an overestimated opinion of their own selves; and they are rebels against God's ways and leadings.

As you spend time with God, you know what you are and what you deserve. It is hard sometimes to understand why God uses men. I have met animals that are better servants to their masters. There are creatures of this earth that seem to give God more glory than the average human, but God has seen fit to use mankind—then we blow it and get arrogant about it. Remain humble before God, and you will keep the proper perspective of sin and holy living.

2. Identify the Problem

And the LORD said unto Joshua, Get thee up; wherefore liest thou thus upon thy face? Israel hath sinned, and they have also transgressed my covenant which I commanded them: for they have even taken of the accursed thing, and have also stolen, and dissembled also, and they have put it even among their own stuff. (Josh. 7:10–11)

As you consider this passage, what were some of the problems?

- Pride—This is seen in the lack of obedience. Pride makes a young person think that he is above God's way of doing things. This must be identified and put out of a Christian's life.

- Presumption—Joshua presumed that everything was okay and proceeded without getting specific directions from God.

- Prayerlessness—Joshua never paused to ask what God would think of his plans. Many times, we as leaders of youth go down our own path. God must always be consulted in all times, but especially when trouble has come.

- No Patience—Joshua needed to wait on the Lord. This is hard for all mankind. There is a desire to get through the difficulty and move on with our lives. However, sometimes God has lessons that can only be taught through a troubling time.

These were some of the problems with the failure of Ai, but they may be different in your life. When we come face to face with defeat in our life, the majority of the time it is our fault. Look at your life; if it is sin, identify the sin—don't keep going. Look internally, not externally (compare verses 9 and 11) and start the process of fixing the problem.

Who Lost the Game? A ball team went to play a game of baseball. Just as the umpire said, "Batter up," the catcher for the home team arrived and took his place. The center fielder and the second baseman didn't arrive until the middle of the second inning. The first baseman didn't come at all, but later sent his regrets and said that he had to go to a chicken dinner at Aunt Mary's. The third baseman likewise failed to show up; having been up too late the night before, he desired to spend the day in bed. The left fielder was away visiting another ball game across town. The shortstop was present, but he left his glove at home. Verily, when the pitcher went into the box he looked around to see his teammates, and lo, his heart was made heavy when he saw the empty places. The game had been announced, and visitors were already in the stands to see the game. There was nothing to do but pitch the ball and hope for the best. Lo, the pitcher tightened his belt, stepped into the box, and did his best to put one over the plate. But for some reason he just couldn't find the groove. Soon some of his team-mates began to ride him for wild pitching, and loud "boos" were heard from the stands. At the close of the game the home team was disgrace-fully beaten. This game caused discussion; and when the rest of the team heard about the defeat, everyone decided to do something about it. They finally reached a decision. A new pitcher must be hired. It was his poor pitching that had lost the game. The team is now looking forward with more optimism. Their new pitcher came well recommended. But who really lost the game?[141]

3. <u>Change Your Behavior</u>

The great character trait that we see in Joshua is that he was willing to change his behavior. We find this in Joshua 7:16. *"So Joshua rose up early in the morning, and brought Israel by their tribes; and the tribe of Judah was taken:"* This means dealing with the problem. Don't "beat around the bush." Don't make an appear-ance or show of repentance. Burn the sin out! Don't be afraid of what others may say or what others may think of you now. We are all sinners, and we all make mistakes. Deal with the sin; burn it deep; pile a heap on the sin to remind you when you come by again.

<u>Teach Them to Work Hard Through the Trial</u>

If a young person will not be diligent in their work, they more than likely will never overcome their faults and weaknesses.

One of the hardest difficulty in not moving on to victory is not that we do not have talents, but that we are not willing to take the time and

---

[141] http://www.jimduggan.org/when-church-is-a-little-like-baseball/. Accessed on September 7, 2018.

effort to root out sin and set in place what is necessary for victory. We are too lazy to get right down to hard work. We are not willing to face the stern problems of life and solve them. We are not willing to put ourselves under the same severe training for our lifework as did those great men of the past who accomplished work for the Lord. We expect somebody to "boost" us, to save us all the painful labor of self-development. It is folly to depend upon "pull." A better method is to have "push"; it is more dependable. The truth is that "what man has done, man can do" provided he is willing to pay the price.

One of the necessary ingredients to overcome sin in our life is a desire to put in work, work, and more work.

IT COULDN'T BE DONE
By Edgar A. Guest

"Somebody said that It couldn't be done;
But he with a chuckle replied
That 'maybe it couldn't,' but he would be one
Who wouldn't say so till he'd tried.
So he buckled right in with the trace of a grin
On his face. If he worried, he hid it.
He started to sing as he tackled the thing
That couldn't be done, and he did it."

Edward Harriman was told that he could not build the railroad across the great Salt Lake in Utah. "All right," said the little giant, "go ahead and do it."

The great tunnels underneath the Hudson River in New York were built by William McAdoo after dozens of attempts had failed. They laughed at McAdoo when he said that intended to go ahead and do it. They do not laugh now, for he did it.[142]

---

[142] Dennis Richard, Above and Beyond: Leading and Managing Organizational Change (Bloomington, Indiana: Author House, 2017), 85.

Let us not consider a thing impossible of accomplishment until we have faithfully tried it. General Grant said, "A man is never whipped until he believes it." The apostle Paul said that he was determined to finish his course. In his dying testimony he tells us that, *"I have finished my course."* That determination carried him through many a hard and difficult place, and he won although many times, no doubt, it looked impossible.

Learn the Balance of Trust and Accountability

The rod and reproof give wisdom: but a child left to himself bringeth his mother to shame. (Prov. 29:15)

In that day I will perform against Eli all things which I have spoken concerning his house: when I begin, I will also make an end. For I have told him that I will judge his house for ever for the iniquity which he knoweth; because his sons made themselves vile, and he restrained them not. (I Sam. 3:12–13)

And his brethren went to feed their father's flock in Shechem. And Israel said unto Joseph, Do not thy brethren feed the flock in Shechem? come, and I will send thee unto them. And he said to him, Here am I. And he said to him, Go, I pray thee, see whether it be well with thy brethren, and well with the flocks; and bring me word again. So he sent him out of the vale of Hebron, and he came to Shechem. (Gen. 37:12–14)

In the passages listed above, we see several examples that show that parents let their children or young people have responsibility. However, some of the parents were chastised because they did not follow up with the trust that was given to the young people. They let the young person run wild without any checks or balances. Remember that the job of parent or pastor is to help guide a young person into the truth. We should be in constant prayer for wisdom in helping our young people realize that the *"eyes of the Lord are in every place beholding the evil and the good."* Don't make the mistake of Eli who knew that wrong was going on but felt it was not his place to stop his sons from doing wrong.

<u>Keep Positive Through the Trial</u>

O God, be not far from me: O my God, make haste for my help. Let them be confounded and consumed that are adversaries to my soul; let them be covered with reproach and dishonor that seek my hurt. But I will hope continually, and will yet praise thee more and more. My mouth shall shew forth thy righteousness and thy salvation all the day; for I know not the numbers thereof. I will go in the strength of the Lord GOD: I will make mention of thy righteousness, even of thine only. (Ps. 71:12–16)

Hope deferred maketh the heart sick: but when the desire cometh, it is a tree of life. (Prov. 13:12)

For whatsoever things were written aforetime were written for our learning, that we through patience and comfort of the scriptures might have hope. (Rom. 15:4)

Now the God of hope fill you with all joy and peace in believing, that ye may abound in hope, through the power of the Holy Ghost. (Rom. 15:13)

But thanks be to God, which giveth us the victory through our Lord Jesus Christ. Therefore, my beloved brethren, be ye steadfast, unmovable, always abounding in the work of the Lord, forasmuch as ye know that your labor is not in vain in the Lord. (I Cor. 15:57–58)

After the defeat suffered by Israel because of Achan, most forget that the rest of the book is still there. Joshua 7 is not the end of the book. Joshua 8 shows us that we can get up and have victory again. Joshua did defeat Ai. He did not stop his forward progress. Yes, there was a time of trouble, but he dealt with it and saw victory again. This positive approach is needed when troubling times come our way. Notice how Joshua saw victory.

Joshua boldly attacked the enemy and after the victory was able to take the spoils of war. (Josh. 8:1–2) This is one of the sad parts about Achan's sin. He could have kept the spoils of Ai without hiding them in his tent! What good is silver that you cannot spend? What good is a Babylonian garment that you cannot wear? He could have had the spoils of Ai if he would have waited on God. God will let you have the spoils of war when you follow His plan.

Joshua never quit in his fight to conquer the land. Don't draw back. We find Joshua's tenacity recorded for us in Joshua 8:18, 22, 24, 26.

And he brought his household man by man; and Achan, the son of Carmi, the son of Zabdi, the son of Zerah, of the tribe of Judah, was taken.

So Joshua sent messengers, and they ran unto the tent; and, behold, it was hid in his tent, and the silver under it.

And Joshua, and all Israel with him, took Achan the son of Zerah, and the silver, and the garment, and the wedge of gold, and his sons, and his daughters, and his oxen, and his asses, and his sheep, and his tent, and all that he had: and they brought them unto the valley of Achor.

And they raised over him a great heap of stones unto this day. So the LORD turned from the fierceness of his anger.

Wherefore the name of that place was called, The valley of Achor, unto this day.

Keep at it until the enemy is hurt. I love the story of this battle. There is strategy, there is thought, and there is a plan. Joshua rallied the troops and told them to conquer.

> There was once a young man who wanted more than anything to take a cruise aboard a luxury liner. He did not have much money, but eventually the young man saved enough to purchase a ticket.
>
> As he packed, the young man knew he would be traveling with no money for food, so he carefully packed some bread and cheese for his meals. Although he truly enjoyed the cruise, as he walked around and watched people eating in the dining and banquet halls of the ship, his joy diminished.
>
> After two weeks, his bread and cheese molding, the young man was starving. As he walked around, people noticed how painfully thin he had become. A gentleman approached and asked the young man if there was anything wrong. Slightly embarrassed, the young man explained that he did not have enough money for food. The gentleman took the young man by the shoulders and explained to him that the food was all paid for in the price of the ticket. The young man was astonished—all the time he could have been enjoying the wonderful banquets, but he sat starving instead![143]

---

[143] https://books.google.com/books?id=rUTxZoHx5WEC&pg=PA8&lpg=PA8&dq. Accessed on September 7, 2018.

Many Christians do not realize that they are more than conquerors through Him that loved us. Christ when He saved us provided all for the voyage—presence, power, provision—we must avail ourselves of these wonderful gifts to win the victory over sin.

Help Them Get Back Up

"For a just man falleth seven times, and riseth up again" *(Prov. 24:16a).*

Once a teen has repented, help them get back up. Parents and youth workers are not a reflection of God's mercy and grace when they keep a teen down. Undue punishment that never ends, never letting go of a previous offense, or "the mark of Cain" can hinder the progress of a teen. There is no teen exempt from problems. Help them live a victorious life!

Picture a basketball with too little air in it. You drop it on the gymnasium floor and instead of bouncing, it lands with a plop. The NBA players won't want this ball. The college hoopsters won't use this ball. Even the kids on the elementary playground will leave this ball behind and choose another. Everyone wants a ball that bounces.

Your kids will have many good days, but if they are normal at all, they will have their share of bad ones as well. What do we want your kids to do after they have a bad day? Have another one? No. We want them to bounce back to respectful behavior as quickly as possible, rather than get stuck in their disrespectful behavior, like a basketball that has no air. Bouncing back is an important life skill, and you can help your kids learn to do it.

So, when you are talking with your kids at the end of a rough day, use words that will help them get moving in a positive direction. Help them see that their negative choices are now over, and the goal is to learn a good lesson from their bad choices and get back to their good choices.[144]

---

[144] Todd Cartmell, 8 Simple Tools for Raising Great Kids (Chicago, Illinois: Moody Publishers, 2016), 153–154.

Chapter 21

U - Understanding the Will of God

Principles for Determining Right and Wrong

As a parent, youth pastor, and pastor, I am glad that I can assure both parents and youth alike that God's will is not mysterious and surely can be found. One can know it, and one can have peace. Peace in this life seems to be lacking; yet in the center of God's will, peace and contentment are found.

I was reading a sermon about God's will by Charles Spurgeon, and it was amazing to see that what he preached about God's will 150 years ago has not changed and still applies today. He told of one man that came to him about some differences in Bible doctrine. The man told Spurgeon that he had read the Bible thirty-four times on his knees and could not find anything that he and Spurgeon agreed on regarding that doctrine in question. Spurgeon said with tongue in cheek that one of the reasons that this man could not find the doctrine in question was probably that he read the Bible on his knees. Spurgeon said that he did not know if he could find anything reading on his knees because of the awkward pain that would be in his back and legs.[145]

We may mock this man, but we do the same thing at times. We miss the obvious because we are so out of sorts with those trying to lead and guide us.

---

[145] https://www.spurgeon.org/resource-library/sermons/gods-will-and-mans-will#flipbook/. Accessed on August 30, 2018.

The idea of finding God's will and direction has been controversial for some in the past. I am hoping to give you some principles to guide you in right and wrong principles found in God's Word.

The Scriptural Test

"Sanctify them through thy truth: thy word is truth" *(John 17:17).*

There are certain things that are just plain black and white. Some folks get upset at our stands against certain sins in this land, but they are clearly defined in Scripture. Let's take two examples.

1. Abortion

Does the Bible have verses that give direction to our thinking on the murder of innocent children?

Thou shalt not kill. (Exod. 20:13)

If men strive, and hurt a woman with child, so that her fruit depart from her, and yet no mischief follow: he shall be surely punished, according as the woman's husband will lay upon him; and he shall pay as the judges determine. And if any mischief follow, then thou shalt give life for life, Eye for eye, tooth for tooth, hand for hand, foot for foot, Burning for burning, wound for wound, stripe for stripe. (Exod. 21:22–25)

For thou hast possessed my reins: thou hast covered me in my mother's womb. I will praise thee; for I am fearfully and wonderfully made: marvellous are thy works; and that my soul knoweth right well. My substance was not hid from thee, when I was made in secret, and curiously wrought in the lowest parts of the earth. (Ps. 139:13–15)

These six things doth the LORD hate: yea, seven are an abomination unto him: A proud look, a lying tongue, and hands that shed innocent blood, An heart that deviseth wicked imaginations, feet that be swift in running to mischief, A false witness that speaketh lies, and he that soweth discord among brethren. (Prov. 6:16–19)

Listen, O isles, unto me; and hearken, ye people, from far; The LORD hath called me from the womb; from the bowels of my mother hath he made mention of my name. (Isa. 49:1)

The Scriptures are clear that God believes that a child is considered life in the womb. Even science can verify these facts today, but man in his limited knowledge wants to reject God's way and establish man's way as the rule of law. This should not deter a Christian from standing true to the Word of God. It is clear that I can tell any young lady or woman that is seeking advice that the Bible says it is not God's will for them to have an abortion—ever.

2. Sodomy

I have known of individuals that have become upset at our church because I or one of the other teachers or pastors have indicated a hatred of sodomy because of God's hatred of it.

If a man also lie with mankind, as he lieth with a woman, both of them have committed an abomination: they shall surely be put to death; their blood shall be upon them. (Lev. 20:13)

Thou shalt not lie with mankind, as with womankind: it is abomination. (Lev. 18:22). And there were also sodomites in the land: and they did according to all the abominations of the nations which the LORD cast out before the children of Israel. (I Kings 14:24)

Know ye not that the unrighteous shall not inherit the kingdom of God? Be not deceived: neither fornicators, nor idolaters, nor adulterers, nor effeminate, nor abusers of themselves with mankind. (I Cor. 6:9)

Look how easy it is to find out what you should believe when it comes to this issue. You can sometimes determine right and wrong that fast. The Bible is not a smorgasbord book of instruction. At a smorgasbord, you can come up to the serving area to pick and choose what you want, then go back and still be fed and refreshed. The Bible as an instruction book is *"Thus saith the Lord,"* it is black and white, it is clear and instructive, it is dogmatic, it is opinionated, it is direct, and it is revealing. Is that descriptive enough for you? The Bible is a guidebook where we can come to get invaluable instruction.

Therefore, like these two examples, there are many other commands in Scripture that leave no doubt to what the will of the Lord is. Go to the Bible first! Consider the instruction from Psalm 1. It is evident that going to Scripture is of utmost importance if a person wants to prosper.

Blessed is the man that walketh not in the counsel of the ungodly, nor standeth in the way of sinners, nor sitteth in the seat of the scornful. But his delight is in the law of the LORD; and in his law doth he meditate day and night. And he shall be like a tree planted by the rivers of water, that bringeth forth his fruit in his season; his leaf also shall not wither; and whatsoever he doeth shall prosper. (Ps. 1:1–3)

THE UNCHANGING WORD
Attributed to Martin Luther

Feelings come and feelings go,
And feelings are deceiving;

My warrant is the Word of God—
Naught else is worth believing.

I'll trust in God's unchanging Word
Till soul and body sever,
For, though all things shall pass away,
HIS WORD SHALL STAND FOREVER!

The Prayer Test

Prayer is vital in a believer's life. Without the habit of prayer, we have one-way communication. Prayer allows us to talk with God.

Then said David, O LORD God of Israel, thy servant hath certainly heard that Saul seeketh to come to Keilah, to destroy the city for my sake. Will the men of Keilah deliver me up into his hand? will Saul come down, as thy servant hath heard? O LORD God of Israel, I beseech thee, tell thy servant. And the LORD said, He will come down. Then said David, Will the men of Keilah deliver me and my men into the hand of Saul? And the LORD said, They will deliver thee up (I Samuel 23:10–12)

And David enquired at the LORD, saying, Shall I pursue after this troop? shall I overtake them? And he answered him, Pursue: for thou shalt surely overtake them, and without fail recover all. (I Sam. 30:8)

And it came to pass after this, that David enquired of the LORD, saying, Shall I go up into any of the cities of Judah? And the LORD said unto him, Go up. And David said, Whither shall I go up? And he said, Unto Hebron. (II Sam. 2:1)

And David enquired of the LORD, saying, Shall I go up to the Philistines? wilt thou deliver them into mine hand? And the LORD said unto David, Go up: for I will doubtless deliver the Philistines into thine hand. (II Sam. 5:19)

And he went a little further, and fell on his face, and prayed, saying, O my Father, if it be possible, let this cup pass from me: nevertheless not as I will, but as thou wilt" (Matthew 26:39).

For we have not an high priest which cannot be touched with the feeling of our infirmities; but was in all points tempted like as we are, yet without sin. Let us therefore come boldly unto the throne of grace, that we may obtain mercy, and find grace to help in time of need. (Heb. 4:15–16)

I have met some folks who say that they pray a lot, but there is no evidence of it in their lives. What do I mean by that? They have no spiritual fruit, wandering aimlessly within the church with no vision or passion for any ministry, and they seem oblivious to the needs of others in the church. These things are evident of a false faith or an empty prayer life. When we go to prayer in God's will, He will give you your marching orders.

There is a silly story about a brother and sister that demonstrate how works need to follow faith or prayer. A little girl and her brother were having a disagreement. She was worried because her brother had built some traps to catch rabbits. She loved rabbits and did not want any of them to be hurt. She tearfully begged her brother not to use the traps, but he refused to change his plans.

The little girl finally chose another course of action—she was going to pray about it, and God would definitely stop it. Later, she explained, "I prayed that God would not let those cute little rabbits get caught in those traps, and then I went outside and broke the traps into a million pieces."

Yes, it's a silly illustration, but the truth is that God will lead us to action when we go to prayer!

The Growth Test

"All things are lawful unto me, but all things are not expedient: all things are lawful for me, but I will not be brought under the power of any" (I Cor. 6:12).

This test is a hard one for most Christians, especially in America. We don't want to look at our lives and root out things that hinder our spiritual growth. However, it is very important that we understand that God desires for us to mature as Christians. Yes, everything may be lawful for me to do, but will I be bettered or improved by this action in my life? We need to be careful about allowing our liberty to limit our spiritual growth in the Lord.

There is a liberty wherewith Christ that made us free, in which we must stand fast. But surely he would never carry this liberty so far as to put himself into the power of any bodily appetite. Though all meats were supposed lawful, he would not become a glutton nor a drunkard. And much less would he abuse the maxim of lawful liberty to countenance other sins of fornication, which, though it might be allowed by the Corinthians' laws, was a trespass upon the law of nature, and utterly unbecoming a Christian. He would not abuse this maxim about eating and drinking to encourage any intemperance, nor indulge a carnal appetite.[146]

We need to be careful that we are not allowing something into our life that will ultimately cause us bondage and will enable the flesh to be

---

[146] Henry, 430.

empowered against the new spirit which lives within us. If it empowers my flesh, if it causes me to stumble, if it dampens my witness—then—it is not the will for God for me.

The Submission Test

And he went a little further, and fell on his face, and prayed, saying, O my Father, if it be possible, let this cup pass from me: nevertheless not as I will, but as thou wilt. (Matt. 26:39)

For I through the law am dead to the law, that I might live unto God. I am crucified with Christ: nevertheless I live; yet not I, but Christ liveth in me: and the life which I now live in the flesh I live by the faith of the Son of God, who loved me, and gave himself for me. (Gal. 2:19–20)

The progression is coming along with our understanding of gaining insight into God's will. We started with the Word of God, prayed about His will, and we then made sure that we would grow through the activity in which we are involved. Now, we come to another level of the Christian life that seems to be difficult—submission. Submission is plainly seen in the life of Christ. Christ is a perfect example of submission. He laid aside His heavenly status and took on the lowly form of man. He humbled Himself, even to death.

We see in the passage from Galatians that Paul claims to be crucified with Christ. This claims a present tense of submission. Submission is found when we understand that our lives are no longer our own. In Christ, we have life rather than in our own self-indulgent ways. Paul found that Christ living in him was the submitted, surrendered life which, in turn, produces victory. For those of us who have young people in our homes or those who are working with young people in churches, we should make them aware of this wonderful truth: submission to Christ brings true freedom.

John Murray has said, "What or whom we worship determines our behavior." When we have a proper understanding of the greatness of God, we will bow before His majesty and glory. This in turn helps us to submit to God's will. He is greater than us, and His sovereignty demands our submission to His desires. Obedience to the commands of God reveals both our submission and our love for the Lord.[147]

<u>The Testimony Test</u>

All things are lawful for me, but all things are not expedient: all things are lawful for me, but all things edify not. (I Cor. 10:23)

But take heed lest by any means this liberty of yours become a stumblingblock to them that are weak. (I Cor. 8:9)

But when ye sin so against the brethren, and wound their weak conscience, ye sin against Christ. (I Cor. 8:12)

These passages discuss a problem that has been around for hundreds of years. It has been debated and argued in halls of universities, in conference rooms of churches, and in living rooms of homes. The debate is that of Christian liberty and Christian stumbling blocks. When considering the passages listed above, the problem is really not that the Christian is doing something wrong. The problem is the perception of those who are not spiritually mature. This makes some situations difficult to discern and understand. A young person is going to argue that we should not live for the applause or approval of men. This is true, but why are we on this earth? To bring glory to God. How is this done?—by bringing folks into a greater relationship with Jesus Christ.

---

[147] Jerry Bridges, The Practice of Godliness (Colorado Springs, CO: NavPress, 1986), 29.

The Evangelism Test

Give none offence, neither to the Jews, nor to the Gentiles, nor to the church of God: Even as I please all men in all things, not seeking mine own profit, but the profit of many, that they may be saved. (I Cor. 10:32–33)

Walk in wisdom toward them that are without, redeeming the time. Let your speech be alway with grace, seasoned with salt, that ye may know how ye ought to answer every man. (Col. 4:5–6)

One of the ways to determine whether an action is right or wrong is to ask if the action will keep people from coming to the Savior by what I am doing. A believer's life is to draw people to Christ. In the book of Matthew, the Bible tells us about the believer being a light to this world. We need to help our young people to understand that accepting Christ as their Savior changes their perspective. One of the changes is that a believer is a beacon to draw people to the Savior. Consider a couple of simple properties of light.

1. Light Dispels Darkness

To give light to them that sit in darkness and in the shadow of death, to guide our feet into the way of peace. (Luke 1:79)

In whom the god of this world hath blinded the minds of them which believe not, lest the light of the glorious gospel of Christ, who is the image of God, should shine unto them. (II Cor. 4:4)

We have also a more sure word of prophecy; whereunto ye do well that ye take heed, as unto a light that shineth in a dark place, until the day dawn, and the day star arise in your hearts. (II Pet. 1:19)

The Word of God uses the picture of light to show that there is a distinction between light and darkness. Most of us do not find this confusing, but when it comes to the Christian walk, we sometimes find this to be not as distinct. When we walk into a room and there is no light, it is obvious. This should become clear to a believer as well. As we walk in the light of the glorious Gospel, the darkness of this world's system should start to slip away. By revealing the light to our young people, we are helping them to learn to find God's will. Choosing light over darkness is always the best decision for a Christian.

2. <u>Light Does Not Mix with Darkness</u>

Be ye not unequally yoked together with unbelievers: for what fellowship hath righteousness with unrighteousness? and what communion hath light with darkness?" (II Cor. 6:14)

For ye were sometimes darkness, but now are ye light in the Lord: walk as children of light. (Eph. 5:8)

This then is the message which we have heard of him, and declare unto you, that God is light, and in him is no darkness at all. (I John 1:5)

But if we walk in the light, as he is in the light, we have fellowship one with another, and the blood of Jesus Christ his Son cleanseth us from all sin. (I John 1:7)

This second aspect of light reveals to the believer the distinction that should be evident in our actions. Light not only dispels darkness, but it is contrary to darkness. It is a contrast. This helps a young person to understand that his life is supposed to be different. Most would not confuse a dark room with a bright room. In the same way, a Christian who cannot be identified as separate from this evil, wicked world is not allowing the light of the Savior to shine through his life. When looking at decisions about which activities to participate in, what clothing to wear, or what friends to have, the light/darkness test can help greatly.

The Authority Test

Remember them which have the rule over you, who have spoken unto you the word of God: whose faith follow, considering the end of their conversation. (Heb. 13:7)

Obey them that have the rule over you, and submit yourselves: for they watch for your souls, as they that must give account, that they may do it with joy, and not with grief: for that is unprofitable for you. (Heb. 13:17)

Some people do not like getting advice from their biblical authority. They say that they can get advice from anyone and then do whatever they want. The problem is that if you are having problems with drug addiction, and you ask your drug dealer if you should stay on drugs, what do you think his advice will be? We must make sure that we are going to the biblical authority in our lives to get advice. Many young people seek advice from their peers who possess the same lack of maturity and inexperience. In essence, we like to find a "yes man" to put a stamp of approval on our wants and dreams. This is not the biblical concept of authority or counsel. We should be finding biblical leadership that cares for our soul and the outcome of our life even if the decision is hard in the short run.[148]

Pastors watch for the souls of the people, not to ensnare them, but to save them; to gain them, not to themselves, but to Christ; to build them

---

[148] Matthew Henry. Matthew Henry's Commentary on the Whole Bible: Volume 6 (Peabody, MA: Hendrickson Publishers, 1991), 777.

up in knowledge, faith, and holiness. They are to watch against everything that may be hurtful to the souls of men, and to give them warning of dangerous errors, of the devices of Satan, and of approaching judgments. They are to watch for all opportunities of helping the souls of men go forward in the way to heaven. The pastor will be watchful of youth going against God's will. Teens should be willing to listen.

The will of God is not always easy, but it is always good and righteous. A young person that applies these seven tests will find that the will of God does not have to be overly complicated. There must be prayer and even times of fasting, but God's will is not mysterious. We serve a wonderful God who is gracious and merciful. His ways are perfect.

> "To know the will of God is the greatest knowledge. To do the will of God is the greatest achievement."[149]

> "To go as I am led, to go when I am led, to go where I am led . . . it is that which has been for twenty years the one prayer of my life."[150]

Someone once said that the easiest thing to decide is what you would do if you were in someone else's shoes.

---

[149] http://www.quoteland.com/author/George-W-Truett-Quotes/8364/. Accessed on September 21, 2018.

[150] Robert J. Morgan, Preacher's Sourcebook of Creative Sermon Illustrations (Nashville, TN: Thomas Nelson Publishers, 2007), 368.

Chapter 22

V - Victory: Helps for Victorious Living

By 1942, the Japanese military had enjoyed almost a half century of military victory after victory. Unstoppable since the Russo-Japanese War of 1895, they later successfully invaded Korea and Manchuria in 1931 and defeated their armies. Then in 1934, they attacked China and continued to defeat them at every turn. In 1941, they invaded Hong Kong, the Philippines, Guam, and numerous islands of the South Pacific. Like an unstoppable army, they handed defeat to the armies of China, Holland, France, England, and the United States. In October of 1942, their imperial presence was being challenged by those angry Americans. The Americans had landed on Guadalcanal and secured Henderson airfield. It was imperative that the Americans were driven off of this airfield and the Japanese regain control. The key to taking Henderson was capturing a small hill that overlooked the field which would allow Japanese forces command of the area below.

On the night of October 25, 1942, the hill was held by ninety-one determined Marines. They suddenly were attacked by over 5,000 Japanese troops. Among the ninety-one was Sgt. Mitchell Paige. Wave after wave of screaming Japanese soldiers smashed into the American lines. Sgt. Paige ran from foxhole to foxhole, dragging dead and wounded Marines and realigning machine guns. As the Marines manning the guns died one by one, Sgt. Paige would fire a few rounds from one gun, then run to another and fire from a different gun to fool the enemy. Hours into the battle, the Marine force had been practically wiped out. With nothing to lose, Sgt. Paige picked up a water-cooled Browning .30 cal. machine gun and started firing from the hip, charging the last of his Japanese attackers.

The next morning when Marines reached the hill, they found every Marine dead or wounded and Sgt. Paige, alone, sitting behind his Browning machine gun, ready for the next attack. Around the hill lay over 2,200 Japanese soldiers. A half century of Japanese military victories had just ended, courtesy of one determined fighter![151]

We are going to consider a passage in Joshua 10 to help us gain some insight for getting spiritual victory. There is a responsibility as parents, pastors, and youth pastors to help our young people to get up after their failures. Some present the Christian walk as a Christian "Disneyland" where there are no problems or woes. This is a false picture and is dangerous for young people. They need to know that the Christian life is a struggle, but there can be victory. The Christian young person does not have to live in defeat or fear of the enemy that he will be facing. Instead, as those who lead young people, we should give them the tools to be able to win victory when the enemy comes for the fight.

I would recommend reading Joshua, chapters 8–10, which will help in setting the backdrop for the reader. Our applications will be taken from Joshua chapter 10. It is a great story of victory. Joshua was not a perfect man or leader, yet he was able to help the children of Israel gain victory. Through the first ten chapters in Joshua, the reader can see a few missteps from Joshua. Joshua was very confident after the battle of Jericho and led his people charging into Ai where thirty-six men were killed. This devastated Joshua, and he was found lying prostrate, crying out to the Lord. The weight of those men's deaths was heavy upon him. Joshua then made a league with the people of Gibeon. Again, a very unwise move on his part, but God in his mercy helped Joshua to pick up and move on.

We come to our narrative in Joshua chapter 10. A group of five kings led by King Adonizedek, king of Jerusalem, join forces and surround Gibeon. As we start these thoughts, one amazing lesson right away jumps

---

[151] Samuel C. Gipp, Fight On!: A Collection of Stories about Those Who Have Persevered Through Hardship and Danger (Miamitown, Ohio: DayStar Publishing, 2004), 55–56.

to the forefront. In dealing with young people, they often are trying to manipulate their friendships to get popularity, prestige, or some type of advantage. The comparable point with the Gibeonites is that they wanted to join the Israelites, not because of the God they served, but because of the might which Israel had. They just did not want to be defeated. Their own crowd quickly turned on them, though. This is the fickleness of the world. One day, they are your ally and the next an enemy.[152]

Another interesting point is the name of the king of Jerusalem. His name Adonizedek means, "Lord of Righteousness."[153] Names are important, but someone can have a name and their character be something completely different. In fact, the Bible tells us that Satan himself can be transformed into an angel of light. This does not mean that Satan is good; he just can appear to be good. Help your young people to see through the charlatans that come with a name of righteousness but who desire to harm their spiritual walk with the Lord. Let's consider some helps for spiritual victory from this event.

Don't Be Afraid of the Fight

"So Joshua ascended from Gilgal, he, and all the people of war with him, and all the mighty men of valor" (Josh. 10:7).

This is the first lesson that we must present to young people. There is a natural fear of facing an enemy. This is not uncommon, but the Lord can give victory if we are relying on him. We also understand that Joshua was shown as being an honorable man. This is very important when facing an enemy. Be honorable. This is a character trait of a godly man. It is never right to cheat, lie, or commit any type of sin knowingly. If you lead young people, be honorable. Joshua could have said that he was tricked or lied to and that he should not have to honor his word. This, however, is not the

---

[152] John G. Butler, Joshua: The Conqueror of Canaan (Clinton, Iowa: LBC Publications, 1996), 224–226.

[153] Ibid., 226.

biblical approach to the problem. There are a number of verses that can bring confidence to a young person when considering the Christian battle.

> *Fear thou not; for I am with thee: be not dismayed; for I am thy God: I will strengthen thee; yea, I will help thee; yea, I will uphold thee with the right hand of my righteousness. Behold, all they that were incensed against thee shall be ashamed and confounded: they shall be as nothing; and they that strive with thee shall perish. Thou shalt seek them, and shalt not find them, even them that contended with thee: they that war against thee shall be as nothing, and as a thing of nought. For I the LORD thy God will hold thy right hand, saying unto thee, Fear not; I will help thee. (Isa. 41:10–13)*

> *Nay, in all these things we are more than conquerors through him that loved us. (Rom. 8:37)*

> *But thanks be to God, which giveth us the victory through our Lord Jesus Christ. (I Cor. 15:57)*

> *For whatsoever is born of God overcometh the world: and this is the victory that overcometh the world, even our faith. (I John 5:4)*

A young person does not have to fear because of the battles that they will have to face in the future. They need to understand that the Lord Almighty is available to assist. The name Lord Almighty was first used to Abraham back in Genesis 17 when God promised Abraham that He would make of him a great nation. This promise to Abraham would only be possible if a God who could fight and have victory would intercede. This promise of God Almighty fighting for the believer is still for us today. Our young people have a triumphant God who can help them defeat the enemy. Christian young people do not have to be afraid of the unknown or worry about the future with El-Shaddai on their side.[154]

Find God for Help in the Fight

"And the LORD said unto Joshua, Fear them not: for I have delivered them into thine hand; there shall not a man of them stand before thee" (Josh. 10:8).

Notice that Joshua goes directly to the Lord to get strength, wisdom, and courage. This is the best place to start. Many times, when the enemy comes to attack, it is sudden and not expected. For this reason, we feel that we do not have time to pause and pray and prepare spiritually like we should. This is an instinct that needs to be overcome. There is never a wrong time to go to the Lord. We should always be seeking His face. We will find courage and gain the insight that we find Joshua has in this fight. Joshua's habit of coming before the Lord was established under Moses.

And the LORD said unto Moses, Behold, thy days approach that thou must die: call Joshua, and present yourselves in the tabernacle of the congregation, that I may give him a charge. And Moses and Joshua went and presented themselves in the tabernacle of the congregation. (Deut. 31:14)

This is an interesting text because the word *present* is used which reminds us of a passage in the New Testament in Romans 12:1 where the believer is to present his body a living sacrifice. The word present in both passages gives us two ideas. One idea is that of an offering, but there is also a military context. In the military context, present was a total allegiance to a commander no matter what the cost.[155]

---

[154] Nathan Stone, Names of God (Chicago, Illinois: Moody Press, 1944), 31–34.

[155] W. Phillip Keller, Joshua: Mighty Warrior and Man of Faith (Grand Rapids, Michigan: Kregel Publications, 1983)

This attitude is what made Joshua such a great leader and commander, but it also made victory possible. Joshua did not present excuses; he instead came to God and asked for strength and wisdom. Those who have influence in a young person's life should help them come to Christ the Mighty Commander and help them swear their allegiance to this Captain of their souls. He will help them fight the good fight of faith.

Keep at the Fight

"Joshua therefore came unto them suddenly, and went up from Gilgal all night" (Josh. 10:9).

There are two thoughts in our text that help us in this understanding—*suddenly* and *all night*. There are times that it is not good to rush in and be overly zealous when you have not prepared for the task. However, that is not the case when it comes to this scenario. Joshua had been at this task for years and was now preparing himself and preparing the people of Israel. The soldiers were trained and prepared, and the Lord had given them the instruction to take the land of Canaan. There was no reason to wait around; get at the fight.

Suddenly is not a complicated word to understand. In the Hebrew it means "instantly or straightaway." [156] Joshua did not waste time in getting at the fight. There are some folks who spend all their time preparing, and they never seem to ever get around to the task at hand.

Bobby Jones arrived at that same conclusion. He did what no other golfer has ever done: win the Grand Slam of golf, which included winning the United States Open, the United States Amateur, the British Open, and the British Amateur. Here's what he said: "It is a fact that I never did any real amount of winning until I learned to adjust my ambitions to more reasonable prospects shot by shot, and to strive for a rate of performance

---

[156] James Strong, Strong's Exhaustive Concordance of the Bible (Nashville, Tennessee: Abingdon, 1977), 97.

that was consistently good and reliable, rather than placing my hopes upon the accomplishments of a series of brilliant sallies."

Bobby Jones did not reach that understanding easily. He had to fight hard against the temptation to push himself beyond his ability. During the early days of his golf career, he was always striving to hit the perfect shot, and when he didn't, he would break clubs and start yelling and sometimes even leave the course. He had such a temper that many golfers wouldn't play with him. Only gradually did he learn that once you hit a bad shot, that shot is over. You must strive to make the next shot as good as possible.[157]

I am not purporting that we do things haphazardly, but many times it is common for people not to get at what they are supposed to be doing. Don't waste time when it comes to getting to the task at hand. Fear can immobilize us, perfectionism can stymie us, and procrastination can deter us.

We also see that Joshua had to travel all night to take his troops up to Gilgal. This was no small feat that he was attempting. It is estimated that this was around a twenty-mile trip uphill from Gilgal to Gibeon. It does not seem like it was a paved, scenic, pre-cut path. Joshua then chose to do this at night.[158] Sometimes, getting to the battle will take some effort and will wear you out. However, this is your calling as a Christian. We are to fight the good fight, endure hardness, and strive for the mastery. All those descriptions listed in the last sentence come from the apostle Paul who knew what it was to be a good soldier.

Don't Be Afraid to Ask for Miracles in the Fight

Then spake Joshua to the LORD in the day when the LORD delivered up the Amorites before the children of Israel, and he said in the sight of Israel, Sun, stand thou still upon

---

[157] B. Eugene Griessman, Time Tactics of Very Successful People (New York, New York: McGraw-Hill, Inc., 1994)

[158] John G. Butler, Joshua: The Conqueror of Canaan (Clinton, Iowa: LBC Publications, 1996), 232.

Gibeon; and thou, Moon, in the valley of Ajalon. And the sun stood still, and the moon stayed, until the people had avenged themselves upon their enemies. Is not this written in the book of Jasher? So the sun stood still in the midst of heaven, and hasted not to go down about a whole day. And there was no day like that before it or after it, that the LORD hearkened unto the voice of a man: for the LORD fought for Israel. (Josh. 10:12–14)

There is an Icelandic fishing captain, Sigurdur Petursson, who is known as the "iceman" because he has no fear of anything. One day in 2003, on a beach in Kuummiut, in eastern Greenland, he was watching his fishing crew as they stood in the shallow water, processing a catch. Suddenly Petursson saw a shark fin in the water. The predator was attracted to the blood from the catch. The deadly killer turned and headed for Petursson's crew. The "iceman" was not about to allow the cold-blooded killer to attack his men. The fearless captain dashed into the shallow water and grabbed the 660-pound shark by its tail. He then wrestled the thrashing beast up onto the beach, pulled his knife, and killed it. His men were safe.[159]

That may sound like a crazy story, but nothing in comparison to what happened in this fight in Joshua's life. What happened is amazing—the sun stood still! Don't be afraid to ask for a miracle from God. He is still in the miracle-working business. Ask boldly of your heavenly Father. Our young people need to see a God who can and will do miracles. There are some folks today who scoff at miracles, and they fritter away with science or technology all the reasoning behind a miracle that might happen in a family, in a salvation decision, or in a medical situation. Don't discount the miracles of God. We live in a skeptical and cynical world. Many say that there is no way that God could care about some of the unimportant matters in a young person's life. However, this is not what Scriptures tell us. Consider the following verses:

---

[159] https://seanpiotrowski.net/2003/10/24/250/. Accessed on September 13, 2018.

Cast thy burden upon the LORD, and he shall sustain thee: he shall never suffer the righteous to be moved. (Ps. 55:22)

Come unto me, all ye that labor and are heavy laden, and I will give you rest. (Matt. 11:28)

These things I have spoken unto you, that in me ye might have peace. In the world ye shall have tribulation: but be of good cheer; I have overcome the world. (John 16:33)

And the peace of God, which passeth all understanding, shall keep your hearts and minds through Christ Jesus. (Phil. 4:7)

Casting all your care upon him; for he careth for you. (I Pet. 5:7)

God is concerned with the young people that we are working with and wants them to come to Him in times of trouble. We can come boldly to the throne of grace. This will allow us to see victory in life. There is so much that is lost in this world because of folks not coming to a miracle-working God. He *"is able to do exceeding abundantly above all that we ask or think" (Eph. 3:20).*

Ask for Wisdom in the Fight

"But these five kings fled, and hid themselves in a cave at Makkedah. And it was told Joshua, saying, The five kings are found hid in a cave at Makkedah. And Joshua said, Roll great stones upon the mouth of the cave, and set men by it for to keep them" (Josh. 10:16–18).

This is an interesting spot in the story. Joshua desired to destroy these kings, but there was a greater priority—the defeat of the whole army.

Sometimes, in the midst of the battle, bad decisions can be made. From personal testimony, I have seen folks lose important spiritual ground in a bad decision made during the battle. It is imperative that we help our young people to know that wisdom should not be left behind in the "base camp." We need to help our young folks to always seek godly wisdom. There should be a constant abiding in Christ. This can help young people gain the spiritual ground that God has for them in their "Canaan land."

Finish the Fight Completely

And all the people returned to the camp to Joshua at Makkedah in peace: none moved his tongue against any of the children of Israel. Then said Joshua, Open the mouth of the cave, and bring out those five kings unto me out of the cave. And they did so, and brought forth those five kings unto him out of the cave, the king of Jerusalem, the king of Hebron, the king of Jarmuth, the king of Lachish, and the king of Eglon. And it came to pass, when they brought out those kings unto Joshua, that Joshua called for all the men of Israel, and said unto the captains of the men of war which went with him, Come near, put your feet upon the necks of these kings. And they came near, and put their feet upon the necks of them. And Joshua said unto them, Fear not, nor be dismayed, be strong and of good courage: for thus shall the LORD do to all your enemies against whom ye fight. And afterward Joshua smote them, and slew them, and hanged them on five trees: and they were hanging upon the trees until the evening. (Josh. 10:23–26)

This last section of Joshua 10 has been preached on for many generations. Listen to a couple of quotes from Christian voices of the past from this passage:

Never conceive that any one of the evils of your nature is so dead that it cannot have a resurrection. Strive against every form of sin, every thought of sin, every carnal tendency, every evil passion, but when you have striven most, never count your victory to be complete, until your feet are within the pearly gate.[160]

In Joshua's requiring the kings to be brought before him, the Christian is taught that he must (in prayer) bring all his foes—be they inward lustings or outward temptations—to the Savior, for it is not by his own strength he can vanquish them. Next, "Joshua called for all the men of Israel, and said unto the captains of the men of war which went with him, Come near, put your feet upon the necks of these kings." And we are told, They came near and put their feet upon the necks of them (verse 24). Very striking is this, and most important the spiritual instruction contained therein. Being dealt with in this manner betokened that these kings were in complete subjugation unto the people of God. And that is the attitude which faith is to take unto all its enemies, regarding them as foes already defeated—not by himself, but by his victorious head.[161]

It is imperative that we finish the job completely. The fight needs began, but we must not let the devil get any advantage later in the struggle. There is a book entitled *Finishing Well* that was written many years ago in the secular world. The purpose of the book is to encourage those that get past their halftime in life to get focused again and accomplish something with the latter years of their lives. As Christians, this should be even more true; we should be a people who not only start a good work but complete the task all the way to the finish line. Challenge your young person not only to get in the battle, but to stay at the battle until God calls them home.

---

[160] C. H. Spurgeon, Exploring the Mind & Heart of the Prince of Preachers (Oswego, Illinois: Fox River Press, 2005)

[161] Arthur W. Pink, Gleaning in Joshua (Chicago, Illinois: Moody Press, 1964), 292–293.

Our seventh president of the United States was Andrew Jackson. He died famous for his poor spelling of many phrases. One such was the phrase "Oll Korrect" which eventually was shortened to "OK." Richard Lawrence hated President Jackson, and thus, he planned a way to assassinate him. One day in 1835, armed with two single-shot shotguns, he concealed himself among some well-wishers. As the president walked by, Richard Lawrence raised his shotgun and pulled the trigger. The gun misfired. He dropped that one and took his other gun, and that one misfired too. Rather than run or yell and scream, President Jackson was enraged and attacked Lawrence with his cane and beat him down until he was arrested.[162] What an interesting story! It shows the stamina of this president. He decided that he was not going to be hindered by someone, and instead, got at the battle.

May the Lord help us to encourage our young people to be in the battle for the Lord and to be victorious for His cause.

---

[162] https://www.history.com/this-day-in-history/andrew-jackson-narrowly-escapes-assassination. Accessed on September 13, 2018.

Chapter 23

W - The Power of Words

"Death and life are in the power of the tongue: and they that love it shall eat the fruit thereof" (Prov. 18:21).

S peech can be misunderstood. Here are a few examples when translation became humorous. These are signs (translated into English) seen in other countries:

1. In a Denmark airline office: "We take your bags and send them in all directions."

2. On the door of a Moscow hotel room: "If this is your first visit to Russia, you are welcome to it."

3. On a Bucharest hotel elevator: "The lift is being fixed for the next day. During that time we regret that you will be unbearable."

4. On a restaurant menu in Poland: "Salad a firm's own make; Limpid red beet soup with cheesy dumplings in the form of a finger; Roasted duck let loose; Beef rashers beaten up in the country people's fashion."[163]

---

[163] https://forum.unilang.org/viewtopic.php?t=35017. Accessed on July 31, 2018.

As you can see, someone should have been a little more careful or should have consulted someone else who understood not just grammar but the vocabulary and nuances of the English language.

So it is in our lives. We should take a little more care in the choice of words that we use both with fellow believers and the world around us. We must understand that words do matter in our relationships with fellow believers and with the community in which we are going to share Christ. A great deal of good or harm can result from how we use our tongues. The Word of God tells us that *"death and life are in the power of the tongue" (Prov. 18:21)*. While a skilled orator can influence vast numbers of people, sometimes it is to their disadvantage. On the other hand, the tongue of a believer, when under the control of the indwelling Holy Spirit (I Cor. 6:19), can be used to bring blessing and happiness to many people. What we say and the things we talk about most frequently and naturally reveal what is in our minds and what dominates our thinking—for as a man *"thinketh in his heart, so is he" (Prov. 23:7)*, and *"out of the abundance of the heart the mouth speaketh" (Matt. 12:34b)*. The Holy Spirit-led and inspired James to write an intensely practical epistle in which he makes several references to the ways we can use our tongues and the consequences that come from these actions. The following references can be used for personal study on this topic: James 1:19, 26; James 2:12; James 3:1–12; James 4:11; and James 5:12.

In James 3, we are given both warning and guidance regarding the use of the tongue. Believers are told that those who teach others the Word of God must teach prayerfully, carefully, and honestly as they are enabled and empowered by the Holy Spirit. They will come under severe condemnation when what they say and teach is not consistent with their manner of life (James 3:1). I would like us to consider some Scripture from the book of Proverbs concerning how our speech reveals what is inside our hearts. For a believer this is important, but for a pastor, youth pastor, or parent, it is imperative to comprehend how words have the ability either to help build or to destroy members.

Consider these verses in relation to how you use words to build the youth that you have contact with.

> *The tongue of the just is as choice silver: the heart of the wicked is little worth. (Prov. 10:20)*

> *The thoughts of the wicked are an abomination to the Lord: but the words of the pure are pleasant words. (Prov. 15:26)*

> *The heart of the wise teacheth his mouth, and addeth learning to his lips. (Prov. 16:23)*

We see from the above verses the relationship of the tongue with the heart and thoughts. The tongue that is continually causing strife and contention is evidence of a heart that dwells on the same. The tongue that is vulgar and vile reveals a mind that is dwelling on impure thoughts. There is a direct correlation between one's thought life and his speech. You may ask then how an unworthy sinner can tame the tongue? Proverbs 16 tells us that a good man teaches his mouth. He decides to ask for God's help in guiding what he says and thinks.

Consider what Charles Bridges says regarding teaching our tongues:

> Man's religion begins, with the head; God's with the heart. "Out of the heart are the issues of life." Let me be careful, in what atmosphere, under what teaching I live. The vivid theory brings me into the icy zone: cold, and clear and cold. The experimental application realizes the glow of evangelical light and warmth. Let me look mainly, not to intellectual or theological attainments, but to heavenly teaching. Let me seek that my heart be first taught. Then

let it teach my mouth, and add learning to my lips for
the praise of my God, and the edifying of His church. [164]

A tongue under control is evidence of spiritual maturity; and if a believer's tongue is controlled by the Holy Spirit, then every other aspect of his life will be under the Spirit's control (v. 2). The tongue is a comparatively small part of the human body, but it has great power. James stresses how a horse is controlled by a small bit placed in its mouth, a large ship is maneuvered by a small rudder, and a small fire can kindle a large, fierce, uncontrolled blaze (vv. 3–5). Men have tamed and controlled all kinds of animals (v. 7), but no man can tame the tongue (v. 8). However, the tongue can be controlled by the Holy Spirit. When a believer is living close to God in submission and obedience to His will as revealed in the Word of God, his tongue will be used to speak gracious words of blessing, comfort, and edification.

Here is another set of verses to further help in this area of the tongue:

> *The mouth of a righteous man is a well of life: but violence covereth the mouth of the wicked. (Prov. 10:11)*

> *A wholesome tongue is a tree of life: but perverseness therein is a breach in the spirit. (Prov. 15:4)*

Let's consider the work of the Holy Spirit and the tongue. I believe that Proverbs 10:11 is referring to the regenerating work that the Holy Spirit can do in a person's heart through the Word of God. The righteous man who is teaching his tongue through the instruments of the Holy Spirit and the Word of God will find his tongue a well of life. In John 4:14 and John 7:38, we find references to the *"well of living water."*

---

[164] https://faculty.gordon.edu/hu/bi/ted_hildebrandt/otesources/20-proverbs/text/books/bridges-proverb-scommentary/bridges-proverbs.pdf. Accessed on August 20, 2018.

*But whosoever drinketh of the water that I shall give him
shall never thirst; but the water that I shall give him shall
be in him a well of water springing up into everlasting life.
(John 4:14)*

*He that believeth on me, as the scripture hath said, out of his
belly shall flow rivers of living water. (John 7:38)*

In both instances, Christ refers to the work of salvation done through Himself, the Living Water. You can see the word picture. Now let's tie in the verse in Proverbs 10. The regenerated man feasting upon the Word of God and invigorated by the water of life can experience a well of life that brings nourishment to others through his conversations with fellow believers as well as unbelievers. This is a wonderful privilege of the redeemed. A mouth supplied from heavenly waters is a well of life.

As we conclude in this specific area of our tongue, consider the references to the tongue in Proverbs 15:1–7: *"a soft answer," "the tongue of the wise," "a wholesome tongue," "the lips of the wise,"* and *"the prayer of the upright."* What a collection of thoughts about our tongues. These key words touch one of the greatest spheres of human influence. If we can rule our speech by surrendering our tongue and lips to the keeping of God's Spirit, we would save ourselves and others a world of trouble. It is imperative that we help our young people learn that frivolity in the area of speech is something to be avoided. Let's help our youth to be ever working to tame that little member which can either curse or bless—the tongue.

Do your words align with the teaching of Scripture? Consider the following verses:

*There is that speaketh like the piercings of a sword: but the
tongue of the wise is health. (Prov. 12:18)*

*Heaviness in the heart of man maketh it stoop: but a good
word maketh it glad. (Prov. 12:25)*

Pleasant words are as an honeycomb, sweet to the soul, and health to the bones. (Prov. 16:24)

Do your words encourage others to move forward for Christ? Do your words help lift the heavy load that others are bearing? It amazes me to see the lack of empathy that the average Christian has for fellow believers. We live in a self-consumed world. How do I know this? Take a look at the average person's Facebook or other social media pages. They are consumed with sharing pictures of their dog, their artwork, their cars, their food choices, and their hobbies. We live in a "selfie" world where most people believe that everything revolves around them.

"My happiness" is the most important thing in this world. Yet, we find more unhappiness and more despondency than ever. Why is this? Because happiness is not found in the *selfie-life*; instead, it is found in a *self-less* life. We should be looking for folks to encourage and help. This is what these verses are trying to encourage us to do with our speech. Is your tongue an instrument that promotes pleasantness, or do your words make others stoop? Let's make sure that our words are there to build up the young person that is in our lives.

Finally, let's consider two more verses from the book of Proverbs:

A man hath joy by the answer of his mouth: and a word spoken in due season, how good is it!. (Prov. 15:23)

A word fitly spoken is like apples of gold in pictures of silver. (Prov. 25:11)

These two verses reveal the satisfaction that words can bring to both the speaker and the hearer. In Proverbs 15:23, the speaker has joy by what he says. He is not getting his satisfaction by tearing someone else down or speaking abusively. The second part of this verse indicates that a godly speaker knows the correct time to say things or the time to refrain from saying something. Having this confidence produces joy in the heart of the speaker.

We then come to Proverbs 25:11. The word *fitly* is a very curious one in the Hebrew. It signifies "wheels" or "revolutions."[165] So what do "wheels" or "revolutions" have to do with speaking? It refers to words which roll smoothly and pleasantly from the lips of the speaker to the ears of the hearer. In that time era, wheels were not used very often, and most things were carried on horseback. On some occasions, makeshift wheels would be needed to ease the burden of travel. Today, we have wheels that are light and smooth so that carrying a burden is easy. The application for a wise man is to learn to "carry" his words with ease so that they are not burdensome to the hearer. The wise man speaks so that his words do not jar or shock the hearer. The speaker's words should not produce hurt by any harshness or roughness, nor should his words leave a painful rut behind in the memory.

Jesus was a great example of words that were fitly spoken. The Lord always spoke graciously; in fact, in John 1:14, He was said to be *"full of grace and truth."* People did not always agree with Him, and there were times that folks were riled up at His speech. However, in John 7:46, we learn that *"never man spake like this man."* There are other references in the Gospels that reveal this as well. One such verse is Luke 4:22 where they *"wondered at the gracious words which proceeded out of his mouth."* Peter says in his first epistle that there was no *"guile found in his mouth . . . when he was reviled, [He] reviled not again; when he suffered, he threatened not."*

The Lord created all things by the power of His word (Ps. 33:6–9; Heb. 11:3). He spoke and a storm ceased (Mark 4:39); He spoke to an unclean spirit, and it came out of a man (Mark 5:8, 13); He spoke, and a man was raised from death (John 11:43–44). For those of us who minister to people, the physical tool that we must use is our words. Let's be sure that we understand the biblical truth of the power of words. The Bible says that we will give an account for every idle word. Christ understood that words count, and He used them wisely to fulfill God's purpose in His life—to bring people to salvation and to teach them His desires for their life.

---

[165] http://www.lexiconcordance.com/hebrew/0655.html. Accessed on August 20, 2018.

Chapter 24

X - eXercise: Developing Spiritual Fitness

We live in a fitness-crazed society. On average, a tennis match lasts about three and a half hours. A long game can go up to five. During the 2010 Wimbledon championships, John Isner and Nicolas Mahut played a match that lasted for over eleven hours. The longest contest in professional tennis history, the match consisted of 183 games held over the course of three days with the longest set going for over eight hours. With twenty-eight different ball boys working in rotation, the players slurped coconut water and munched on chicken to keep their energy up over the exhausting playing period.

The next time you're finishing up an exhausting round of laps at your local gym, think of Benoit Lecomte. One of the greatest long-distance swimmers to ever live, the Frenchman is credited with being the first person to successfully swim across the Atlantic Ocean without the benefit of a kick board. Doggy paddling for around seventy-three days, Lecomte covered approximately 3,716 miles of deep-sea to complete this mammoth task in 1998. Beginning in Hyannis, Massachusetts, the athlete swam in two hour sessions for up to eight hours a day until he reached his goal over two months later in Quiberon, Brittany, France. (And if you're wondering how Lecomte avoided becoming great white food, he was tailed by a boat with an electromagnetic field that warded off sharks!)

Considered to be the best endurance runner on earth, Dean Karnazes was covering ridiculous distances from the time he was in grade school. As he grew, so did his accomplishments; and on October 18, 2005, the California native completed one of the most awe-inspiring runs of all time when he pulled off a nonstop, 350-mile run around the San Francisco Bay area. Beginning his trek on a Wednesday afternoon, Karnazes pushed himself for over eighty hours of relentless pavement pounding until he finally finished his journey on Saturday night.

By traveling from the southwestern point of Land's End to John O'Groat in the northeast, it is possible to cover all of Great Britain in an uninterrupted trip. This course, popular with tourists, takes about three months to cover on foot and about two weeks on a bicycle. But in 2001, cyclist Gethin Butler conquered the whole journey in only two days. Racing across 874 miles of terrain, the extreme cyclist spent a little over forty-four hours on his bike, vigorously pedaling with little rest until his astonishing trip was complete. An extreme rider, Butler has also cycled 1,000 miles in two days, seven hours, and fifty-three minutes.[166]

> If thou put the brethren in remembrance of these things, thou shalt be a good minister of Jesus Christ, nourished up in the words of faith and of good doctrine, whereunto thou hast attained. But refuse profane and old wives' fables, and exercise thyself rather unto godliness. For bodily exercise profiteth little: but godliness is profitable unto all things, having promise of the life that now is, and of that which is to come. This is a faithful saying and worthy of all acceptation. For therefore we both labor and suffer reproach, because we trust in the living God, who is the Savior of all men, specially of those that believe. (I Tim. 4:6–10)

While we do need to take care of our physical bodies, more importantly is to keep our spiritual lives in shape. In this passage of Scripture, Paul gives us some principles for maintaining spiritual strength. What I am going to try to look at in this chapter is both ideas. We will try to take

---

[166] https://www.mensjournal.com/health-fitness/amazing-feats-endurance/. Accessed on August 30, 2018.

a physical aspect of exercise and discipline, which seems to be missing in a lot of teenagers today and then also make a spiritual application to the fitness that is necessary to keep one's spiritual life in shape.

Eat Well
(Verse 6)

The phrase *"nourished up"* means that we should watch what we eat. This is a very important physical point. I remember in high school taking a programming class for computers. The teacher would tell us over and over the following acronym, GIGO. What does that mean? Garbage in; garbage out. In the computer world, that was important to know, and it is also important to know in a physical world. Our bodies have been given to us to be stewards over for furthering the kingdom of God. How will that happen if you do not watch what you eat? There are passages in the Bible about gluttony and moderation. We should be careful of having a lack of self-discipline in physical food. Most importantly, we should be constantly feeding on the words of God—soul food.

> *Neither have I gone back from the commandment of his lips; I have esteemed the words of his mouth more than my necessary food. (Job 23:12)*

> *These were more noble than those in Thessalonica, in that they received the word with all readiness of mind, and searched the Scriptures daily, whether those things were so. (Acts 17:11)*

What are you feasting on spiritually? Do you use the down time to fill your carnal flesh yet starve your spirit? You then wonder why you are not spiritually strong and seem to have less resistance to temptation. Look at what you are eating, spiritually. If you are having a steady diet of the world, then more than likely you are going to want more of the world. We acquire tastes, don't we?

A great man had a camel that was wasting away, until it seemed at the point of death. "See," cried he, to the simple son of the desert, "here is my camel: I have tried cordials and elixir, balsams and lotions. Alas! all are in vain." The plain man looked at the hollow sides, the staring bones, the projecting ribs. "Oh, most learned philosopher," said he, "thy camel needeth but one thing!" "What is it, my son?" asked the old, wise man, eagerly. "Food, sir—good food, and plenty of it." "Dear me," cried the philosopher, "I never thought of that!"[167]

Give your starved soul more prayer, more communion with God, more meditation on the Word. That's the sure cure for a miserable spiritual life. You have feasted on the world, tasted of its dainties, and then come up empty spiritually. This should not shock us.

Exercise Regularly
(Verses 7–8)

From the Greek word *exercise* we get our word "gymnasium." [168] Just as physical strength requires constant physical exercise; it is necessary to apply spiritual exercise to gain spiritual. The Bible does not necessarily command a young person or older person to go out for a walk, but the Bible seems to imply that a Christian should take care of their physical well-being. It is important that as parents, we create opportunities for our young people to be active physically. This may be in some organized athletic endeavors, or it may be on an individual level within the family unit. I enjoy taking hikes, riding bikes, and doing other physical activity with my young people. It is good for the body, mind, and emotional well-being. I don't think that I must go to the numerous studies that have been published over the last couple of decades that show that sitting in front of a television screen, playing video games, or just sitting doing nothing is detrimental to good health.

---

[167] Mark Guy Pearse, Homely Talks (Nabu Press: Charleston, South Carolina, 2010), 45.

[168] W. E. Vine, Vine's Expository Dictionary of Old and New Testament Words: Volume 2 (Iowa Falls, IA: World Bible Publishers, 1981), 59.

The passage says, though, that godliness is the most profitable effort. The Christian is referenced as an athlete and soldier both in Corinthians and Timothy. This means that the Christian must train himself and exercise himself for a lifelong contest. He will be required to wrestle and fight with the powers of evil that he may win a crown of glory that fadeth not away. How natural then that the apostle Paul, having just spoken of spiritual exercise for the attainment of godliness, should go on to glance at bodily exercise to point out the superiority of the one over the other. Let us consider Paul's words and see what meaning they may have. "*Bodily exercise profiteth little.*" It is not saying that physical exercise is a worthless endeavor. Instead, it says that there is some profit to exercise. So, in its proper place, it has value. Taken in moderation, physical exercise tends to preserve health and increase strength.

So, if physical exercise is a little profitable and we should do that, what would spiritual exercise be worth? It would be of MORE worth. What can be the worth of spiritual exercise?

1. **Spiritual Exercise Will Limit Your Flesh**

It is the direct effect. Not that man is wholly without restraint, but the carnal man will find that there is so much power in his flesh. Remember the Apostle Paul noticed this effect when he was discussing the disappointment of the flesh in Romans 7. The many pronouns in this section indicate that the writer is having a problem with self. This is not to say that the Christian is a split personality because he is not. Salvation makes a man whole. But it does indicate that the believer's mind, will, and body can be controlled either by the old nature or the new nature, either by the flesh or the Spirit. The statements here indicate that the believer has two serious problems: (1) he cannot do the good he wants to do; and (2) he does the evil that he does not want to do.[169] Paul gave us a key in

---

[169] Wiersbe, 428.

Romans 8. He said that the Holy Spirit of God can give victory. This comes through spiritual exercise.

Spiritual exercise is not easy; we must *"labor and suffer reproach"* (*I Tim. 4:10a*). The word *strive* is an athletic word from which we get our English word agonize. Here the words, *"suffer reproach"* are used. It is the picture of an athlete straining and giving his best to win. A Christian who wants to excel must really work at it, by the grace of God and to the glory of God.[170] Our flesh is greatly assisted by powerful allies. The flesh loves to allow Satan access to sit at the right hand of the human heart, blowing upon the coals of evil which a person allows into their heart. The world is quick to assist in this as well. But spiritual exercise can be helpful in counteracting these enemies. By applying Bible truths and disposing the mind to be sober and vigilant against the wiles of the devil, we can learn to resist the devil, the flesh, and the world.

2. Spiritual Exercise Will Give You Right Priorities of Action

The discipline of godliness, temperance and spiritually uplifting activities enables the mind to conquer its enemies. Keeping eternity in the forefront of a life keeps the temporal at bay. Godly religion tends to guide the mind aright. What is that which can help decide the direction of the whole life? The apostle has stated it—*"Whatsoever ye do, do all to the glory of God"* because all that is not done according to this motive is not done according to the will of God. When a teen is allowed to do whatever he pleases because it is what he wants, his flesh will prevail and his new man will pine away.

3. Spiritual Exercise Renews the Mind

Your brain is no different than the rest of the muscles in your body— you either use it or you lose it. You utilize the gym to stimulate the growth

---

[170] Ibid., 761.

of all muscle cells. You can actually get an additional brain boost by donning your sneakers and hitting the gym. The benefits of physical exercise, especially aerobic exercise, have positive effects on brain function on multiple fronts, ranging from the molecular to behavioral level. According to a study done by the Department of Exercise Science at the University of Georgia, even briefly exercising for twenty minutes facilitates information processing and memory functions.[171]

Physical exercise affects the human brain in several areas. It increases heart rate, which pumps more oxygen to the brain. It also aids the bodily release of a plethora of hormones, all of which participate in aiding and providing a nourishing environment for the growth of brain cells. Exercise stimulates the brain plasticity by stimulating growth of new connections between cells in a wide array of important cortical areas of the brain. Recent research from UCLA demonstrated that exercise increased growth factors in the brain—making it easier for the brain to grow new neuronal connections.[172]

From a behavioral perspective, the emotions can be affected by physical exercise. An article published in *Time Health* magazine list multiple studies showing the antidepressant effect of differing types of physical exercise.[173]

The spiritual mind can also be renewed by spiritual exercise. Remember the occasion of how Moses was taken up to converse with God? He seemed to come down from the mountain energized for the fight with those that wanted to choose another god instead of Jehovah. Also, recall the time of fasting and prayer that Christ took in the wilderness? Yes, he was tempted, but his time of spiritual exercise allowed him to face the devil with fervor. We need to have spiritually refreshing times of renewal

---

[171] https://www.brainhq.com/brain-resources/everyday-brain-fitness/physical-exercise. Accessed on July 31, 2018.

[172] http://newsroom.ucla.edu/releases/researchers-link-sedentary-behavior-to-thinning-in-brain-region-critical-for-memory. Accessed on August 30, 2018.

[173] http://time.com/4752846/exercise-brain-health/. Accessed on August 30, 2018.

for our minds. The study of God's Word tends to strengthen the mind; and that which strengthens the mind improves it.

Exert Yourself
(Verse 10)

The word *labor* is an athletic term. Just as athletes exert energy to win a competition, so we are to give all we have in service to God.

On September 11, 2001, Muslim terrorists attacked America. Soon thereafter, their compatriots in Afghanistan were scurrying from cave to cave, trying to avoid the wrath of the US military under *Operation Enduring Freedom*. While taking part in that operation on December 16, 2001, Marine Sgt. Christopher Chandler stepped on a land mine near Kandahar. He lost his left leg below the knee from the explosion. Such an injury spells the end of a military career, but Sgt. Chandler, known to his friends as a "can do" type individual, didn't want out of the Marines. He fought to remain on active duty and won. But that wasn't enough for Chandler. He enrolled in airborne jump school, finishing at the top of his class. On November 10, 2003, less than two years after his injury and on the birthday of the Marine Corps, he became the only service member ever to become jump-qualified with a prosthetic leg.

Sgt. Chandler took the accomplishment in stride. "I figured I had an advantage. After all, I have one less ankle to break."[174]

What is the purpose of this story? The man had to exert himself and force himself physically to get out of his comfort zone. The same is true spiritually. Many a young person is aching, having spiritual problems that can be corrected if they would start exerting themselves.

You may be having spiritual ailments—bad spiritual posture (you limp instead of walk erect; you drag your feet and walk slow and undeliberate), spiritual headaches (your mind wanders to the world; your mind is consumed with self). You need to exert yourself spiritually to get out of the

---

[174] Sam Gipp, More Fight on! Stories (Miamitown, OH: Daystar Publishing, 2008), 41.

lethargy. As physical strength takes effort to build and maintain so also does spiritual strength. Spiritually speaking, we need to eat well, exercise regularly, and exert ourselves. Let's not let our young people become out-of-shape Christians. Help them to take the time to be in God's Word and apply the Word that has been given to them. They will become spiritually fit.

Chapter 25

Y - Youth and the Church

Why Have a Youth Pastor?

The first of the seven famous debates between Abraham Lincoln and Stephen A. Douglas took place on August 21, 1858, in Ottowa, Illinois. Their arrangement was that Douglas would speak first, for one hour; Lincoln would take an hour and a half to reply; Douglas, a half hour to rebut Lincoln's reply. This debate was considerably shorter than those to which the two men were accustomed. In fact, they had tangled several times before, and all their encounters had been much lengthier and more exhausting. For example, on October 16, 1854, in Peoria, Illinois, Douglas delivered a three-hour address to which Lincoln, by agreement, was to respond. When Lincoln's turn came, he reminded the audience that it was already 5 p.m., that he would probably require as much time as Douglas and that Douglas was still scheduled for a rebuttal. He proposed, therefore, that the audience go home, have dinner, and return refreshed for four more hours of talk. The audience amiably agreed, and matters proceeded as Lincoln had outlined.[175]

This excerpt is amazing to read. Can you imagine this occurring today in a teen meeting or youth conference across America? I believe that the average teenager could not last for an hour of intellectual conversation. Some fault must lie with us as parents, pastors, and youth pastors. We have "babied and coddled" our young people by giving them watered

---

[175] Neil Postman, Amusing Ourselves to Death (New York, NY: Penguin Books, 1985), 44.

down doses of scriptural knowledge. For those teenagers who have grown up in our churches, they should be able to reason and be scripturally logical. Years ago, as a youth pastor, I was with a group of our teens, and we were doing a study on authority. At the end of the night, I was thrilled to see the conclusions that the teens could draw from Scripture regarding the biblical concept of authority. They were diving in and enjoying the study!

I believe this is what Paul was instructing Timothy about in II Timothy 2:15. He tells Timothy, a young pastor, to *"study to shew himself approved."* As we start to think of youth and the church, let me clarify that I enjoy a good time and having fun. I am not saying that we must stop fun activities with our teens and start youth group convents. However, we need to have a balance and make sure there is ample time given to the study of God's Word. Our teenagers need to mature in the Word of God. For this reason, it is important who we get to lead the activities of the youth. We need to understand that those that we put before our youth will have an influence.

As a pastor and youth pastor, I received countless invitations to bring our teens to youth explosions, youth manias, and youth spectaculars. The invitations all seem to be striving to create a party atmosphere. As independent, fundamental Baptist churches, what type of atmosphere will be created by the leader of the youth? We should refrain from this wild, rebellious, worldly college campus atmosphere. Our job is to train soldiers for Jesus Christ. Is the youth program preparing the teens to endure hardness or scoff at seriousness?

Qualifications

The first item of consideration is choosing the right person to work with the young people. Some churches use lay folks to work with youth, I am not opposed to this if the pastor is very involved with much of the detail. There is a difference between a called person and a parent helping with the youth. For this reason, I am addressing more specifically a person who feels called to the ministry. Among the most important are his spiritual, personal, and educational qualifications.

1. Spiritual Qualification

Know and Love Christ

This is obvious if he is to lead others to know Him. It is imperative that there is a God-given love in the one leading the group. He must have a love for God, for His Word, and for those who have been committed to his care.

Consistent, Exemplary Christian Living

This must go hand in hand with salvation. Youth are quick to detect—and despise—hypocrisy. The inconsistency of adults was the second-ranked complaint made by the church dropouts surveyed by the National Sunday School Association.[176]

Call of God

Before considering giving his life as a youth pastor, he must feel a call of God to that phase of Christian work. As it is true in any other field of service in the Christian realm, this is not a position in which one becomes rich materially. He must perform his work out of a love for God and the souls of men, remembering that his rewards are eternal and spiritual. The call may not be such as Saul had on the road to Damascus; but when the call comes, he will know it to be a call to serve.

2. Personal Qualifications

Humility

A proud person will never get along with the pastor, teen parents, or the teens themselves. There should be no spirit of superiority. Pride and self-importance separate; humility unites. The youth pastor will have real humility if he is willing to help others succeed to a point higher than even he has attained—and do it without jealousy.

---

[176] http://www.ccel.us/youtheducation.ch11.html. Accessed on August 21, 2018.

Emotional Maturity

The person who is on the mountaintop of elation one day and down in the valley of despair the next will not become a safe and sane director of youth. Emotional stability does not mean a person is devoid of emotion, but one whose emotions are subject to intelligent control.

Forethought and Initiative

He should anticipate some problems and aggressively intercept others. The results of his actions should be thought out before he acts. He should direct the present with an eye on the future.

Self-Control

If the youth pastor cannot control himself, he will not be able to control others. Along with self-control comes patience. He should be tolerant, but not lax in discipline; forgiving, yet frank in discussing failures of conformity to Christian standards. This is even explained in the qualifications of a pastor, "not a striker." This does not necessarily mean that the man is a pacificist and that there is no animation of opinions. However, "flying off the handle," "seeing the red dot," and "loud and boisterous" should not be attributes of the youth pastor.

Burden for Youth

There should be a genuine burden for youth. Some do not relate well to teenagers. If a person does not relate well, then I would not recommend that they work with teenagers. God puts a love for the folks that a minister is called to work. This does not mean that everything is always smooth sailing, and it does not mean that the man who is called will know everything about youth. For one who is just starting into the ministry, this would be impossible. There will have to be learning, reading, and studying. However, there should be a love for the people—in this case, the youth of the church. We see this displayed in the life of Christ. Yes, Christ had conflict, but he wept, prayed, and ministered continually with a burdened heart for those He came to seek and to save.

3. <u>Educational Qualifications</u>

We are living in an age when academic degrees and professional training have become the measuring stick, even in church vocations. Education, per se, will not give us adequate youth leadership. Proper, biblical education will help us get adequate youth leadership. A youth pastor must have a special interest and desire to work with the youth, and this position of youth pastor should not be looked on as merely a steppingstone into the regular pastoral ministry. This may occur in time, but looking at the youth group as an "incubator" for the real ministry is diminishing the role that a youth pastor can have on impressionable minds. There should be training in understanding how to teach young people, how to relate to parents, and how to help the youth develop in the church and in their homes.

There should also be adequate Bible training. A youth pastor will teach and preach to his youth group every week. He cannot come in as a novice when it comes to God's Word and being able to "rightly divide." Some may not want specific Bible college training but be careful of scoffing at this extra effort that a young person may put into getting qualified. Training is necessary and beneficial for doing any work, secular or spiritual. It is necessary to be active in helping young men who desire the work of the ministry to be helped in the area of youth. All through Scriptures, you will find the importance of training youth and the development of youth. For this reason, training those who lead youth is important in steering young people down a godly path.

<u>Relationships</u>

The job of youth pastor is often left undefined; but because of the necessity of spiritual harmony within the church, the relationship of the youth pastor to the pastor, the congregation, and the youth of the church cannot be overlooked.

1. <u>To the Pastor</u>

He is responsible directly to the senior pastor. The youth pastor holds his positioning trust to the senior pastor. His ministry is an extension of the pulpit ministry of the senior pastor of the local church. The youth pastor is subordinate to and shares in the senior pastor's ministry. The pastor and youth pastor should share their viewpoints on doctrines of the Bible and the church. If the director finds his beliefs at odds with those of the senior pastor, he should not go behind his back and seek to rally support for some controversial feature in the youth program. If the pastor cannot support the youth pastor in several programs, it is up to the two of them to get together and reconcile matters or make provisions to go their separate ways. *"And if a house be divided against itself, that house cannot stand" (Mark 3:25).*

It is necessary for the pastor and youth pastor to have a clearly defined division of responsibilities to function effectively. This assignment of responsibilities should be made, based on job analysis. Such factors as abilities, knowledge, aptitude, and the common purposes in the light of the church needs are the primary considerations. The youth pastor should never develop plans or announce policies without first consulting the pastor and securing his advice or approval, and he should make no important decisions without being in perfect harmony and agreement with the pastor.

2. <u>To the Parents</u>

The youth pastor should remember that he is there to assist the parents. Pitting a teenager against his parents is a dangerous tactic. This should be avoided at all costs. There will be times that a youth pastor will come to an end of being able to help a young person because the parent intervenes and puts a stop to the spiritual direction that the young person wants to go. This can be disheartening, but the parent will ultimately give an account for the life of their child. A youth pastor can sit down with the parent and explain the wrong path choices, but then he must step away.

On the other hand, there are times that the parent may need to come to the youth pastor and mention some concerns that they may have with activities, discipline, or behavioral concerns. The parents and youth pastor should have open communication so that it is a team effort regarding direction in a young person's life.

3. To the Young People

Earn Their Respect

The teens are the ones that he is to minister to, and winning their respect is basic to a lasting, fruitful relationship. The youth pastor should make these young people his life. He must be open to listening to them as well as counseling them. He must be concerned and show it. They must be understood and loved.

Tactful Discipline

Youth respect the leader who will kindly but firmly insist on what is right, yet at the same time helps them develop their own standards. Building such a relationship will take time and effort, but the influencing of one's life by another cannot be done by remote control. It will require personalized attention of the leader to each youth.

The Duties of a Youth Pastor

1. Supervision in General

Adult workers should not be judged by how much they do for the young people, rather they should be judged by how much they can get the young people to do for themselves.

Supervision is needed after the work has been assigned to assure the best results. Young people must be reminded again of their responsibility and be helped with the problems that arise from the assignments given. The youth pastor is not merely a chaperone but is chosen to render encouragement as well as instruction.

2. Other Responsibilities

These responsibilities may take some time to develop so be slow and steady in the implementation.

Soul winning—creating opportunities to see teens get a burden. This can be done through going with individuals and showing one at a time how to be a soul winner. Classes can be taught on how to know the Bible and lead someone to the Lord. There can be organized Sundays for teenagers to bring the lost and then organized soul winning times for the Parents and teens to go door-knocking together. All these items will cultivate a right burden for the lost.

Example—It is important that the youth pastor be a godly example. A lot of damage can be made to a church when they put an unspiritual man into a place of leading young people. There can be a worldly, materialistic philosophy if the man is carnal and greedy. All the requirements for a godly person should be portrayed in the youth pastor.

Disciplinarian—This does not mean that the youth pastor must be dull and dry. However, he must understand the authority that he has and that sometimes the youth will test this authority. I don't know of any pastor that has not been tested. Usually, all authority is tested at some point, so the youth pastor must understand some concept of discipline. This means maintaining control of a youth meeting, dealing with a rebel, dealing with unruly parents, and restoring a repentant teen.

Counselor—The counseling that a youth pastor does with his teens takes place on many levels. Some of it is very informal. It might take place out on the athletic field, over a Coke, or just when the teen drops by the youth pastor's office or home. It may also be scheduled. It may take only one good session together or the counseling may extend over a long period of time with many sessions.

With any one student, the ability to provide this help depends on a combination of things—attitudes, methods, techniques, procedures, and philosophies. While all these things are significant, the relationship is the most important of all. If a youth pastor has a good relationship with a teen, the counselee will be helped, even if the counselor makes mistakes in his technique. If he has a poor relationship with the teen, even the best techniques will become mere mechanics.

Instructor—One of the main jobs that a youth pastor will be doing is teaching. The teen years are some of the most formative years of life. Be careful of getting someone into leadership, who is not able to rightly divide the Word of Truth. It is an important aspect of the job and treating this area lightly can have grave results for the future of any church. With weak teaching on biblical doctrines, separation and moral issues, a youth group can be led into neo-evangelicalism or even apostasy. This is why the listing of requirements is thought through and some type of Bible training should be necessary. It takes time and practice to rightly divide the Word of Truth. Putting someone into a position just because it needs to be filled can be very dangerous. There are many pastors and youth pastors who have been at this ministry for many years and can help a young man develop teaching skills and teaching topics that can benefit the youth and the church.

Why Have a Youth Group?

It is not:

- A social group (dating club, hangout)

- A substitute for the home

- A "baby sitting" service

It is:

- An extension of the home

- An extension of the pastor

- An opportunity to learn service principles

- An opportunity to learn social skills–treating the opposite sex, where their friends should be

- An opportunity to learn to love God's Word

As we conclude with these final thoughts, I understand that there are differing opinions. One author made the following conclusion which I believe can be helpful. "The church is God's family for eternity. The Christian family has present ties which should be maintained in such a way as to strengthen and support the ties in God's family. By working together, the church and the home can mutually benefit one another—the home supporting the church, and the church providing spiritual guidance and stability for the home. A good working relationship between the home and the church is maintained by mutual respect and wholesome communication between parents and ministers."[177]

Within an independent local church, there should be a unified understanding of what the purpose of the youth pastor's job is and what the youth group is trying to accomplish. If the church has a youth group, the parents should get behind that ministry and help their youth be involved. A youth group that is functioning spiritually can be a huge help to the godly home.

---

[177] John Coblentz, Christian Family Living (Harrisonburg, VA: Christian Light Publications, 2002), 244–245.

Chapter 26

Z - Zealous for the Right Things

For Sparky, school was all but impossible. He failed every subject in the eighth grade. He flunked physics in high school, getting a grade of zero. Sparky also flunked Latin, Algebra, and English. He didn't do much better in sports. Although he did manage to make the school's golf team, he promptly lost the only important match of the season. There was a consolation match; he lost that, too.

Throughout his youth, Sparky was awkward socially. He was not actually disliked by the other students; no one cared that much. He was astonished if a classmate ever said hello to him outside of school hours. There's no way to tell how he might have done at dating. Sparky never once asked a girl to go out in high school. He was too afraid of being turned down.

Sparky was a loser. He, his classmates—everyone knew it. So, he rolled with it. Sparky had made up his mind early in life that if things were meant to work out, they would. Otherwise, he would content himself with what appeared to be his inevitable mediocrity.

However, one thing was important to Sparky—drawing. He was proud of his artwork. Of course, no one else appreciated it. In his last year of high school, he submitted some cartoons to the editor of the yearbook. The cartoons were turned down. Despite this rejection, Sparky was so convinced of his ability that he decided to become a professional artist. After completing high school, he wrote a letter to Walt Disney Studios. He was told to send some samples of his artwork, and the subject for a cartoon was suggested. Sparky drew the proposed cartoon. He spent a great deal of time on it and on all the other drawings he submitted. Finally, the reply came from Disney Studios. He had been rejected once again. Another loss for the loser.

So, Sparky decided to write his own autobiography in cartoons. He described his childhood self—a little boy loser and chronic underachiever. The cartoon character would soon become famous worldwide. For Sparky, the boy who had such a lack of success in school and whose work was rejected again and again, was Charles Schulz. He created the "Peanuts" comic strip and the little cartoon character whose kite would never fly and who never succeeded in kicking a football was Charlie Brown.[178]

Motivational stories such as the one above can inspire and teach some practical lessons to all of us. Pastors, youth pastors, and parents do not want their kids just to "feel good" and "believe in themselves" and "follow their heart." This is the mantra that is touted day in and day out by Hollywood stars and athletic stars. There is guidance that can be given to our young people to help them to be zealous and persevere for the right things. Psalm 16 offers us some help in finding some guidelines for our young people. In this chapter, we see David asking God to show him the path that he should take.

> *I have set the LORD always before me: because he is at my right hand, I shall not be moved. Therefore my heart is glad, and my glory rejoiceth: my flesh also shall rest in hope. For thou wilt not leave my soul in hell; neither wilt thou suffer thine Holy One to see corruption. Thou wilt shew me the path of life: in thy presence is fulness of joy; at thy right hand there are pleasures for evermore. (Ps. 16:8–11)*

Let's take some time to consider some helps to reveal "the path of life" for our young people.

---

[178] Alice Gray, Stories for the Family's Heart (Sisters, OR: Multnomah Publishers, 1998), 73.

<u>Planning—Soundness in Our Steps</u>

We see this in the idea phrase, *"I have set the Lord always before me:"* In the context of Psalm 16, the writer indicates that there was some decision-making done ahead of time. Planning ahead is a primary trait of intelligence. A wise person knows that the major plan must be sound, or the minor plans will fail. The soundness of step is in following the guidance of the Lord. The Lord, through the guidance of the Word of God, must be before a young person or they will not succeed in their path.

> In the summer of 1988, three friends and I climbed Mount Lyell, the highest peak in Yosemite National Park. Two of us were experienced mountaineers; two of us were not. I was not one of the experienced two . . . The climb to the top and back was to take the better part of a day due, in large part, to the difficulty of the glacier that one must cross to get to the top . . . As the hours passed, and we trudged up the glacier, the two mountaineers opened a wide gap between me and my less-experienced companion. Being competitive by nature, I began to look for short cuts I might be able to take to beat them to the top. I thought I saw one to the right of an outcropping of rock—so I went up, deaf to the protests of my companions . . .
>
> Thirty minutes later I was trapped in a cul-de-sac of rock atop the Lyell Glacier, looking down several hundred feet of a sheer slope of ice, pitched at a forty-five-degree angle . . . I was only ten feet from the safety of a rock. But one little slip and I wouldn't stop sliding until I had landed in the valley floor about fifty miles away! I was stuck and I was scared.[179]

---

[179] https://www.sfchronicle.com/news/article/Witness-to-death-plunge-of-2-climbers-on-El-12982924.php. Accessed on August 21, 2018.

As a leader of youth either in a home or in a church, let's direct young people's steps by the clear teaching of the Word of God. Youth will be tempted to take short cuts. It is imperative that proper planning is done before each decision or, like the illustration above, disastrous results may follow. Tie the young person to the unchanging words of God in the Bible. We do not desire our youth to be carelessly climbing and then be put into harm's way. The devil has many paths that seem innocent and would lead to a successful end, but they are slippery slopes to destruction.

Prudence—Wisdom in Our Choices

False choices may appear wise and will beguile for the moment. Youth must learn to have the long look when making choices. Christianity helps to form standards and clarify judgments in making choices. It adds power for deciding when decisions are significant. Our Christian faith is an accurate signpost pointing the way. "Character is the momentum we gain from past acts of choices" (George Eliot).[180]

There are four areas that we must consider for any Christian to establish what God's will is for their lives.

1. God's Word

Zeal for the study of the Word is essential to spiritual transformation. Most people are too lazy to study. They'd rather drift or be entertained. That's why Disneyland and the rubbish on TV is so popular. A large number of people read because they enjoy it. And it may even be good reading, reading on the truth—but few people *study*. Study is effort and digging and concentration, and a methodical going over and over to get things clear and fixed in the mind. Reading can be a mere passing pleasure, a lazy relaxation but it is not necessarily studying. Study is disciplining the mind to consistent, purposeful labor and accomplishment. The motive

---

[180] https://www.goodreads.com/book/show/304.Daniel_Deronda. Accessed on September 13, 2018.

must be love. If we do not love God enough to *want* to study and learn all we can about His Word and work, then we are of no use to Him. Be sure your reading is purposeful, beneficial study.

The word *study* in II Timothy 2:15 is defined as "endeavor, do diligence, be diligent, give diligence, be forward, labor, or study."[181] Look at the other uses of the word *study* in Scripture:

- "*Endeavoring* to keep the unity of the Spirit in the bond of peace" (Eph. 4:3).

- "Do thy *diligence* to come shortly unto me" (II Tim. 4:9).

- "When I shall send Artemas unto thee, or Tychicus, be *diligent* to come unto me to Nicopolis: for I have determined there to winter" (Titus 3:12).

- "Let us *labor* therefore to enter into that rest, lest any man fall after the same example of unbelief" (Heb. 4:11).

These other uses of the word *study* indicate to us what we should be trying to accomplish in the lives of our teens. We need to teach them to labor, strive, and endeavor to further their knowledge of the Lord Jesus Christ. We should be working with our teens to help them "rightly divide the truth."

2. God's Voice, the Holy Spirit

And the LORD went before them by day in a pillar of a cloud, to lead them the way; and by night in a pillar of fire, to give them light; to go by day and night: He took not away the

---

[181] W. E. Vine, Vine's Expository Dictionary of Old and New Testament Words (Iowa Falls, IA: World Bible Publishers, 1971), 311.

pillar of the cloud by day, nor the pillar of fire by night, from before the people. (Exodus 13:21–22)

In the Old Testament, God showed His presence to the Israelites by overspreading the tabernacle with fire (Num. 9:14–15). This fiery presence provided light and guidance (Num. 9:17–23). In the New Testament, God guides and comforts His children with the Holy Spirit dwelling in our bodies—the *"tabernacle"* and the *"temple of the living God"* (II Cor. 5:1; 6:16). It is imperative that those who lead teenagers help them to understand the guiding direction that the Holy Spirit can have in their life. Samuel learned to listen to God's voice at a very young age. Our teens should be able to learn His voice as well.

3. <u>God's Authority</u>

Remember them which have the rule over you, who have spoken unto you the word of God: whose faith follow, considering the end of their conversation. (Heb. 13:7)

Obey them that have the rule over you, and submit yourselves: for they watch for your souls, as they that must give account, that they may do it with joy, and not with grief: for that is unprofitable for you. (Heb. 13:17)

There are other verses that could be listed, but for sake of space only two are listed that show the importance of godly authority in a young person's life. Soundness comes in heeding advice. Some attend church because it is necessary, but they have no desire or zeal to ever listen to the pastor or youth pastor. When planning our path, my question then is, where is the separation in a person's life that separates the secular and the spiritual? According to I Corinthians 6 and Romans 12, all a Christian's life is to be given over to God with the realization that he is owned by God. This would mean that there is no separation, and thus godly authority should be sought. There should be some time of fasting and prayer as one heads into a large decision.

4. <u>Godly Counsel</u>

Blessed is the man that walketh not in the counsel of the ungodly, nor standeth in the way of sinners, nor sitteth in the seat of the scornful. (Ps. 1:1)

Where no counsel is, the people fall: but in the multitude of counsellors there is safety. (Prov. 11:14)

The way of a fool is right in his own eyes: but he that hear-keneth unto counsel is wise. (Prov. 12:15)

Without counsel purposes are disappointed: but in the multi-tude of counsellors they are established. (Prov. 15:22)

Hear counsel, and receive instruction, that thou mayest be wise in thy latter end. There are many devices in a man's heart; nevertheless the counsel of the LORD, that shall stand. (Prov. 19:20, 21)

Counsel in the heart of man is like deep water; but a man of understanding will draw it out. (Prov. 20:5)

Every purpose is established by counsel: and with good advice make war. (Prov. 20:18)

There is no wisdom nor understanding nor counsel against the LORD. (Prov. 21:30)

Many take these verses and do not align them with the previous points. This is dangerous because one of the keys to counsel is that it is godly. There are thousands of opinions that one can get regarding almost everything that one can think about: home repairs, vehicle purchases, job opportunities, vocational choices, and on and on. However, a Christian has a responsibility to try not just to find someone who agrees with their decision so that a stamp of approval can be obtained. Gaining godly counsel means that this person is mature spiritually and has evidence of the Holy Spirit in their life.

Preserve me, O God: for in thee do I put my trust. O my soul, thou hast said unto the LORD, Thou art my Lord: my goodness extendeth not to thee; but to the saints that are in the earth, and to the excellent, in whom is all my delight. Their sorrows shall be multiplied that hasten after another god: their drink offerings of blood will I not offer, nor take up their names into my lips. The LORD is the portion of mine inheritance and of my cup: thou maintainest my lot. The lines are fallen unto me in pleasant places; yea, I have a goodly heritage. I will bless the LORD, who hath given me counsel: my reins also instruct me in the night seasons. I have set the LORD always before me: because he is at my right hand, I shall not be moved. Therefore my heart is glad, and my glory rejoiceth: my flesh also shall rest in hope. For thou wilt not leave my soul in hell; neither wilt thou suffer thine Holy One to see corruption. Thou wilt shew me the path of life: in thy presence is fulness of joy; at thy right hand there are pleasures for evermore. (Ps. 16)

Notice that the Psalmist chooses to take God's way of living, and he does not want to be moved from that choice. This is a sign of wisdom. We should desire to develop in our young people the helps for getting wisdom and understanding in their lives.

Two paraplegics were in the news recently. One was Kenneth Wright, a high school football star and later, an avid wrestler, boxer, hunter, and skin diver. A broken neck sustained in a wrestling match in 1979 left him paralyzed from the chest down. He underwent therapy, and his doctors were hopeful that one day he would be able to walk with the help of braces and crutches. The former athlete could not reconcile himself to his physical disability. He prevailed upon two of his best friends to take him in his wheelchair to a wooded area where they left him alone with a twelve-gauge shotgun. After they left, he held the shotgun to his abdomen and pulled the trigger. Kenneth Wright, twenty-four, committed suicide.

The second paraplegic was Jim McGowan. Thirty years ago, at the age of nineteen, Jim was stabbed and left paralyzed from the middle of his chest down. He is now confined to a wheelchair. He recently made the news when he made a successful parachute jump, landing on his target in the middle of Lake Wallenpaupack in the Poconos. Reporters learned a number of things about Jim. He lives alone, cooks his meals, washes his clothes, and cleans his house. He drives himself in his specially equipped automobile. He has written three books, and he did the photography for our country's first book on the history of wheelchair sports.[182]

Two men with handicaps: one chose life and the other one didn't. As Robert Frost wrote, "Two roads diverged in a yellow wood, and I took the one less traveled by—and that has made all the difference."

If our learning succeeds only in making us wealthy or famous, our studying has not been of the fullest benefit; but if it enables us to be of higher service to God and man, it is worth all the years of effort it has cost us.

PATIENCE—THOROUGHNESS IN OUR TASKS
By Edgar Albert Guest

Who does his task from day to day
And meets whatever comes his way,
Believing God has willed it so.
Has found real greatness here below.

---

[182] Sidney Greenberg, Say Yes to Life: A Book of Thoughts for Better Living (Lanham, Maryland: Jason Aronson, Inc., 1982), 100–101.

Who guards his post, no matter where,
Believing God must need him there,
Although but lowly toil it be,
Has risen to nobility.

There are a couple of indicators in Psalm 16:9 which reveal that the Psalmist had patience. First, he was willing to wait on the Lord. Then, he was willing to rest in the Lord—that the author's soul would not always be in hell. Both ideas convey the patience that must be implemented in a young person's life for them to be zealous in finding the right path. Zeal does not mean haste. The easy path will many times be convenient and offer immediate results, but disaster awaits around the unseen corner of life. We must continually be presenting this concept of patience and thoroughness in tasks and disciplines as well as in personal perseverance through each area of the young person's life. We live in the world of the immediate. We have "microwaved" the life out of almost anything. We are not willing to let something simmer and roast for an hour or two so that we can enjoy the fruit of the tasty marinade. The immediate satisfaction in the fast-food industry has transferred to the everyday mundane tasks that are required for long-term success.

Faithfulness every day in every job of each day is essential to worthwhile success. Patient, persistent, and thorough work is the only way for achievement. This is especially true in the realm of ideas and ideals. Never give up. Never give in. If we learn how to tackle a task with patient thoroughness, we have mastered one of life's greatest secrets of successful living.

A poor woman had a supply of coal laid at her door by a charitable neighbor. A very little girl came out with a small fire shovel and began to take up a shovelful at a time and carry it to a sort of bin in the cellar.

I said to the child, "Do you expect to get all that coal in with that little shovel?"

She was quite confused by my question, but her answer was very striking, "Yes sir, if I work long enough."[183]

Make up for your lack of ability by abundant continuance in well-doing, and your life's work will not be trivial. The repetition of small efforts will accomplish more than the occasional use of great talents.

Priorities—Adherence to God's Path

The Psalmist again gives us this instruction in some of the verbiage that we find in this text: *"I have set"*; *"I shall not be moved"*; *"at my right hand"*; *"evermore."* What do these phrases have in common: A desire to constantly set God first in the writer's life. How often do we find that a young person's priorities are not truly lined up with godly principles? We must help young people develop a godly criterion for finding God's path for their lives. They then will be zealous for the right things in the right order.

In the Library of Congress, on the plaque above the statue of religion, are inscribed the words of the prophet Micah: *"What doth the Lord require of thee, but to do justly, and to love mercy, and to walk humbly with thy God."* Not in pride and power but with deep humility, we must teach our youth to strive to root out injustice and to show a life of good conversation that righteousness is the path to be chosen. Here is where our unselfish devotion to things that matter most springs into life and deed. Christian youth will stand in array for battle, not with arms, but rather girded in the full armor of God to fight for peace, truth, justice, joy, and the spiritual furtherance of His kingdom. Our Christian young people need to be trained as the future defenders of our spiritual heritage. They need to understand that they must find God's purpose through God's book so that they can sure up the walls that keep out tyranny, hate, immorality, materialism, and atheism. They are the future.

---

[183] M. C. Hazard, The National Sunday School Teacher (London, United Kingdom: Forgotten Books, 2017), 237.

There's a true story that comes from the sinking of the Titanic. A frightened woman found her place in a lifeboat that was about to be lowered into the raging North Atlantic. She suddenly thought of something she needed, so she asked permission to return to her stateroom before they cast off. She was granted three minutes, or they would have to leave without her.

She ran across the deck that was already slanted at a dangerous angle. She raced through the gambling room with all the money that had rolled to one side, ankle deep. She came to her stateroom and quickly pushed aside her diamond rings and expensive bracelets and necklaces as she reached to the shelf above her bed and grabbed three small oranges. She quickly found her way back to the lifeboat and got in.[184]

Now that seems incredible because thirty minutes earlier she would not have chosen a crate of oranges over even the smallest diamond, but death had boarded the Titanic. One blast of its awful breath had transformed all values. Instantaneously, priceless things had become worthless. Worthless things had become priceless. And in that moment, she preferred three small oranges to a crate of diamonds. This is what we must do for youth of our age. We must help them understand that right choices come from being zealous about the right perspective on situations. Godly priorities will establish a godly path that produces rich rewards.

---

[184] https://www.christianity.com/devotionals/insights-from-bill-bright/the-woman-on-the-titanic-feb-25. html. Accessed on August 21, 2018.

Conclusion

The world and the devil are after young people. They desire to make a young person disabled and defeated in the Christian life. As parents and church workers who work with teens, we must help a young person fight valiantly for right. The pull on a young person to leave the right paths they have received from godly parents is great. Teens are deceived to pursue temporal things. These temporal "things" leave a young person unhappy and dissatisfied. We need a young person to understand that they are not in this fight alone.

Take time to instruct the young people that God has given you in each of the areas in this book. Also, do not be afraid to add some of your own instruction. The Word of God is inexhaustible in its instruction. It will never run dry. May the prayer of our hearts for our teens be: *"Let no man despise thy youth; but be thou an example of the believers..."*

Hopefully, after reading Teens from A to Z, you are more equipped to help a young person reach more maturity in Christ. The design of each chapter was to help either a parent or pastor tackle some of the hard issues that young people face in these transitional years. There are much more than 26 issues which face teens. This is just the beginning. As you work in guiding young people, may it be that the Word of God is the first source of instruction. God desires young people to grow in grace and in the knowledge of the Lord Jesus Christ. He will help guide you along the path of life. May God raise another generation of young people with great zeal for the Lord and His Word.

A Youth that God Builds
By Steve Damron

A youth that God builds is different than your average teen.
He is not proud or arrogant but can humbly submit to his authority.
He is pliable and eager to learn though the path may be rough.
He has vigor and life to persevere when the going gets tough.

A youth that God builds is not perfect at all.
He will mess up, be tempted, and sometimes fall.
He will rise again with godly help and face the storms that often come.
The clouds will not damper his spirit though wet and fearful he
may become.

A youth that God builds will learn to face the battle fierce.
His metal will be tried and tested to temper his sword to be sure.
Though Satan try to stunt his growth, the Spirit's help will victr'y gain.
The teen years will pass, and the seasoned youth will be warrior strong.

Be brave, young man, young woman though teen you may be.
God has a plan that often you cannot see.
God desires to build a man or woman to endure for length of days.
So, stay true to God, His Word and His Church.
You can always trust in His Infinite Ways.

About the Author

S teve Damron grew up in Cleveland, Ohio, under the ministry of Dr. Roy Thompson. His youth pastor, Pastor Dan Wolvin, was instrumental in steering him to God. Steve served as an associate pastor for twenty years where his primary responsibility was as youth pastor. It was during this time of his life that God developed a strong love for young people. His desire was to reach as many young people as possible for the

Lord and bring them to a point of full surrender to Him. God blessed that desire. Many who came through his youth group not only have a deep love for the Word of God but have surrendered their lives to work for the Lord in full-time ministry.

Steve Damron also served as senior pastor of Fairhaven Baptist Church for ten years. He graduated from Fairhaven Baptist College in 1993 with a bachelor's degree in theology and continued his education earning a master's degree in Biblical Exposition. Later, he pursued an earned seminary degree, a PhD in Religious Education that he received in 2019. Steve and Becky Damron were married in December of 1994 and have been blessed with four children—Jennifer, Sabrina, Jake, and Clint. Steve's materials can be located at stevedamron.com and baptistpulpit.com.

The desire of this book is to be a help to parents and young people to show them a few areas of study that can shore up weak walls in one's life. There have been many times that a young person or a parent has asked me when it (referring to the trial) would be over so that life could be easier. Sometimes, I would have to shrug and say that life is not always easier. I know of some dear saints of God that every day endure hardships physically, emotionally, or financially. However, those saints of God are experiencing God's blessing and see His power through their life. Every day may be a tough day, but it does not have to be a day of defeat. Every day can be a victorious day!

(Steve Damron)

I thank the Lord for the blessing of preaching. Good, Biblical preaching helps the Christian to learn more about God's Word, how to walk in the Word, how to stay in love with the Word, and how to pass on the Word to fellow believers and to a lost and dying world. As I have shared some of the people and memories from my life that have contributed to my own love for preaching, my prayer is that God will use these simple thoughts to encourage lay folks to love preaching more and for preachers to be more dedicated to Biblical preaching. May the messages found in this book be an encouragement to all who read them.

(Steve Damron)

The most important of all lessons are those which teach us how to live. There come points and experiences in every young person's life when a word may give help, save from mistake, and make the way plain and clear. It is in the hope of throwing light on some of the questions which are sure to arise in young people's lives, that these chapters have been written. It is not claimed that all the "problems" are here considered; but perhaps

those eager to make life beautiful and rich will find a
little help in some of these pages
(J. R. Miller)

CPSIA information can be obtained
at www.ICGtesting.com
Printed in the USA
BVHW071530200223
658845BV00007B/380